DISCARDED

Water Politics and Public Involvement

The fourth in a series entitled
Man, The Community and Natural Resources
Donald R. Field, Series Editor

Water Politics and Public Involvement

John C. Pierce
Harvey R. Doerksen

HD
1694
A17
P5

665826

ANN ARBOR SCIENCE
PUBLISHERS INC
P.O. BOX 1425 • ANN ARBOR, MICH. 48106

LAMAR UNIVERSITY LIBRARY

Copyright © 1976 by Ann Arbor Science Publishers, Inc.
230 Collingwood, P.O. Box 1425, Ann Arbor, Michigan 48106

Library of Congress Catalog Card Number 76-1723
ISBN   0-250-40128-2

All Rights Reserved
Manufactured in the United States of America

Preface

Public involvement is central to water resource politics. The purpose of this book is to approach public involvement from a variety of perspectives, for only from diverse viewpoints can the full complexity of public involvement be understood. Thus, the chapters in this book range widely in their content and style. Public involvement is examined in terms of theory and methodology, asking some of the following questions: What are the alternative mechanisms for public influence? How does public involvement fit into administrative decision-making? How can individual preferences be aggregated into public policy? What can public involvement provide in the way of information helpful to policy formation? And, how can the level of public representation in water resource policy be measured? Public involvement also is examined in terms of practice: On what bases does the public actually form its water policy preferences? On what bases does the public actually participate in water politics? What are the consequences of public involvement programs on the attitudes of the participants? Does a specific form of public involvement affect representation of the public? And, what kinds of public involvement programs have been used in the natural resources arena?

The book is potentially useful to a wide range of audiences. For social scientists, it demonstrates the application and importance of social science concepts and methods in an important area of public policy traditionally dominated by technical expertise. The hard scientist (the water engineer, the environmental scientist) will find information here about the political and social forces with which they are increasingly being confronted. Students in social science and natural science disciplines alike will find several things here. First, there is information about the politics of water resources and the forces that constrain water resource policy formation. Second, there are examples of different analytical and methodological approaches to the study of important public policy problems. Third, the materials are drawn from a wide variety of sources; students and researchers should increase the range of materials seen as relevant to the problem of water resource policy. Finally, we hope that political decision makers, both those in the water resource area and those with more general responsibility, will find the book useful. It should provide them with information about the kinds of programs available, the success of some programs, and the alternative perspectives from which that success can be evaluated.

In sum, we have tried to bring together here materials that will be useful to the interdisciplinary audience concerned with public involvement in water resource policy formation. It is increasingly clear that solutions to policy problems in natural resources are social, political, and technical. Each has implications for the other. Nowhere is that more clear than in efforts to make government policy more responsive through public involvement. That policy cannot be responsive—except by chance—without the development of a sensitivity to the conceptual, methodological, and pragmatic problems involved. We hope this book increases that sensitivity.

April, 1976

J. C. Pierce
Pullman, Washington

H. R. Doerksen
Fort Collins, Colorado

Acknowledgments

As in any project, the editors owe many debts. The authors who contributed to the volume have been cooperative and amiable in response to details and deadlines. We appreciate their work and their support. Chapters of the book authored by the editors were supported in part by several sources: a grant jointly received from the Department of Interior Office of Water Research and Technology; a grant to Pierce by the Washington State University Graduate School; released time to Pierce through the Washington State University Social Research Center; and released time to Doerksen provided by the State of Washington Water Research Center. Without support from those diverse sources, the material included in those chapters could not have been obtained, processed, or written.

The editors have been supported by a highly competent group of assistants. Two research assistants contributed invaluable aid to the project: Richard Childs in the earlier stages and Kathleen Beatty in the later ones. In particular, Kathleen Beatty consistently demonstrated wit, intelligence, and forbearance. Judy Bhagat and Sandy Meyers handled the coding chores quickly and competently. Linda McKenzie, Dell Day, Teena Bechard, and Kathy Stark not only provided secretarial help, but also their usual encouragement and good humor. Teena Bechard typed the manuscript and assisted with many of the editorial chores. Linda McKenzie's organizational skills and political expertise kept the project above water. Our wives, Ardith Pierce and Diana Doerksen, sympathized, encouraged, and cajoled at all of the right times.

Contents

I. INTRODUCTION

1. Citizen Influence in Water Policy Decisions: Context, Constraints, and Alternatives
   Harvey R. Doerksen and John C. Pierce 3

II. ANALYTICAL FRAMEWORKS

2. Participation and the Administrative Process
   Norman Wengert 29
3. Identification of Publics in Water Resources Planning
   Gene E. Willeke 43
4. The Politics of Information: Constraints on New Sources
   Helen Ingram 63
5. Individual Preferences and Group Choice
   Nathaniel Beck 75
6. Measuring Political Responsiveness: A Comparison of Several Alternative Methods
   Anne L. Schneider 87

III. PARTICIPATION PATTERNS AND EVALUATION

7. Methods for Acquiring Public Input
   John C. Hendee, Robert C. Lucas, Robert H. Tracy, Tony Staed, Roger N. Clark, George H. Stankey and Ronald A. Yarnell 125
8. Codinvolve: A Tool for Analyzing Public Input to Resource Decisions
   Roger N. Clark, John C. Hendee and George H. Stankey 145

9. Rational Participation and Public Involvement
   in Water Resource Politics
   *John C. Pierce, Kathleen M. Beatty,
   and Harvey R. Doerksen* 167
10. Public Opinion and Water Policy
    Douglas D. Rose 179
11. Participatory Democracy in a Federal Agency
    Daniel A. Mazmanian 201
12. Prospects for Public Participation in Federal Agencies:
    The Case of the Army Corps of Engineers
    Daniel A. Mazmanian and Jeanne Nienaber . . . 225
13. Citizen Advisory Committees: The Impact
    of Recruitment on Representation and Responsiveness
    John C. Pierce and Harvey R. Doerksen 249

IV. ANNOTATED BIBLIOGRAPHY

14. Public Participation in Water Resource Policy Making:
    Selected Annotated Bibliography
    Kathleen M. Beatty 269

Index 289

Part I

Introduction

About the Contributors

John C. Pierce is Associate Professor and Director of the Division of Governmental Studies and Services for the Department of Political Science, Washington State University. He earned his PhD at the University of Minnesota and previously taught at Tulane University and has been an American Political Science Congressional Fellow (1970–71). He is the editor of several books, and the author of articles appearing in professional journals, including *The American Political Science Review, The Public Opinion Quarterly, The American Journal of Political Science,* and the *Water Resources Bulletin.*

Harvey R. Doerksen is Western Water Allocation Project Leader for the Western Energy and Land Use Study Team of the U.S. Fish and Wildlife Service in Fort Collins, Colorado. He received his PhD in 1973 from Washington State University and worked for three years with the State of Washington Water Research Center. He has coauthored several articles on water politics and is author of *The Columbia River Interstate Compact: Politics of Negotiation.*

1. Citizen Influence in Water Policy Decisions: Context, Constraints, and Alternatives[1]

Harvey R. Doerksen and John C. Pierce

PUBLIC PARTICIPATION IN WATER RESOURCES PLANNING

The concept of public participation has a long history in both governmental theory and practice. The focus of participation is by no means limited to water resources planning, but that area faces several unique problems. First, many agencies that traditionally have been viewed as "conservation" oriented now have the appropriateness of their mission seriously questioned. Second, the substantial lead time from planning to implementation and the tremendous monetary investments render these agencies particularly susceptible to extreme losses caused by delay. Third, the many quantitative and qualitative demands for water cause conflict to be the rule, rather than the exception. Thus, special problems in the water resources policy arena make the question of public participation particularly salient and conflict-producing.

Questions as to the public's role in the formulation and execution of water resources policy surface in two broad areas. First, *should* the public be involved? Second, *how* should that involvement occur? The resolution of the conflict over these two questions is hindered severely by the generally narrow perspective within which the problem has been approached. This chapter attempts to expand that perspective substantially by placing the

---
[1] Published previously in *Water Resources Bulletin* 11, 5 (1975).

problem of public participation in water policy in the context of (1) the nature of the current controversy over whether the public should or should not be directly involved and (2) the variety of political processes through which the public might be linked to policy and the requisite conditions for each "linkage process."

THE CURRENT CONTROVERSY

The demand for increased public involvement in the water resources arena has many sources. The importance of some form of citizen participation was recently recognized at the national level by the National Water Resources Council and the National Water Commission. The need for public participation has been echoed in some fashion by numerous water resources agencies, such as the multiple objective planning program of the Bureau of Reclamation, and the Susquehanna Communication-Participation study by the Corps of Engineers. State agencies across the country have followed suit by attempting through various means to involve larger segments of the public than had participated previously in agency program planning. Advocates of a greater degree of public participation include many scholars as well.

Unfortunately, many of the political ramifications of current proposals for increased public participation in water resources planning have not been explored fully by either proponents or opponents. First, as Wengert (1971) pointed out, a wide range of motives exists for advocating increased public participation, from strong ideological beliefs in public participation as a democratic goal to "...jumping on the band wagon." Second, proposed participation procedures also vary widely in terms of the range of political system change that will be required, from simple modification of the planning process to radical change in the basic political system (Hart, 1972). Third, most recent discussions of increased public participation have expressed a simplistic view of the "public" and the role of the citizen in the American political system. Finally, many discussions of increased public participation concentrate upon the participatory process with respect to planning and operating *agencies* and ignore many of the other access points to the governmental process, such as Congress and the executive.

The narrow conceptions of the problem by people on both sides of the issue require a more systematic integration of public par-

Historical Context

The activities of water resources planning and development agencies in past years have not been conducted in a political vacuum. There has been substantial input and support from *segments* of the public. Indeed, the activities in water resources development on the part of such agencies as the U. S. Army Corps of Engineers and the Bureau of Reclamation would have been impossible without strong support from influential publics. The Corps of Engineers, for example, received much of its support from the National Rivers and Harbors Congress, composed of member organizations representing "local interests which included state and local officials, local industrial organizations, and contractors" (Maass, 1951). Similarly the Bureau of Reclamation has maintained close liaison and received support from such water development interests as the National Reclamation Association and its local affiliates (Allee and Ingram, 1973). Whether these publics represent that amorphous entity known as *the public,* of course, is one of the major issues in the present controversy.

Redford (1969), Maass (1951), and Freeman (1955) all have noted the manner in which agency relationships with local interests have been linked with the interests of the congressional public works committees, and how those linkages have become institutionalized over the years. Decisions on water development have been based on interactions among three groups—congressional committees, agencies, and interest groups. Bureaus thus were encouraged to become relatively independent from the executive department hierarchy, becoming more responsive to the legislative committees. In addition, agencies solidified and sometimes institutionalized their relationships with particular interest groups that were supportive of the agencies' programs.

Due to the general "development" bias of the prevailing agency-committee-interest group troika, and the emphasis placed on locally controlled water development decisions, certain publics have been systematically excluded from the decision-making process. Most notably, these included the conservationist and preservationist interests whose values often appear to be (1) antidevelopmental and (2) nationally or regionally (as opposed to locally) oriented.

After operating for many years under a decision-making system quite functional for the agency, committee, and interest groups, agencies now are pressed from all sides by persons advocating increased public participation. According to Ingram (1972), decision rules that had applied for years are changing. Agencies now face less certain local support, an increase in controversy and conflict, the inclusion of noneconomic criteria for project evaluation, inclusion of all "relevant" interests in the decision-making process, and consideration of values and priorities in place of the older "objective" benefit-cost ratio.

Current Context

The events of the past can be viewed with a certain amount of clarity, but the future is much less certain. The manner in which decision rules are changing portends a period of uncertainty. At present there is no sign that the "public" is involved to any large extent in water resources development decisions or that a new set of relationships has been institutionalized. Rather, the current situation is one of change, jockeying for position, uncertainty, and conflict.

Dreyfus (1973) unequivocally pronounces that "the public, from this point on, is going to intrude in public decisions." He is joined by many others in predicting a radical change in the extent to which the public will be involved in water resources decisions. (For examples, see Cole, 1974; Dodge, 1973; Burlee, Heaney, and Pyatt, 1973; Wandesforde-Smith, 1971.)

Not all observers, however, are in agreement that radical and lasting change is in the future of water resources agencies. Anthony Downs (1972) describes what he calls the "issue-attention cycle" in which public interest moves through five stages: preproblem, alarmed discovery and enthusiasm, cost realization, decline in public interest, and postproblem stages. He predicted that the environmental crisis would move through the same cycle but that the postproblem stage would come less rapidly than for certain other issues. It might now be argued that the energy crisis has prematurely moved even the environmental crisis into the "postproblem" stage. Whether demands for increased public involvement in water resource decision-making will follow the same pattern remains to be seen.

Why Public Participation?

David Hart (1972) raises a very basic question that must be addressed regarding increased public participation: Why should people participate? Obviously, this question has many answers. For example, one might expect a very different response from an agency head facing a bombardment of opposition than would be expected from a private citizen who felt strongly that his rights had been violated by an agency decision.

Most reasons for seeking increased public participation can be placed into one of three categories: self-fulfilling, symbolic, and instrumental. Self-fulfilling reasons relate to the benefits the individual derives from participating in decisions that affect him personally. Participating in such decisions, it is argued, make the individual a more fulfilled person by allowing him to use the attributes given him as an individual to control his own environment. Symbolic reasons for citizen participation essentially result in legitimizing the process. It is not necessary, in this thinking, for decisions to be influenced as long as people have the feeling that they are able to provide their input and that their input will be heard. It may not even be required for all persons to participate, as long as the opportunity is available if one wishes to participate. Instrumental reasons for participation relate to outcomes from the policy process. It is argued that wrong policy decisions have been reached in the water resources area, and these decisions are the consequence of the biases of those who make them. If citizen participation is broadened, then, better decisions will be made because of interaction with and perhaps alterations in the composition of effective policy-makers. Citizen participation thus is instrumental to change in policy outcomes.

Why Not Participation?

Arguments against substantial public participation relate both to institutions and to individuals.

Institutional Constraints

Hart (1972) draws a direct connection between a participatory system and governmental decentralization and suggests that the "iron law of oligarchy" and "tyranny of expertise" favor decision-making by an administrative elite. The iron law of oligarchy—the tendency of organizations to become controlled by a few—is a difficult problem at best. Perhaps even more difficult in modern society, and to no small extent in water resources planning, is the tyranny of expertise, in which the expert becomes powerful on the basis of his specialized knowledge.

The problem of expertise is compounded by the tendency of most professions to adhere to certain value premises and policy outcomes that are considered to be the "right" ones for society. Such professional biases often are narrow in the sense that other policy preferences somehow are perceived as less good, or even based upon "subjective" rather than upon "objective" criteria. When a particular professional group becomes entrenched in an agency, having power because of expertise, change may become extremely difficult.

Helen Ingram (1973) points out that agency personnel—experts—often have extreme difficulty in relating to new input especially when it is nonsupportive because of the "costs" of receiving and assimilating it, and because it strikes at the heart of agency goals, values, and programs. But the impact of public participation programs may be very limited because opposition may be received only when backed by sufficient political clout to demand attention.

Individual Constraints

The problems of participation for the individual citizen similarly are enormous. It certainly is not unusual to find some citizens involved in public hearings, writing letters to congressmen, and visiting City Hall. However, the numbers of people who participate only minimally—to the extent of voting—is small compared to what one might call a democratic ideal. And of course, the amount of information about specific water resource planning issues possessed by the general public may be biased and inadequate. What information is possessed is, to a large extent, generated by policy-makers. Some scholars take the view that widespread public participation in any policy area is to be avoided at all costs. Dye and Zeigler (1972) found evidence to suggest "... that large numbers of the electorate are politically uninformed and inarticulate and generally unsupportive of democratic values." In any case, the question of whether and how the public ought to participate is far from resolved.

Given the background conditions and the nature of the current controversy, we are still left with the problem of just how the public *can* influence public policy in the water resources arena. The limitations imposed by traditional practice, the institutional environment, and the behavior and information of the public means the problem is a difficult one. There exists a need to outline the alternative ways in which the public can influence policy and to find out what the requirements for such influence are.

LINKAGE PROCESSES

Observers of public policy formation stipulate a variety of processes through which political outcomes *may* reflect public preferences. These processes concern *political linkage*. Political linkage is "...the mechanism that allows public leaders to act in accordance with the wants, needs, and demands of the 'public' in making governmental policy" (Luttbeg, 1974). Analyses of citizen participation in the making of water policy, however, generally discuss only a few of the alternative linkage processes and very seldom explicitly. In some instances the conceptual context of citizen participation is ignored entirely. Yet, in order to clarify differences among alternative modes of citizen participation the full range of linkage processes must be systematically considered. Thus, this section reviews those linkage processes in terms of (1) the meaning of public, (2) the proximity of the public to actual policy decision, and (3) the role of actual public preferences relative to the public's best interest.

The linkage processes described below are pure types in that they represent abstractions from sets of recommendations for public influence and involvement.[2] Nonetheless, they can impose some order to the complexity and diffusion in current debate over public participation.

Direct Participation

In the direct participation form of public-policy linkage, the public makes policy decisions directly (although some variations

---

[1] The typology owes a great deal to the work of Norman Luttbeg (cited above). Our divisions among the linkage processes, however, do not correspond precisely to his and we have added several processes because of specific developments in the water policy area.

allow for public formulation of *guidelines* within which others make the actual decisions). Specific examples of direct participation are the town meeting, referendum, initiative, and, in a special sense, public opinion polling.

Direct participation allows for the greatest public penetration of policy-making, but each variation also has its obvious limitations. The town meeting form allows only a relatively small "public" to participate effectively. For large publics, the referendum, initiative, and public opinion poll appear more appropriate. However, these latter methods are inflexible in the options they provide and in the negligible opportunity they allow for individuals to interact. Moreover, when large numbers of people participate in a policy decision, one is confronted with the problem of aggregating individual choices. There is no clear-cut way to handle questions on whether each person's choices should count the same, or whether those with more information, interest, or greater stakes in the outcome should have greater weight (Wildavsky, 1973). Once individual preferences are identified, the choice of which decision rule to apply is difficult. Should public policy in water allocation problems, for example, depend on a plurality choice among many options, a simple majority, or an extraordinary majority of $2/3$ or $3/4$ on a single alternative? When large majorities are required to make policy decisions, a minority is able to prevent the policy decision, which itself establishes policy.

All forms of the direct participation model depend extensively on certain assumptions about the characteristics of those participating: (1) that people care about the policy problem, (2) that people have information about the policy area and how it affects them, (3) that people have opinions about the issues, and (4) that people have the motivation to participate in the policy decisions on the basis of the interest, information, and opinions.

While members of the general public may meet those conditions in the water policy area on some very broad questions, it is unlikely that anything other than a small minority is capable of meeting such requirements for specific applications and issues. The source for much of the public expertise in more specific and technical areas, such as instream flow, nitrogen supersaturation, or channelization, will of necessity be the policymaker experts themselves, the ones the public is influencing.

Nevertheless, the apparent general sensitivity to water issues may be a launching pad for intense public involvement in specific issues affecting the people more or less directly, as when a dam is proposed in a wilderness stretch of river. When such episodal participation is stimulated by a latent concern, it is unclear how much technical information the general public brings to the policy process. People stimulated to particpation may, however, possess a unique type of information about the personal impact of the policy, and there is often a self-selecting process in which the uninterested and the uninformed do not participate in direct involvement programs.

The choice among alternative direct participation mechanisms is partially a function of perceptions of what constitutes the relevant public (Warner, 1971). Limited notions of a participatory public argue that only individuals immediately affected by a policy should be involved in its formulation. More broadly based conceptions include anyone who might even be tangentially affected by the decisions. It is possible, of course, to construct some *a priori* hierarchy of publics and to weigh their involvements accordingly. But, a decision on the nature of the hierarchy would be subject to the same political pressures and demands for citizen involvement it would be designed to accommodate. Regardless of the form, however, direct participation models are based on the affirmation of the importance of the public's *preferences;* the proposals are designed to reflect what the public wants, *as the public sees it.* The assumption is that the public knows best its own best interest, and self-interest will be expressed in choices among available alternatives. Thus, support for public *preference* in the abstract presupposes a simultaneous expression of public *interest*. Preference and interest are inextricably intertwined; the public knows best the probable impact of alternative policies.

Indirect Participation Models

Citizen Advisory Committees

In the Citizen Advisory Committee (CAC) model, a group from the affected citizenry represents the public in making water policy or in advising policy-makers. This option is partially in response to the problems of direct participation models, such as the difficulty of coherent, efficient, and economical decision-making when all members of a large public are eligible to participate (Miller and Rein, 1969). Thus, CACs are formed to link the public to the policy process by being a representative microcosm of the larger public. The assumption is that a smaller group of people with preference and interest distributions similar to the public's will ensure the desired public input without creating unnecessary bottlenecks.

Two crucial links prevail in the process by which the CAC places the public near the decision-making locus. The first is the extent to which selection procedures produce committees representative of the public, either in preferences or in interests. The second crucial link is the impact of the CAC on those who make decisions. Generally the public possesses no real sanction by which to ensure representation.

CAC models contain two primary notions of public, depending on the mode by which CAC members are chosen. If members are elected by some expression of the larger public, such as a public hearing, the public comprises everyone actively interested in the substantive policy area; the public represented is self-selected. If CAC members are chosen by the policy-makers, the definition of public is likely a function of the policy makers' perceptions of the community's important interests. Policy-maker definitions of public thus will be based on their perception of the differing substantive interests affected by the decisions and their perceptions of the numerical or political importance of those holding those interests in the public.

Citizen Advisory Committee linkage models combine an emphasis on public preference and an emphasis on public interest. To be sure, they are designed to obtain information about the preferences of the public. However, because public representatives are "advisors," the implication is that preferences must be balanced against other considerations. Thus, CACs provide perfect public policy linkage only when the preferences of CAC members match the preferences of the public and the policy of the elite reflects the input of the Citizen Advisory Committee.

Pressure Group Model

The pressure group model has its source in general "group theories" of politics in which political outcomes are the consequence of interaction and competition among groups and organizations. Group interaction is structured by formal political processes, but public policy only represents the outcome and legitimizes the result of the group conflict (Latham, 1952). In the pressure group model, citizen involvement in policy-making has no meaning except when it takes place within the context of group activity. And, as Betty Zisk (1969) argues, "... such groups can act as a major link between the citizen and his government."

Water policy typically has been the result of group interaction. Helen Ingram (1969), for example, stressed that consensus building among groups historically has been an important prerequisite to congressional approval of water development projects. In his study of water pollution control and the U.S. Congress, Jennings (1973) concluded that the "... most influential interest groups were the state officials and the conservationists." And, Paulsen and Denhardt (1973) write that "... pollution policy is likely to be determined by a special type of interaction among special types of interest groups." In each case, groups are a dominant, if not exclusive, determinant of public policy.

Much of the clamor for greater public representation in water policy-making is the result of perceptions that water policy is the domain of special interests. There is the criticism that group politics omits the larger public. The counter-argument, though, pleads the adequacy of the group process in representing the important elements of the public.

Pressure group models generally consider the "public interest" to be the result of compromise among groups. Important citizen interests do not exist independently. The public as a whole benefits from the compromise and bargaining attendant to group interaction and to shifting coalitions of groups.

The roles of preference and interest in the pressure group model are unambiguous. Policy is supposed to reflect the preferences of groups as they are moderated by the interaction of the groups. The group interests are reflected in the articulated group preferences.

Electoral Model

According to the electoral model of political linkage, the public influences policy through its choice among candidates and parties in elections. The perfect case of electoral linkage contains: clear policy differences among the election alternatives, concerned citizens with informed policy preferences, citizen vote choices based on the meshing of their preferences with the policy positions of the alternatives, and election winners who make policy in accord with their campaign positions (Sullivan and O'Conner, 1972).

This model additionally requires that the electoral alternatives differ with regard to water policy solutions. The only evidence readily available indicates that they do. Doerksen (1972) has found party affiliation to be a good predictor of Washington State legislators' positions on the Columbia Interstate Compact. And, in votes on water pollution control in the U.S. House of Representatives, M. Kent Jennings (1973) concluded that partisanship was more closely related to voting patterns than was type of district. In both cases, the party differences apparently stemmed not from shared interests in water policy *per se*, but from overall ideological differences between the parties within which the water policy alternatives fit. Generally speaking, little information is available on party or candidate differences on water policy issues.

Many of the requirements of the public in this model are similar to those in the direct participation model—a well-informed public that votes on the basis of water policy choices. Typically water policy issues are not stated as clearly defined electoral alternatives. Rather, they become intermingled with all other salient political issues. Thus, it is unlikely that many people vote primarily on the basis of water issues, except, perhaps, in very unusual circumstances. Recent studies of the electorate have shown an increasing inclination to choose candidates and parties on the basis of general ideology and issue positions (Pomper, 1972; Kirkpatrick and Jones, 1970). For the electoral model to apply in the water resources arena, people would have to share water policy positions of the candidates they chose as well.

The adequacy of the electoral model also turns on the "role" orientation of the elected representatives, and the role they take will have a large impact on the influence of the public in their behavior. Representative role orientations have been classified into two polar styles: the delegate who behaves in policy-making according to what he perceives to be the preference of his constituents, and the trustee who acts according to what he perceives to be the best interest of his constituents, even if widely divergent from the public's preferences (Wahlke, Eulau, Buchanan, and Ferguson, 1962). Previous research shows the role orientations taken by "representatives" to vary across issue areas (Miller and

Stokes, 1963). Generally speaking, the more salient the issue area is to the public, the more likely it is that the representative will take a delegate role, and hence the greater the public influence or link to the policy outcome. Given the lack of general on-going salience of most water issues to the public, it is likely that elected representatives would most often adopt trustee roles, unless on a very specific issue the constituency is immediately affected and communicates intense preferences.

Bureaucratic Model

The bureaucratic model of linkage places the locus of policy-making with permanent and technical experts in formal administrative agencies. The experts make decisions in terms of what they perceive to be in the best interest, rather than the preferences, of the public and in the form the public would prefer if it had the necessary information and perspective. The model is based on the assumption that in many policy areas a large portion of the public does not have the information available for making reasonably intelligent policy decisions.

There is little *direct* accountability built into the bureaucratic model. It does share with the electoral trustee role orientation a certain commitment to act in the best interest of the public even if the public disagrees. When bureaucrats interact with clientele groups, it shares a certain commonality with the pressure group model, depending on how the bureaucracy responds to the group pressures. However, the groups directly interacting with the agencies normally have had shared, rather than conflicting, values and goals.

Public involvement is not necessarily absent from this model. Through its own initiative in the political process the public can set general policy guidelines within which the bureaucracy will make specific decisions. The public's tenuous control over legislative action may extend one step further to the legislature's ability to influence the bureaucracy. Moreover, the bureaucracy may be willing itself or required by legislative mandate to search out and determine public preferences. As noted earlier, however, agencies often find it extremely difficult to assimilate and act on input which conflicts with the agencies' traditions, goals, and mission orientations.

Much of the movement for public involvement in water policy-making is in response to recent criticisms of bureaucratic agencies and to a realization that the solutions to policy problems "... rest fundamentally on the *interplay of technical and political forces*" (Paulsen and Denhardt, 1973). Whether that interplay takes into account the preferences of the public depends both on the procedural mechanisms established for ensuring public input and on the orientations the bureaucrats themselves have to the public. The bureaucratic model is based on the assumption that sensitive, public-minded officials can establish mechanisms for integrating public preferences into their decision-making and thereby both maintain the essential elements of the democratic system and carry out efficient, economical, and correct policy decisions.

IMPLICATIONS FOR WATER RESOURCE POLITICS

Defining a series of alternative processes by which the public *might* influence policy formation in the water resource area is important for several reasons. First, it illustrates the wide range of ways the public can influence public policy while focusing on the differences in the meaning of public and the conditions on which public influence depends in each case. It thereby expands the context within which discussion and conflict can take place by defining options and the dimensions on which the options can vary. That there exists a variety of processes through which the public could have some influence obviously is no guarantee that the influence will obtain through any or all of the linkage processes.

Second, noting the variety of linkage processes demonstrates that public influence is a political problem, one that must be examined within a political context. The choice of the linkage process for public influence and policy will substantially determine who wins and who loses when policy decisions are made. Political processes are not neutral. They benefit people who possess the resources to exploit the process. Not all processes are exploitable by the same resources, and thus people will support the process that is most amenable to the resources they hold. Thus, judgment of the "best" ways for public participation must take into consideration their impact on "who gets what, when, and how" (Lasswell, 1965).

Third, in the long run, if general public influence prevails in the making of water policy, it probably will be the result of interaction among the different linkage processes. The processes are not mutually exclusive and can work simultaneously but independently of each other, or can in several ways be intermingled. Assessment of whether the public does or does not influence policy must be based on the extent to which the processes work together with a cumulative impact or whether they conflict with each other. That multiple processes are simultaneously at work makes judgment about the extent of public influence much more difficult. The alternative processes may begin with different assumptions and work toward divergent goals.

Fourth, the entire discussion of the role of the public in making decisions about water policy rests on the assumption that in fact there exist real policy alternatives. Obviously, to the people involved in controversies about specific water policy decisions and to the people involved in the arguments about citizen influence in policy-making there are indeed variable consequences of decisions. The presence and nature of these choices, of course, are limited by natural resource availability, technical feasibility, traditional decision patterns, and economic costs. Less obviously, but equally as important, is whether the public *believes* there is a real choice it can make if the procedures for making the choice are present. Political and cognitive constraints on choice among policy alternatives will have just as important an impact on the success of citizen participation processes as the material, economic, and technical constraints.

ACKNOWLEDGMENTS

The research on which this paper is based was supported jointly by Washington State University and the U.S. Department of the Interior, Office of Water and Technology Research as authorized under the Water Resources Act of 1964 (P.L. 88–379).

REFERENCES

Allee, D., and H. Ingram. "Authorization and Appropriation Processes for Water Resource Development," a report prepared under contract with the National Water Commission, 1973.

Burke, R., J. P. Heaney and E. E. Pyatt. "Water Resources and Social Choices," *Water Resources Bull.* 9 (3), 433 (1973).

Cole, R. L. *Citizen Participation and the Urban Policy Process* (Lexington, Massachusetts: Lexington Books, 1974).

Dodge, B. H. "Achieving Public Involvement in the Corps of Engineers, Water Resources Planning," *Water Resources Bull.* 9 (3), 448 (1973).

Doerksen, H. R. *Columbia River Interstate Compact, Politics of Negotiation* (Pullman, Washington: State of Washington Water Research Center, 1972).

Downs, A. "Up and Down with Ecology—the 'Issue Attention Cycle,'" *Public Interest,* 29, 38 (1972).

Dreyfus, D. A. "Competing Values in Water Development," *J. Hydraulics Div.* 99 (HY9), 1599 (1973).

Dye, T. R. and L. H. Zeigler. *The Irony of Democracy,* 2nd ed. (Belmont, California: Wadsworth, 1972).

Freeman, J. L. *The Political Process: Executive-Bureau-Legislative Committee Relationships* (Garden City, New York: Doubleday and Co., Inc., 1955).

Hart, D. K. "Theories of Government Related to Decentralization and Citizen Participation," *Public Administration Review,* 32, 603 (1972).

Ingram, H. *Patterns of Politics in Water Resources Development: A Case Study of New Mexico's Role in the Colorado River Basin Bill* (Albuquerque, New Mexico: University of New Mexico, Division of Governmental Research, 1969).

Ingram, H. "The Changing Decision Rules in the Politics of Water Development," *Water Resources Bull.* 8 (6), 1177 (1972).

Ingram H. "The Politics of Information: The Social Well-Being Objective," *Proceedings, Conference on the Social Well-Being/Quality of Life Dimension in Water Resources Planning and Development,* Logan, Utah (July, 1973).

Jennings, M. K. "Legislative Politics and Water Pollution Control," in *Pollution and Public Policy,* David F. Paulsen and Robert D. Denhardt, Ed. (New York: Dodd, Mead and Co., 1973).

Kirkpatrick, S. A., and M. E. Jones. "Vote Direction and Issue Cleavage in 1968," *Soc. Sci. Quart.* 51, (4), 689 (1970).

Lasswell, H. *Politics: Who Gets What, When, and How* (Cleveland: The World Publishing Co., 1965).

Latham, E. "The Group Basis of Politics: Notes for a Theory," *Amer. Pol. Sci. Rev.* 46 (2), 376 (1952).

Luttbeg, N. R., Ed. *Public Opinion and Public Policy,* revised ed., (Homewood, Illinois: The Dorsey Press, 1974).

Maass, A. *Muddy Waters* (Cambridge, Massachusetts: Harvard University Press, 1951).

Miller, S. M., and M. Rein. "Participation, Poverty, and Administration," *Public Admin. Rev.* 29 (1), 15 (1969).

Miller, W. E. and D. E. Stokes. "Constituency Influence in Congress," *Amer. Pol. Sci. Rev.* 57, (1) (1963).

Paulsen, D. F. and R. D. Denhardt, Eds. *Pollution and Public Policy* (New York: Dodd, Mead and Co., 1973).

Pomper, G. M. "From Confusion to Clarity: Issues and American Voters, 1956–1968," *Amer. Pol. Sci. Rev.* 66 (2), 415 (1972).

Redford, E. S. *Democracy and the Administrative State* (New York: Oxford University Press, 1969).

Sullivan, J. L. and R. E. O'Connor. "Electoral Choice and Popular Control of Public Policy," *Amer. Pol. Sci. Rev.* 66 (4), 1256 (1972).

Wahlke, J. C., H. Eulau, W. Buchanan, and L. C. Ferguson. *The Legislative Systems: Explorations in Legislative Behavior* (New York: John Wiley and Sons, 1962).

Wandesforde-Smith, G. "The Bureaucratic Response to Environmental Politics," *Natural Resources J.* 11 (3), 479 (1971).

Warner, K. P. "A State of the Arts Study of Public Participation in the Water Resources Planning Process," a report prepared under contract with the National Water Commission, 1971.

Wengert, N. "Public Participation in Water Planning: A Critique of Theory, Doctrine and Practice," *Water Resources Bull.* 7 (1), 26 (February, 1971).

Wildavsky, A. B. "Aesthetic Power or the Triumph of the Sensitive Minority Over the Vulgar Mass," in *Pollution and Public Policy*, David F. Paulsen and Robert D. Denhardt, Eds. (New York: Dodd, Mead and Co., 1973).

Zisk, B., Ed. *American Political Interest Groups: Readings in Theory and Research* (Belmont, California: Wadsworth, 1969).

Part II

Analytical Frameworks

About the Contributors

Norman Wengert is Professor of Political Science, Colorado State University. His PhD and JD degrees were earned at the University of Wisconsin. Major research interests include environmental policy and law, and natural resources administration. Part of Dr. Wengert's time is allocated to the Colorado Extension Service involving community development and public policy education. He is associate editor of the *Water Resources Bulletin* published by the American Water Resources Association. Under a long-term arrangement with the Colorado Experiment Station, Dr. Wengert is concentrating on water-land relationships and legal problems of land use planning and control. He is a member of the Wisconsin Bar, and has had over ten years of service with various federal agencies dealing with natural resources.

Gene E. Willeke is Associate Professor of Public Works Planning at the Georgia Institute of Technology. He received his PhD in Civil Engineering from Stanford University, where he also served on the Civil Engineering faculty. His research interests and recent publications are largely in the areas of social, political, economic, and environmental aspects of public works planning and management. He has been a consultant to several federal, state, and regional public agencies on public participation in planning and social impact assessment. He is a trustee and member of the Executive Committee of the Georgia Conservancy, Inc.

Helen Ingram is Associate Professor of Political Science and Director of the Institute of Government Research at the University of Arizona. After earning her PhD from Columbia, she has spent much of her career in research and writing on the politics of water resources. Following a monograph on the Grand Canyon Dam controversy, *Patterns of Politics in Water Resources Development: The Case of New Mexico's Role in the Colorado River Basin Bill,* she served a year as staff political scientist at the National Water Commission. She has been a consultant to the New England River Basin Commission, the U.S. Water Resources Council, and the National Commission on Water Quality. Dr. Ingram has written a number of articles on public policy issues in natural resources and the environment.

Nathaniel Beck is Assistant Professor of Political Science at Washington State University, where his specialties are political methodology and public choice models. His PhD was earned at Yale University. He has published in several professional journals, including *Public Choice* and the *American Political Science Review*. Currently, he is working in the area of formal models of political development.

Anne L. Schneider is a research scientist at the Oregon Research Institute. Dr. Schneider received her PhD in political science from Indiana University, joined the political science faculty at Yale University and began her research in policy analysis and evaluation at ORI in 1973. She has directed a crime analysis and victimization survey project in Portland, Oregon, and has been involved in education policy research as well as water quality policy problems.

Part II

Analytical Frameworks

The question of public involvement in water resource policy formation is many-sided. No single paradigm is widely accepted as the dominant perspective by which to examine citizen participation. Part II provides alternative ways of looking at public involvement in water resource policy-making. Together, the selections demonstrate that there is much to be gained from placing public involvement in different contexts, each illuminating a particular facet.

Norman Wengert has observed water resource politics for several decades. He also has had over ten years' service with federal natural resource agencies. Thus, he has a unique perspective from which to evaluate the impact of public involvement on the administrative process. In Chapter 2, Wengert confronts this question: what is the impact of participation on bureaucratic decision processes and what conditions constrain that impact? He argues that the impact of participation depends on the stage of the policy process, the level of participation (geographic or functional), the perspective one takes (agency or public), the definition of the public, and one's concern with the future. The response of the administrative process to public involvement is the consequence of the intermingling of all those forces.

Gene Willeke, in Chapter 3, examines the planner's problem of identifying the "public" in public participation. He argues that there exist many publics. How does the planner identify and communicate with them? Willeke offers some alternative theoretical bases for identifying publics. Some publics can be identified by geographic location, others by policy interests, and still others by social and demographic characteristics. Willeke then surveys methods of identifying different publics and the resources that are needed to employ each technique. Overall, he provides a sensitivity to both the theoretical and the practical perspectives that the water resource planner must consider in developing public involvement.

Helen Ingram (Chapter 4) examines public involvement by considering the water policy process in terms of *information*. Public involvement is viewed in the light of the ability of new information to penetrate decision-making and the kinds of impact that information can have. Information from the public must contend with other information; decision-makers presently hear more information than they can use. The success of public-generated information depends on the context of the issue, the source of the information, the context of information, the characteristics of the decision-maker, the rules and regulations surrounding the decision process, and timing. Ingram then argues that information's impact depends on its costs and utility. There are costs of acquisition, consumption, and value conflict. The information is useful if it can justify actions the agency wants to take, and if it can help the agency politically. She concludes that information generated by public involvement will affect decisions only when decision-makers perceive benefits as greater than the costs.

In Chapter 5, Nathaniel Beck considers the problems of aggregating individual policy preferences into actual public policy from a social choice perspective. The problems in that aggregation are important for several reasons. First, they should be considered when designing policy once the public's preferences are known. Second, they are important in evaluating whether present policy actually reflects the public's preferences. Both are crucial to the evaluation of the need for and success of public involvement programs. Beck's chapter specifies some of the conditions that make aggregation difficult (*e.g.*, intransitive preference orderings and irrelevant alternatives), provides some ways of obviating those difficulties, and demonstrates the usefulness of logical analysis of political problems.

Anne Schneider (Chapter 6) also is concerned with the problem of aggregating public preferences into policy, with the focus on representation. In her chapter, which is more methodological, she examines the various methods available for deciding the extent to which policy or policy-makers are representative of the public. Schneider describes the problems with each measure of responsiveness as well as its theoretical implications. The question of "concurrence" is important because it reflects on the need for public involvement programs and the success of those programs. Her chapter should be helpful to individuals who are looking for ways to study the impact of the public in water resource policy processes.

2. Participation and the Administrative Process

Norman Wengert

INTRODUCTION

Public participation and citizen involvement are terms with many meanings and connotations, depending on the situation, and on the ideological motivations and practical orientations of the users. They are terms used in the context of political determinations of government structure and of the content of public programs. But they are also applied to more or less routine processes of political activity, elections, program planning, and day-to-day administration. Demands for more public participation and citizen involvement in decision-making may be motivated by desires to alter significantly the power structure and to weaken "the establishment," or they may merely seek better information inputs and more effective, responsive, and acceptable public service. From each of the many usages and situations flow different consequences, different emphases, and different procedures.

At least since the French Revolution of 1789, the slogan "Power to the People" has served to rally those who may seek to overthrow an existing regime and who desire to change the power structure and power relationships in the social, economic, and political system. While the concern of this paper is by definition not directed to violent and revolutionary mass participation, it is nevertheless important to be aware of this dimension of the subject, which may often lie behind pressures for greater participation, and to recognize that some of the rhetoric and polemics of those most vociferous in expanding citizen roles in government may often be borrowed (knowingly or unknowingly) from the slogans of revolution.

It is important, too, that while much of the administrative concern for increased participation is based on desires for efficiency, better information flow, greater responsiveness to citizen interests, and the like, the processes of participation are not necessarily politically neutral. They can and do challenge preconceptions and previously accepted ways of doing things. They can and do bring program goals and objectives into question. They can and do affect power relationships and may introduce perturbations into otherwise stable societal systems and situations.

Bureaucratic support for increased participation may in part be motivated by a desire to increase program and agency support—what sociologists have designated "legitimation." "Efficiency and participation do not necessarily converge" (Miller and Rein, 1969). Nor does increased participation mean a reduction in conflict and social tension. Public preferences rarely reflect consensus for in most situations, even with complete participation, there will be "winners" and "losers." Participation may clarify and alter social issues, and it may contribute to a better understanding of differences, but it rarely serves as a means for conflict resolution; in most cases it will make the task of the planner and administrator more difficult.

In terms of administrative decision-making, one of the difficult problems associated with public participation is what to do with citizen or public inputs. To begin with, even when all of the groups and individuals who should participate have been involved, it will be a rare situation in which any kind of consensus will prevail. Thus the public servant is confronted with the need to weigh and choose from among the viewpoints presented. These he must balance against his professional and technical judgments and responsibilities. In particular, in most instances, he alone can speak for the future, since to do so responsibly requires high levels of intellectual input and rigorous analysis. Very often, though, he alone can recognize indirect effects and assess secondary and tertiary consequences.

The balance of the chapter is devoted to evaluating public participation and the administrative process as related specifically to the planning, implementation, and management of water resources development projects and to environmental improvement.

STAGES OF DECISION-MAKING AND PARTICIPATION

Public participation and citizen involvement, if it is a controlled part of the administrative process, will vary over time along the total decision-making continuum.

To begin with, program formulation and the definition of agency missions is primarily a function of the political system, and citizen involvement will have to occur in accordance with the participatory procedures of that system. With respect to water resources development activities, the political system must identify needs for development and for the products of development, such as flood control, more food, more electrical energy, navigation improvement, and water supply. At times, major disturbances such as might result from a flood or other natural catastrophe will provide the stimulus for action. And the definition of agency missions may be preceded by a wide variety of organized and unorganized participatory activities. In highly volatile situations, demonstrations and protests may be a part of this initial stage in decision-making. Once agency missions have been set in general terms, the agencies themselves become involved in developing and implementing their programs, drawing on their employees and support groups as need and opportunity suggests. Here a variety of sociological bureaucratic influences may become apparent, and the limitations of specialized professional training and biases evident. It is at this stage too that a variety of participatory techniques may prove useful.

A first stage in the development of public projects (when general authority has been provided) might be designated the reconnaissance stage. Here an opportunity should be provided for large public inputs as the responsible agencies explore both technical and popular preference alternatives. The goal of participation at this stage is to secure the best planning information so that from such reconnaissance activities the agency may move to the preliminary planning stage.

Next, as goals and objectives begin to be narrowed, alternative schemes may be considered and alternative consequences and solutions evaluated. It is at this point that research studies on environmental impacts would best be undertaken, and an assessment of alternative solutions together with alternative costs and benefits be considered.

At this preliminary planning stage, large public inputs would also seem to be desirable. But now the difficult question arises of identifying and weighing those who have an interest in particular projects or in a set of project alternatives. In many cases, if intelligent citizen contributions are to be secured, they must be preceded by citizen education on goals, objectives, problems, alternative solutions, costs and benefits and their distribution—without which alternative proposals may not be understood. Unless deliberate steps are taken to overcome this difficulty, the participants may consist primarily of those who expect to benefit from project proposals, with no one speaking for those who will bear the costs and negative consequences. Again the fact of the silent majority must be noted, for it is to this majority that professional civil servants must speak.

After the preliminary planning stage has been completed, including in this stage extensive coordination with other agencies and consultation with a variety of public and private groups, a tentative *decision to proceed* may be made. It is assumed, of course, that financing is available to undertake whatever has been decided upon. Once the tentative decision to proceed has been made, more formal hearing procedures would seem to be appropriate, both as a kind of safety valve and as a way of identifying those who may not be happy with a particular proposal, seeking to determine whether their unhappiness is due to value conflicts, ignorance, or whatever.

Once the decision to proceed with a project has been made, detailed design analyses can begin. Not infrequently, these detailed studies may reveal the need for further exploration of alternatives for citizen participation and will certainly also suggest the needs for continuing educational programs. The next stage, then, might be designated the construction period, which might, of course, extend over a very long time, particularly if a project with many components is involved. Presumably while construction is going on, continuing education, assisting in adjusting to project impacts and opportunities, would also move ahead, with public participation being structured to deal with the details of project impacts and consequences. One possibility at this stage is to utilize the work force as a communication channel with the region to be effected by the project, particularly if that work force has been locally recruited.

Finally, the operational stage is reached. Depending on the nature of the project, a variety of participatory activities might be planned, focusing on adjustments to the impact of the project as well as on the effective use of the benefits that flow from the project and the mitigation of adverse effects.

LEVELS OF PARTICIPATION

It is clear that public participation can be classified both according to *geographic* and according to *functional* levels. Essentially, geographic would be the following: (1) the family, (2) the neighborhood, (3) the community, (4) the village, (5) the region, and (6) the state or nation. While the first three of these are more sociological and less geographic, they nevertheless do have strong spatial relationships, whereas the latter three are dominantly spatial in orientation.

In most societies, participation on a spatial basis has been well accepted. It should be noted, however, that as the area involved increases in size, the diversity of problems and of interests tends to increase and the possibility of gaining an areal consensus diminishes. For this reason, some theorists have stressed the most local organization as the basis for participation, often ignoring the need for coordination among small geographic entities, and the very difficult problems of externalities and spillover effects from one community to another. One of the consequences of modern transportation and industrialization is that the spatial basis for organizing human activity has become larger and larger, making meaningful public participation difficult, if not impossible, except in the most formal sense.

Functional participation does not avoid the problems of coordination, but it places less emphasis on geographic entities and uses program similarities as a basis for organizing what in effect are group activities. In most societies, participation in functional organizations is pluralistic, that is, individuals may be involved in more than one functional organization. A partial list of such organizations would include: (1) political parties and political meetings, (2) work-skill related organizations such as labor unions and professional societies, (3) general membership organizations that can have a wide variety of purposes and programs, (4) economic groups, including cooperativies, consumer groups, and business groups, (5) social groups of which there can be very many, including religious organizations, and (6) groups organized on an age and sex basis.

The more fluid a society, the more shifting will be its group structure. There is some research indicating that *ad hoc* (as contrasted with permanent) groups have relatively short life spans, and there is evidence to suggest that as group activity evolves, the group itself develops a kind of bureaucracy that places great emphasis upon convincing the members as to the importance of continuing group activities and upon issue-oriented positions on policy questions.

PERSPECTIVES

How one regards public participation and citizen involvement depends to a great extent on one's point of view or perspective, and this in turn is determined to a large extent by the role one fills in society. Clearly, political decision-makers will have one view of public participation, at times utilizing and manipulating citizen activities and at other times seeking to restrain or direct them. One is reminded of the story about the French politician who gazed out of the window to see a mob pass by and exclaimed, "Those are my people, I am their leader, I must follow them."

Government agencies (*i.e.*, the bureaucracy) will regard public participation in a different perspective. Self-preservation, an important bureaucratic value, may result in regarding participation as a way of gaining legitimacy and public support. To the planners, who are members of the bureaucracy, public participation may be important for information purposes. Depending on how closely the planning process and program objectives are directed towards meeting the needs of the people, securing positive inputs from the public can be very important.

To the member of the public, participation may be important for personal ego reasons or to seek to frustrate plans and proposals regarded as unsound or undesirable. At this point, basic freedoms of speech, press, and petition come into play as individuals seek to persuade decision-makers as to the rightness of particular actions or causes.

DEFINITION OF THE PUBLIC

Much of the discussion of citizen participation and public involvement in water resources development activities moves forward without facing up to the questions of "Who is the public?" and "What public should be involved?" Since water in many of its aspects is so strongly related to topographic features, it is easy to assume that the appropriate public is the population living in a given watershed or river basin. At least two problems are involved in this simplistic view. The first is that even within a very small watershed, there is no reason to assume that consensus (in its true meaning of full agreement) is likely to exist. There will be differing interests, differing attitudes, differing perceptions, and differing values and goals. It is important to be reminded of the conclusion:

> In all societies, and under all forms of government, the few govern the many.... Because the symbols and concepts of American politics are drawn from democratic political thought, we seldom confront the elemental fact that a few citizens are always called upon to govern the remainder.
> It is somehow undemocratic to think of elites and masses and to differentiate between them ... [yet] elite-mass interaction is the very heart of the governing process (Zeigler and Dye, 1969).

The point simply is that in all social organizations, even in the family, leader-follower relationships are universal, and while who is the leader and who is the follower need not be a permanent relationship but may depend on the issues involved and on time considerations, nevertheless, the fact of these relationships in all human organizations cannot be denied.

A second characteristic or problem is that of boundary determinations in relation to interests in and consequences of water development decisions. To be sure, for example, people living in the watershed have an interest in what may happen to the water in that watershed. But ground water, for example, does not necessarily follow surface water flow. Actions in an adjoining watershed may have spillover or externality effects on ground water flow.

An American governmental administrator, in discussing man-induced precipitation, stated that the man on whose land such precipitation falls has a right to be involved in the decision as to whether rainmaking techniques should be applied. It is difficult to quarrel with such a comment, but clearly it is not *only* the man on whose land the man-induced precipitation falls who has an interest in the situation. All those in the watershed where such induced precipitation will influence flow have an interest, and if the induced precipitation is designed to reduce drought or to increase crop production, many need to be involved, including those concerned in the marketing and ultimately in the consumption of the crops. And clearly participation cannot be limited to those who volunteer. Responsible professionals must assume the task of identifying interests that should participate.

Theories and practices of representative government have for centuries been so closely tied to geographic patterns of representation that there is an understandable tendency to assume that this is the only way to identify constituent interests. The small but significant literature on functional or economic representation (that of the Guild Socialists in Britain and the Syndicalists in France) points to the limitation of the geographic approach. As suggested above, the intimate relationship of water flow patterns to geography tends to reinforce a reliance upon geographic definitions of interests and, hence, of public involvement and participation. But a careful review of modern water development systems also suggests some of the limitations involved in simple geographic organizational patterns. In terms of water supply, for example, trans-basin diversions are common, and most urban residents are only vaguely aware of the watersheds from which they draw their water supplies or from which their food may come. This is particularly true of urban centers on the seacoast where residents do not identify with specific watersheds.

Similarly, hydroelectric energy produced at water development projects is distributed without regard to the river basins concentrating the water so that it can be used to generate power. Irrigation water also may be diverted from one watershed to another depending in this case on the availability of irrigable lands rather than on any special relationships to designated watersheds. Wastewater management, both of sanitary wastes and storm waters, is probably somewhat more closely related to natural physiographic features of particular watersheds since gravity flow has been an important practical consideration. Until quite recently, the tendency throughout most of the world has been to pass pollution consequences to downstream areas. But as a part of the environmental movement such spillover or externality effects have begun to attract engineering, economic, and legal attention. The very nature of pollution problems, however, points to the difficult questions of how to identify the constituent public. Is it those who pollute a stream or those who are affected by pollution? And how are the often conflicting views to be reconciled?

Perhaps the most directly watershed-oriented aspect of water development is flood control, since floods by definition are watershed phenomena. But even here the consequences of floods are more widespread than simply the area that might be inundated. Where prime agricultural lands are flooded, where industrial plants are put out of commission, or where transportation routes are disrupted the consequences of flooding and hence the interests in the flood problem may often transcend simple watershed boundaries.

And finally in our complex and interconnected society, most public actions involve a "taxpayer" interest that is not simply the issue of tax rates and burdens involved in water development, but the effects on the national economy of such development, as well as spending priorities.

To illustrate, some years ago an eminent American economist, in criticizing some U. S. irrigation programs, pointed out that per acre investments of a far lower magnitude in the humid northeastern and north-central United States would result in far larger returns than proposed expenditures for irrigation in the semiarid western regions. Thus he posed the critical issues of regional priorities. The priority issue is important in all countries, but in countries with limited capital resources the problem is particularly acute. And yet how should participation be structured in these situations of competing priorities? How should different views be weighted?

The difficulties of identifying the concerned public (or the appropriate public for participation and involvement) is perhaps suggested by a significant experiment in this field conducted by the U. S. Army Corps of Engineers in connection with the formation of a development program for the Susquehanna River Basin (Havlick, 1970; Borton *et al.*, 1970).

The approach used by the Corps was unique in several ways. First, instead of simply developing a single plan for the river basin, the Corps formulated three alternative plans, each one resting on different development assumptions and goals. The next step in its approach was to learn the preferences of Susquehanna Basin residents with respect to the three alternative plans. It was immediately clear, of course, that ordinary opinion polling techniques would not have been appropriate since preferences with respect to the plans required an understanding of them. To achieve better public understanding, the Corps undertook an intensive program of informing the residents with respect to the three plans. But for reasons of time and cost, formal research on citizen preferences was limited initially to five Pennsylvania counties (and subsequently extended to several additional counties in New York State).

A basic assumption of these investigations was that those who happened to live in the watershed were the people with a major concern. But this is a dubious assumption. To illustrate: water supply from the Susquehanna is of major importance to the one million people living in the Baltimore area, which is not in the Basin; the recreation potential of the Basin is probably of greater importance to urbanites living just outside the Basin in cities like Buffalo, Pittsburgh, Washington, Baltimore, Philadelphia, and New York City. And as suggested above, the entire nation has a vital stake in the economic development of the Susquehanna Basin, both from the viewpoint of taxpaying and in terms of the interest in establishing a sound economy in the region.

THE MANY PUBLICS

The literature on public opinion and governmental processes has for at least fifty years stressed the idea that there is rarely *one* public, but rather *many publics*. In this view, society is composed of a web of formal and informal groupings. Clearly, this pluralistic view of societal organization complicates problems of involvement and participation. To make the situation even more complex, it has been recognized that many individuals are members of many groups, and that the intensity of commitment to the viewpoints and interests of any particular group will vary considerably among its members, being a function of time and the particular issues on the current action agenda.

The relationship of the individual to the group is further complicated by questions of levels of knowledge and information. And perhaps the most important limitation is that of the span of attention of all citizens. No matter how much one might emphasize that a citizen *should* be interested in and involved with particular public policy and social policy issues, the sheer number of these issues requires him to make choices and set priorities, so that at any one time an individual can only give attention to relatively few public issues. What determines his selection at any one time undoubtedly is based on a very wide range of interests and perceptions on his part. There is, in short, a silent majority on many issues, and this fact certainly creates both conceptual and practical difficulties in the design of involvement and participation systems.

"AFFECTED" AND "INTERESTED" CITIZENS

One of the most important distinctions frequently not included in discussions of citizen involvement and participation is the distinction between *affected* parties and *interested* parties. Basically, the affected party has no alternatives. For example, his land might lie at the bottom of the proposed reservoir. He has no real alternative but to move. Depending on the size of the project, there are many persons who are affected by it both *directly* and *indirectly* but who have little or no choice with respect to how the project will change their way of life. Participation may give them a veto. But more often it simply provides a way by which they find out what will happen.

Interested parties, on the other hand, include those who look to the project for employment or who expect to sell equipment or raw materials (such as pumps or cement) for a project, as well as the obvious *direct* beneficiaries. Others interested may be those who expect an increase in productivity in the area and in the Gross National Product from a particular project.

Most difficult to deal with is that class of persons who may be benefited by a particular project but who would not be directly injured by the failure to complete the project. Perhaps typical of the latter is the person who uses a project reservoir for boating. Clearly this provides leisure-time recreation. But if the leisure time is available to him in any case, that individual would use it in some other way, and it is therefore difficult to say whether he gains or loses by virtue of a particular reservoir project. Yet in many areas of the United States, beneficiaries in this category may be particularly demonstrative. How should their interests be weighted?

A difficult problem in citizen involvement and participation concerns the presentation of numerous alternatives for discussion and consideration including, as a matter of logic, the alternative of doing nothing. This is difficult because most of the agencies and bureaucracies concerned with water resources development (or any other kind of development) are mission-oriented. Their existence is determined by an assumed need for projects of a certain kind, and their success is measured by the number of projects constructed. This characterization applies, for example, to the U. S. Army Corps of Engineers and to the U. S. Bureau of Reclamation, two of the major water resources development agencies in the United States. It probably applies with equal validity to similar organizations in other nations and cultures.

It is because of such mission-orientation that an approach involving the decision to do nothing may be regarded with hostility and may be viewed as politically untenable. When an agency is created to build river structures to control floods, it is difficult for such an agency to contemplate nonengineering solutions to flood problems. It took almost one hundred years for the U. S. Army Corps of Engineers to accept the idea that in some situations nonengineering solutions might be preferred to engineering solutions. Yet the broader the scope of systems analysis, the more logical it is to ask difficult questions of this sort. Certainly involving citizens can result in these "embarrassing"-type questions being raised with some frequency. At the same time, it may be difficult to involve people in "doing nothing."

WHO SPEAKS FOR THE FUTURE?

Water development projects almost by definition involve substantial capital expenditures and have very long-term effects. In many cases, water development projects will remain for centuries. It has been estimated, for example, that Norris Dam in the Tennessee Valley Authority system will have a useful life of at least 800 years *i.e.*, it is estimated that it will take 800 years before the dead storage in the reservoir will be filled with silt). Few Americans, only now contemplating the 200th anniversary of the Republic, can think in terms of 800-year time spans. To a certain extent, the time question may be dismissed simply as a matter of "sunk costs" to use an accounting term. At the same time, the environmental concerns of the recent past have rested on a belief that many development decisions have been unsound just because they did not consider long-term consequences. And while it must be admitted that no one possesses a very clear crystal ball, the case has been well stated for a greater consideration of longer range effects and impacts.

But this poses a very real dilemma when related to questions of public participation. There is reason to believe, for example, that most members of the public (all of us, in effect) tend to discount the future and may even be unable to look very far ahead. Referenda and plebiscites might be decided against the future. Who then can speak for those yet unborn? How do planners take into account the interests of those who obviously cannot be assembled in a citizens' meeting? Here again the professional responsibility of the planner is part of the answer. Another part is political and requires farsighted political leadership. Important to decision-making for the long-range future is the fact that large public works projects tend to illustrate the self-fulfilling prophecy phenomenon. Once a project has been completed, it is difficult, if not impossible, to reverse the course of events and to return to a previous condition. And at that point, the questions of alternatives become irrelevant. This lends weight to the arguments of environmentalists that irreversible decisions should only be made after most thorough investigation, and doubts should be resolved in favor of the environment, in favor of the future, in favor of the people.

REFERENCES

Borton, T. E., K. P. Warner, and J. W. Wenrick. *The Susquehanna Communication Participation Study* (Springfield, Virginia: Clearinghouse for Federal Scientific and Technical Information, 1970).

Havlick, S. W. "The Construction of Trust," *Water Spectrum*, 1, (2), 13 (1969–1970).

Miller, S. M., and M. Rein. "Participation, Poverty, and Administration," *Public Admin. Rev.*, 29 (1), 15 (1969).

Zeigler, H., and T. R. Dye. "Editor's Note," *Amer. Behavioral Scientist* 13 (2), 167 (1969).

3. Identification of Publics in Water Resources Planning

Gene E. Willeke

THE NATURE OF PUBLIC PARTICIPATION IN PLANNING

Direct participation by the public has come to be a key part of water resources planning in recent years. It was incorporated originally to increase public understanding of projects and to speed up the implementation process. Public demands for such involvement had become so strong that projects and programs were either being slowed down, halted, or subjected to intense adverse publicity.

Beginning in the late 1960s, a series of federal laws required public participation in the planning of federal water resource projects and programs, including projects that received federal funding or required federal licensing. The three most important federal laws are the National Environmental Policy Act of 1969, the 1970 Rivers and Harbors Act, and the 1972 Amendments to the Water Pollution Control Act.

As public participation in planning of water projects became more common, the objectives were modified. In addition to the early objective of speeding up and easing the implementation process, some planners came to feel the plans were actually better because of public participation. Conflicts among different groups were brought into the open and sometimes resolved during the planning process, rather than being left to a political decision or a difficult planning agency staff decision. More and better information was used and impacts were assessed better.

The incidence of costs and benefits on societal groups could be more equitable.

Still later, it became evident that public participation enhanced the prospects of potential beneficiaries actually receiving the benefits intended for them by the planners. With sufficient lead time, local residents could get a higher percentage of construction jobs because they were prepared to take them. The often disruptive effects of construction could be planned for and mitigated. When other, related programs were necessary to make a water project work at something approaching its optimum, the public could play a role in ensuring that those other programs did, in fact, take place in a timely manner.

The conceptual base for public participation was also expanded and refined. In the early public participation efforts, there was a strong emphasis on public information and education. The public was generally thought of as being a unitary *mass*. Engineers stressed *measurement* of public desires so that the planners could meet those desires. There was heavy stress on *input* from the public.

From direct field experience, most planners learned that the public was not a unitary mass. At about the same time, academics were borrowing the concepts of audience segments from communication researchers and market segments from market researchers. These two concepts refer to identifiable but not necessarily socially connected groups that have similar behavior patterns relative to communication in the first case and a marketable product in the second. With few exceptions, both audience and market segments were defined in terms of demographic and geographic characteristics.

The field experience of planners and the conceptual contributions of academics happily coincide. The two groups now talk of segments of the public or, simply, publics. Having accepted the concept, the planner is faced with the task of locating those publics. The researcher, in turn, is asked to provide methods of locating, identifying, and/or describing publics. A subsequent step is to find ways of communicating with each public. If a communicator wishes to get a particular message across to some audience segment, he must choose the right channel or channels of communication and he must code the message in appropriate symbols. If a *person* is to do the communicating, the right person must be selected.

Here are two probably extreme examples. One would likely

not choose a Cambridge don to lecture on stock cars over a classical music radio station in the evening if one wished to promote a stock car race in Georgia. Likewise, one would not have Lawrence Welk read a major address by the president of the New York Stock Exchange on the state of the stock market, intended to reach stock brokers, over a major television channel at 2:00 p.m. on a weekday. In both cases, the communicator, the channel, the timing and the symbol coding are likely to be very inappropriate.

In the late 1960s two more concepts were incorporated, largely by academics, into the theory of public participation. The first was the concept of planning as a social process. It followed some definable stages, was subject to the rules of group interaction behavior, and was dependent on the mix of participants. The second was the concept of two-way communication.

The importance of conceiving planning as a social process is that there may need to be a somewhat different set of participants in each stage, and that the mode of participant interaction is likely to influence the outcome of the process. In addition, if the mix of participants does indeed make a difference, we need to be concerned about getting an optimal mix of participants.

The concept of two-way communication means essentially that the two parties to a communication should both communicate with each other. Two-way communication is ordinarily more effective in accurately conveying a message and is ordinarily more persuasive than is one-way communication. In order to have two-way communication, it is almost always necessary to identify the second party, so that the communication may be carried out. In one-way communication, it is possible to disseminate a message on some channel without regard to the receivers. These concepts underscore the need to identify publics as a means of achieving better public participation in the planning process.

THEORETICAL CONSIDERATIONS IN IDENTIFYING PUBLICS

This general background on public participation in planning provides the basis for considering the theoretical aspects of identifying publics. The discussion examines the purposes of identifying publics, components of the identification process, and the fundamental concepts that guide the identification process.

Purpose

The principal reason for identifying publics is so that they may, if they wish, be involved in the planning process. Clearly, not all of the publics want to be involved in a given water resources planning venture, even if they are affected by the plans. The reasons for nonparticipation are many. Whether or not certain segments of the public wish to be involved in planning should not negate the need for a thorough effort to identify each relevant segment of the public.

A second reason for identifying publics is to be aware of, and account for, those segments of the public that are affected but do not choose to be involved in planning. The planner must more explicitly account for those interests not having a spokesperson or advocate than for those segments that can and do choose to speak for themselves.

Many planners consider the silent public as the really important segment. Those holding such views look upon organized, vocal groups as minorities who don't speak for many people and whose views, therefore, should be given little consideration. This view is erroneous for two reasons. First, those who are vocal and active have usually adopted such a role because they are acutely affected by a proposed section. Second, as Ragan (1974) points out, such groups can be effective surrogates for the general public. When actions have low level and/or invisible impacts on a population segment, a surrogate may be the only reasonable course of action because individual citizens cannot individually bear the costs of full participation. An organized surrogate group can, on the other hand, do the necessary research, present the case to the responsible decision-makers, and muster the necessary political support. This is analogous to the classic consumer problem in which no individual is hurt very much by a questionable trade practice but the aggregate effect is enormous.

Components of Identification

As there are many publics, there are many ways of defining and describing those publics. Identification methods vary in the degree of specificity from very broad amorphous categories to discrete units. Identification should be brief enough to be manageable and complete enough to be useful.

Location

One part of public segment identification in water resource planning and management is locating the segment. Some segments have a definite geographic location, such as a town, those living in a flood plain, those living below a dam, those living on either side of a river, those living around a lake, or those inside the project boundaries.

Other public segments do not have a specific geographic location. They derive their significance to planning from some characteristic other than locale. For those segments, a part of the identification process is to explicitly recognize the lack of a geographical characteristic and concentrate on the characteristics that do relate to the planning process.

Interests

A segment of the public identified as having some relevance to water resource planning would ordinarily have some particular interest in the planning process or the outcome. This interest might be economic benefit or loss, environmental protection, concern about governmental process, historical or archeological values, or attachment to property.

To some extent, the interest of an identified segment would be known to the planner. However, for completeness and accuracy, an explicit statement of interest should be secured from the segment, if possible. This statement need not be complete at the early stage of identification, but should be complete and accurate before concluding the identification.

This step in identification has ultimate importance *to the segment itself* because the segment has been assisted in clarifying its role. It is important *to the planner* because he knows why a segment is being involved and what some of the issues are. It is important *to the other participants* because they can know the relationship of each segment to the planning process and because segments with common interests can work together. Also, conflicting interests may be more easily determined at an early stage when there is more opportunity to solve conflicts.

Social Characteristics

In order to involve effectively some segment of the public in the planning process, it is desirable to know something of the social characteristics of the segment. There is a strong tendency to say *necessary* rather than *desirable*, but unless there are major cultural differences among segments and planners, generalized approaches to involvement may be used that do not require a high degree of specific knowledge.

Since a public segment may or may not be a social group, one of the first social characteristics to be determined is whether a *social group* exists. Where the segment does comprise a social group, the group goals, history, boundaries, reasons for existence, size, structure, mode of organization and operation, and communication behavior patterns may be determined.

Demographic Characteristics

Such things as age, sex, race, education, income, and occupation are commonly referred to as demographic characteristics. While the amount of information they convey about segments of the public is obviously limited, much of water resources planning is oriented toward use of highly aggregated demographic data as primary components of project or program development.

Demographic description is easiest when a public segment can be associated with some geographic territory because the best sources of demographic data are organized in that manner. Survey research is the most common technique for determining demographic characteristics of segments with other than geographic bases.

As in the case of audience and market segments, some public segments are defined almost entirely in terms of demographic characteristics. Such groups as the elderly, the young, low, high, or middle income, racial/ethnic groups, and occupation groups are all examples of public segments defined in terms of demographic characteristics. Demographic characteristics often are used as proxies or surrogates for other cultural traits. Thus, low income people in a small city may mostly reside in a particular territory, belong to certain voluntary associations such as churches and community groups, and share common problems. Communication behavior may be quite similar among most members of a segment defined in demographic terms. (Indeed, marketers of consumer products stake much of their advertising budget on the belief that this is the case.)

Fundamental Concepts

In sifting out the theoretical concepts useful in formulating approaches to identifying publics, it seems most valuable to work with simple concepts. The concepts presented here seem to be the most useful with regard to identification of publics.

Groups

This concept begins with the basic assumption that society is, with some exceptions, organized into groups. Thus, most of the basic work in identifying publics is to locate those preexisting identifiable groups. Most individuals are members of more than one group. This allows a person to express more fully the different aspects of his own personality and to work on different goals simultaneously. On the one hand, this would seem to complicate the task of identifying publics in a comprehensive manner. On the other hand, there is the distinct advantage that if some group is not identified, the individuals in the group may have access to the planning process through another identified group.

A group may be thought of as being bounded by group goals. Persons who do not share those goals either do not enter the group, leave the group, or have weak ties to the group. Thus, it is possible to reach effectively individual members of the groups by having direct contact with only a small percentage of the population. Some consider the leader of the group generally to exemplify the goals of the group. This is, of course, not always true, but is true often enough to make it a good working rule-of-thumb. There should be provisions in the planning process to ascertain whether the leader does or does not adequately represent the group.

Rules and Roles

In dealing with the identification of publics, it is useful to add some discussion of rules and roles. Each group operates by some set of formal and informal rules. Since public participation in planning entails interaction between the planners (presumed not to be part of the group) and the group, it would be desirable for the respective parties to have some knowledge of the rules under which each is operating.

The planner's choice of techniques should be influenced by this information so that he can approach them in the best way. The planner can routinely set forth some of the rules under which he operates. He can describe the planning process and then promulgate it to each of the groups and individuals to be involved in the planning process.

The more formidable task would be obtaining and recording the rules under which each of the publics operates. From a theoretical standpoint, it is sufficient to say that the interaction characteristics of each public should be known. This may be approximated by knowing the general interaction characteristics or the rules under which most groups within a given society function. If the rules are found not to apply in a given situation, the necessary information about that public may be sought.

A simple example of how groups adopt a general set of rules is the widespread adherence to some form of parliamentary procedure. It is also customary for voluntary associations to accomplish much of their work through the use of committees and the elected officers of the group. Thus, if the planner interacts with the committees and elected officers, he usually has adequately contacted that group. When relationships with a group seem to be unsatisfactory, it may be because such interaction is not sufficient for any number of reasons. Others in the group may need to be directly contacted, perhaps by a presentation to the entire group.

In addition to the rules of conduct for a public, the roles of groups should be considered. For example, some groups will not intervene in political matters. Others choose to lobby. Some groups are entirely educational, some social, and others promotional. The importance of this concept is that the planner may need to relate to the group in accordance with the role the group chooses rather than the role the planner would like to see the group adopt.

The League of Women Voters, for example, is a study and issue group. It has built its reputation on thoroughness and accuracy. Its positions (consensus) are taken with great deliberation, according to a prescribed procedure. This process is slow. Few issues can be expected to reach the stage of consensus in less than a year. If the planner wants to have an official position from a group like the League, he cannot expect it quickly (unless the position has previously been taken) and may not get it at all. Conversely, a group that relies heavily on Executive Committee action may be able to reach a group position in a matter of hours, days, or weeks.

Generalizability

The process of identifying publics will not yield a complete, comprehensive list of relevant publics. Moreover, even if the list *were* complete, there would be no reliable way to weight the concerns of each identified group or public segment in such a way that a composite assessment of preferences would be possible.

Sample survey work, it might be argued, provides precisely such a tool. Such an argument is fallacious. While a properly selected and executed probability sample would indeed be representative of the general population, it is so only for the purpose of getting answers to questions for which the respondents are able to formulate an adequate answer. The general public is ordinarily able to supply adequate answers to very general questions, questions of facts about personal traits and practices, and specific, detailed questions about which there has been a high level of public discussion and/or information on which opinions might be based. For detailed questions on which there has not been a high level of public discussion and information, responses to a sample survey may be of little value.

This discussion is not an indictment of survey research. The survey is admirably suited for use in water resources planning. Whenever information of the three types cited above is needed, there is probably no better method. However, for other types of information its usefulness is very limited.

If we cannot get a good composite assessment of public preferences either from identifying publics and interacting with them or from sample surveys, what then do we get from public groups that is useful to a planner?

In regard to issues and concerns, public involvement increases the *range* and *richness* of issues and concerns brought to salience in the planning process. If a planner doesn't *know* what the issues are, he probably won't *deal* with them. A number of issues have been brought to the attention of water resources planners in such areas as water quality, urban erosion, use of free-flowing streams for recreation, public access to reservoirs built under the P.L. 566 program of the Soil Conservation Service, public access to and use of shorelines in the Great Lakes and the ocean fronts, and water utility pricing policies.

Consideration of these types of issues is becoming almost routine in water resource planning. Within a few years, it probably will be routine. As more publics are identified and their concerns probed, the range of issues will increase further; the quality of planning should increase accordingly.

In addition to expanding the *range* of issues and concerns, one can also increase the *richness* of content in an issue. In other words, more facets of an issue become known. A broad, mushy concept such as land use planning becomes explicated and refined into more useful categories. The richness comes in part from simply talking with more groups. It also comes from the promotion of interaction among identified groups. As their respective concerns become known, those with interest in similar issues (though they may be on opposite sides of the issue) can be brought together for discussion of the issues.

One effect of bringing more richness to public works planning is likely to be spillover into other areas of public policy. Public works themselves are blunt, crude instruments and cannot be expected to cope with the myriad of public concerns that might be raised during the course of public works planning.

THE PRACTICE OF IDENTIFYING PUBLICS

The practice of identifying publics builds on the theoretical base described above, but is modified somewhat by limitations of staff, budget, information, and personality characteristics of participants on all sides. The approaches may generally be classed as self-identification (with and without staff intervention), third party identification, and staff identification. In general, a mix of all three approaches, though not necessarily each technique, would be appropriate to any given public participation program.

Self-Indentification

There has always been some opportunity for self-identification either of groups or individuals, in water resources planning. Laws at all levels of government have usually contained provisions allowing for petition, appeal, public hearing, election, suit, protest, and publicity. While these vary considerably and some laws do not allow for even these means of citizen access, there is at least some means by which a citizen or group may enter the planning process. Each of these methods is still a legitimate avenue that need not and should not be abridged.

Legal Actions

The laws governing citizen-initiated access mechanisms are so variable from place to place that citizens may be unaware of what must be done to intervene in governmental action. This, of course, applies primarily to such mechanisms as petition, appeal, public hearing, election, and suit. For example, a Vermont statute provides that adoption of rules for municipal shoreland zoning be considered at public hearing on a petition of ten freemen (Vermont, 1971). To use such a statutory provision a citizen needs to know what a freeman is, the form of the required petition, and what kind of action might be taken as a result of public hearing.

Elections have not often been used as a means of identifying publics or even as a means of public participation in planning. There is a substantial precedent, however, in the Project Area Committees used in urban renewal programs where there is participation by the U. S. Department of Housing and Urban Development (National Urban League, 1973).

Protest and Publicity.

Protest and publicity are theoretically available to anyone with the inclination and resources to engage in such activities. Their effectiveness derives not from any legal power, but from exposing the general public to activities and issues considered important by the exposers. From a practical standpoint, there are numerous societal sanctions available to restrict protest and publicity. Economic threats, such as loss of job or promotion may be used, directly or indirectly to sanction such activities. Social snubs and so forth are also used.

There are two possible roles for the planner in enhancing the usefulness of these methods of self-identification. He may publicize the legal requirements for petition, appeal, public hearing, election, and suit. He may also seek to reduce the incidence of sanctions imposed on those who use protest and publicity. Often, the planner has little control over such sanctions. However, if he expresses an openness and receptiveness to dealing with the protest and publicity, he may set a tone of softness that reduces the imposition of sanctions.

Correspondence

Citizens also identify themselves by corresponding, by letter or telephone, with the planning agency or a related agency and by appearing at public meetings dealing with water resources planning. The usefulness of such means can be enhanced with little effort and cost. At public meetings, identification cards with space for supplying information useful in categorizing and correctly corresponding with the person or group can be used. In newsletters and general circulation newspapers, advertisements may be taken with the same kind of information requested. A toll-free telephone number may be established for those who would prefer to communicate by telephone. Radio and television announcements may be used to publicize the willingness and desire on the part of the planner to have people identify themselves.

In recent years, radio and television programs operating in a two-way communication mode have been adopted. Listeners may telephone directly to the station and talk on the air, with a moderator or panelist. While not ordinarily used for this purpose, this format could be adapted to identify interested parties, especially if the radio or television program were supplemented with a phone bank. This approach has been used in fund-raising drives and religious programs for essentially the same purpose.

An important ingredient in facilitating self-identification approaches is the use of multiple channels of communication to and from the public so that maximum opportunity for self-identification is afforded, and so that the publics have a number of ways to self-identify themselves with little cost and effort.

Third Party Identification

Third party identification is much like self-identification except that it is done by a third party. The Seattle District of the U. S. Army Corps of Engineers uses Citizen Committees for this purpose (Ragan, 1974a). One purpose of citizen committees is to identify those groups and individuals who should be involved in planning or who are affected by proposed plan alternatives. This principle can, of course, be extended further. Any person who is aware of the planning effort and knows of some other individual or group that should be involved may identify that person or group to the planner.

Staff Identification

The planner plays the role of facilitator in both the self-identification and third party identification approaches. Staff time requirements and budget requirements are generally low. However, in the initial stages of establishing a mailing list and processing requests to be involved in the planning process, there may be a substantial amount of time and money involved. During the early stages of involvement there frequently are requests for information about what is happening. Mailing reports and other material to individuals, answering questions on the telephone, and accepting speaking requests are all time-consuming. Sufficient money and other resources must be budgeted for the task.

In staff identification, nearly all the work involved in identifying publics is done by planning staff. Though there may be contact with other persons and groups to perform the function, the other persons and groups bear little of the responsibility. The principal techniques and approaches to staff identification are described below, with some appraisal of their effectiveness and appropriateness in water resources planning.

Analysis of Associations

Analysis of associations is a process of consulting available lists of organized groups and picking out those that appear to the planner to have possible interest in being involved. The groups then are contacted and queried about their interest.

Lists of associations are usually available in any community, though the lists are almost always incomplete. The Yellow Pages of the telephone directory, the Chamber of Commerce, newspaper lists, city and county directories are all ready sources. In addition to these lists, which are free and available to anyone, there are lists available on a national and state basis, sorted by ZIP code, and categorized by type. The cost for these lists usually is quite low. Small lists are somewhat more expensive. Sociology and political science departments at local colleges and universities often maintain lists of organizations in a particular area.

Analysis of associations is always an appropriate method of beginning to identify publics. It is fast, inexpensive, and prompts thought about possible interested and affected groups. Moreover, it provides a guide to the general social organization of the area. It is also, however, approximate and incomplete.

Geographic Analysis

Geographic analysis involves study of maps and photographs to determine areas that should be singled out for special attention in the planning process. As mentioned earlier, flood plain dwellers, those downstream from a dam or sewage treatment plant, and those displaced by a reservoir are obvious groups to be identified from map studies.

Other groups that may be identified from geographic analysis are those who live in a certain relationship to the proposed projects or programs. Ordinarily, those closest to a project have the most interest, though this is not always the case. Geographic territories such as market and economic areas have been established for the entire United States, especially by demographers. Social area analysis has been done in many urban areas and, to some extent, for states and multi-state regions.

Demographic Analysis

Demographic analysis may be used alone or in combination with geographic analysis. When it is used alone, a public is defined as that group of persons having a given set of demographic characteristics. When used in combination with geographic analysis, one might look for those territories containing unusually high percentages of elderly, nonwhite, middle income, or any other demographic characteristics of interest.

When demographic analysis is used alone, its value is primarily as a tool to be used on one-way, mass media communication. Thus, certain channels of communication might be selected to reach a particular audience.

The more useful application of demographic analysis is in combination with geographic analysis. This coincides with the usual approach in water resources, in which subareas are defined and a project or program is analyzed in terms of the effects on groups of persons with given demographic characteristics who reside within those areas.

The U. S. Census is the primary source of information on demographic traits. It may be supplemented with special surveys or field work. Demographic analysis can ordinarily be done entirely as an office study, without extensive interaction with the public. This has the advantage of speed and low cost, but it has the disadvantage that no public contacts are made until the study is completed.

Historical Analysis

Most water resources projects and programs have a history that is documented by reports, correspondence files, and newspaper accounts. Reference to such data can provide a means of discerning what the various publics have been in the past, relative to water resources issues.

Historical analysis is made somewhat easier when clipping files are available. Some water resource planning agencies make extensive use of such files and they are available to the water planner. Newspapers also keep such files, but they are not always open to the public. When they are open, they are a gold mine of information. Libraries likewise keep such files on particular projects. The Atlanta Public Library, for example, has extensive files on the Chattahoochee River, the principal river in the Atlanta area.

Comparative Analysis

A fruitful source of information about publics is the record of studies and projects in fields closely related to water resources, such as HUD 701 planning, land-use planning, forestry planning, outdoor recreation, and transportation. The public hearing transcripts, clippings, reports, and correspondence files on such studies may yield information about groups that would be interested in a water resources planning effort. When comparative analysis is used, interviews with the study managers should be conducted in addition to simply reviewing documentary materials. Such interviews give insight into the contemporary situation, rather than what the situation may have been a few years ago (Arnstein, 1974).

General Lists

A recent tendency in some water resource studies, especially those conducted by the Federal Government, is the use of standard categories of publics. In the Atlanta Water Resources Management Study, three levels of publics were used. Level I publics include "all major units of government." Level II publics include special interest organizations. Level III publics include local public interest groups. Peavy (1974) has added a fourth level of publics, consistent with the earlier theoretical base, of "the unreachables"—people who may have a stake in water resources planning and, for whatever reason, do not wish to participate or to be informed about the study or the issues.

Developing a good, accurate mailing or correspondence list is an essential part of a public involvement program and, as it is developed, is a partial means of identifying publics. To be really effective, it needs to be regularly updated, categorized in a way that mailings can be made to selected persons or groups on the list, and prepared in a fashion permitting easy use. The computer is a useful tool for handling mailing lists.

There is a considerable risk of coming to believe that the mailing or correspondence list *is* the identification of publics. In a recent study done for the U. S. Army Corps of Engineers, it was found that most lists are over 70 percent dominated by governmental interests (Ragan, 1974). Their purpose was primarily for notification of public meetings. While it is acknowledged that a list of those interested in and affected by water resource plans normally includes a number of public agencies, their importance as publics should not be weighted so heavily.

Field Interviews

The field interview has been much discussed as a method of identifying publics. There are essentially two approaches used in field interview work. The best known is often referred to as the snowball. In the snowball methods (in a sense, a special case of third party identification) the planner begins his work by interviewing a group of people known to have some interest in the field and asking them to identify others likely to be interested in the water resources planning study. Those persons are subsequently interviewed and asked the same question. The process is repeated until no more new names are received.

Much of the reported work on snowball methods has concentrated on "water resources influentials" or prominent people. While this is certainly an important part of those who should likely be involved, it is by no means the only segment. Essentially the same methods could be employed with people not ordinarily considered part of the "water resource influential" group.

Success in doing snowball work depends upon capable interviewing and receptive respondents. Among prominent people, a great deal of snowball work has been done in recent years in the United States as part of examinations of decision-making and "power structure." Almost immediately after an interview begins, the respondent is likely to recognize he is being asked snowball questions. While this is not necessarily a handicap, it can be. The importance and worth of the study must be demonstrated to the respondent before he is willing to go on. The planner must be alert to the possibility he is being given incomplete information, inaccurate information (perhaps deliberately), and that in some cases, securing accurate information in this way may even harm the respondent (Maruyama, 1974).

Snowball methods will identify those persons who have in the past been interested in and/or influential in a particular issue area. It will not easily identify persons who are not well-known but who have a legitimate interest in participating. It can be an expensive, time-consuming method. There is a definite advantage to doing snowball interviews in such a manner that the planner gets information about more than publics. Indeed, this type of field interviewing should be used to understand social structure and planning issues, uncover data sources, and ascertain something about goals, objectives, and problems.

The other approach to doing field interview work concentrates more on understanding the community and its problems than it does identifying publics. As the community and its problems are studied, publics are identified as a matter of course.

Field interviews should ordinarily be a part of any identification of publics work. It will be remembered that identification is more than naming; it includes knowing something about the identified segment. This can best be done by field contacts.

Affected Publics

At each stage of the planning process, the planner should be able to identify in some form those groups of people who in some way are likely to be affected or impacted by the proposed project or program. As the planning progresses, the identified groups will change, but even at the very beginning the planner should have some idea about the nature of probable impacts and, therefore, the groups affected.

Examples of groups that could be identified in this way include those who would gain or lose economically, those physically in the path of some project element, and communities whose pattern of activity would have to be changed in some way. In part, these groups would be recognized from economic, demographic, or geographic studies. Others would be recognized from staff discussion. Indeed, an alert group of planners sensitive to the local social-political-economic situation should be able to acquire a good deal of knowledge of relevant publics just by being observant and by thinking about the probable consequences of proposed actions (Wenrich, 1974).

Analysis of affected publics should be part of any attempt to identify publics. Indeed, it should also be part of any planning effort. After all, planning seeks to reduce adverse effects and increase beneficial effects to various segments of the public. If these groups are not brought into the planning study in some way, it is doubtful the full planning job can be done.

Selecting the Mix of Techniques

It should be apparent that not all the techniques described above should necessarily be used in any one planning study. Rather, those techniques should be selected that are appropriate to any given planning situation. It would be rare, however, to find a situation in which one of the three general approaches was inappropriate. Self-selection and staff identification are clearly appropriate anywhere, though not all the techniques under these general approaches are. Third-party identification, probably the least used of the three approaches, is a highly cost-effective method because the output is so good and the cost is so low.

The most important point is that explicit consideration be given to identifying publics and that a strategy for doing so be developed. In the absence of such a strategy, there will be the possibility of great gaps, surprises, and an inability to communicate effectively with some publics.

CONCLUDING REMARKS

This state-of-the-art report contains both theoretical and practical considerations for identifying publics in water resources planning. Readers from other fields will observe that much of what is said about water resources planning will likewise apply in other kinds of public works planning. As is the case in many fields, the difficulty of identifying publics lies more in the practice than in the availability of methods and theory. Many practitioners are not aware of the theory or the variety of methods.

Variations in local culture, in the personalities of the practitioner, and in the planning situation require that a somewhat different strategy for identifying publics be employed for each planning effort. These variations are too great to be covered in a general fashion. Even such matters as relative cost of using various techniques can be discussed in only the most general way. For example, self-identification and third-party identification methods are usually less costly than field interviews by staff.

The researcher can usually supply a theoretical framework into which various aspects of the subject may be placed (*e.g.,* the three approaches to identification: self, third-party, and staff). He also can attempt to determine what techniques various practitioners have tried. Perhaps of most importance, he can think about the subject in some logical fashion for longer periods of time than the practitioner can usually afford.

On the other hand, the ingenuity of field-level practitioners in devising new techniques, hopefully assisted by a theoretical framework and an inventory of techniques used by other practitioners, is more likely to advance the field than is any effort by the researcher (unless the researcher becomes, for a time, a practitioner). With timely reporting of new techniques and the results obtained by their use, we may go forward.

Finally, it is important to reemphasize that identifying publics is only one part, albeit an important part, of the entire process of public participation in planning. Public participation, in turn, is only one part, albeit a vital part, of the entire planning process. We may do a superb job of identifying publics and a poor job of planning. This would be tragic. We must seek to integrate fully all the needed pieces into a useful whole. Water resources planning is an ill-defined problem, and public participation in planning is a means of bringing some clarity and definition to the process so that planning may be a means of reaching our desired societal goals and objectives.

ACKNOWLEDGMENTS

The work on which this project is based was partially supported by the Environmental Resources Center and the Graduate Program in City Planning, Georgia Institute of Technology, and by the Department of the Interior, Office of Water Resources Research as authorized under the Water Resources Act of 1964 (P.L. 88–379). The project was administered through the Environmental Resources Center of the Georgia Institute of Technology under provisions of P.L. 88–379.

REFERENCES

Arnstein, S. Personal Communication, July 2, 1974.

Baur, E. J. *Assessing the Social Effects of Public Works Projects*, Research Paper No. 3, Resident Scholar Program, Corps of Engineers, Board of Engineers for Rivers and Harbors, Fort Belvoir, Virginia (June 1973).

Maruyama, M. "Methods in Obtaining Grass-Roots Epistemology, Relevance Structures and Opinions Concerning Water Resources Projects," unpublished Manuscript, Portland State University (1974).

National Urban League Urban Renewal Demonstration Project, *Toward Effective Citizen Participation in Urban Renewal* (June 1973).

Peavy, J. R. *The Who of "To Whomsoever They May Accrue:" Identification of Publics in Water Resources Planning*, Special Problem Masters Paper, Georgia Institute of Technology (May 24, 1974).

Ragan, J. F., Jr. Personal Communication, July 12, 1974.

Ragan, J. F., Jr. *Public Participation in Water Resources Planning: An evaluation of the Programs of 15 Corps of Engineers Districts*, Review draft of report submitted to U. S. Army Engineer Institute for Water Resources, Fort Belvoir (July 1974).

Vermont Stat. Ann. Tit. 10, Secs. 1100–1105 (Supp. 1971).

Wenrich, J. W. Personal Communication, July 5, 1974.

4. The Politics of Information: Constraints on New Sources

Helen Ingram

Opportunities for the participation of new publics are greatest when decision-making arrangements are in flux. This is precisely the current situation in water resources where the past pattern of politics is in a state of disarray. Once it was possible for water development agencies to continue and prosper by following certain well-accepted rules about building public support. Agencies selected projects on the basis of the unity and strength of local, pro-development publics. Multi-purpose projects were designed to serve a variety of interests, and agencies dealt with dissent by adding a new project feature or sweetening the offering by more generous cost-sharing. The way the pattern of water politics worked in the past, national consent for locally based projects was constructed by stringing projects together in packages as omnibus rivers and harbors bills or basin-wide development acts and logrolling them through Congress. Today these rules no longer create political consent (Ingram, 1972).

Old formulas no longer work for water development agencies because their traditional public support has deteriorated and their current critics cannot be appeased by the old bundle of benefits such as flood control, irrigation, power, water supply, and recreation that agencies have had to offer. The results have been increasing conflicts and problems in getting water projects approved and growing disappointments at backlogs and low budgets. Frustration has fostered a receptivity to change within water development agencies. At present they are open to, indeed searching for, new combinations of supporting interests that will restore their ability to authorize and fund projects. Publics not previously represented have a unique opportunity to assert their goals, objectives and preferences into the decision processes.

The extent to which a new pattern of politics based on the representation of new publics eventually emerges from the present state of flux will depend on the extent to which the information generated by these different publics is in fact assimilated into the decision-making process. There is a good deal of resistance among governmental decision-makers to the collection and utilization of information that they find diversionary, antagonistic, or threatening. Their mind-set is not likely to be altered by arguments counter to the agency's internal goals and objectives, whether the arguments are couched in terms of broad national interests or in terms of utility to a specific public. Governmental decision-makers will integrate new kinds of information into the decision-making process only when they can see a positive utility to themselves.

Policy-makers are eclectic. They utilize many different kinds of information: press headlines, quotations from speeches and private conversations, administrative reports, and numerical data. At the same time policy-makers do not by any means assimilate all possibly relevant data in decision-making. Lindblom's now classic formulation of incremental problem solving illustrates that, to be seriously considered, information on alternatives must deviate only slightly from past patterns of decision. Further, not all the consequences of any alternative are, in fact, taken into account. There is a tendency among decision-makers to concentrate on direct and immediate effects of decisions, discounting the remote and imponderable, the intangible, and the poorly understood. As a rule the incremental decision-making strategy dictates that a decision-maker attend to the short run consequences in hope that the long run will take care of itself, or that some other decision-maker in another setting will take care of it (Braybrooke and Lindblom, 1963).

The general proposition of this paper is that inputs from new publics will be used when their *utility* to policy-makers is greater than the *cost* of using them (Rose, 1972). It has been demonstrated that policy-makers are receptive to new environmental information generated by environmental impact statements only when they see clear advantages. New rules and regulations requiring increased public involvement in agency decision-making are not likely, by themselves, to force decision-makers to take into account interests and concerns they would not otherwise consider (Ingram, 1973). Any attempt to anticipate how policy-makers will react to public inputs from new sources must try to do three things: (1) identify those factors to which decision-makers will listen and be receptive, (2) enumerate the costs in terms of resources of incorporating new kinds of information into decision-making, and (3) predict the utility that new sources of information may have for decision-makers.

FACTORS AFFECTING WHAT DECISION-MAKERS HEAR[1]

Decision-makers are barraged by more information than they can actually use, even as the information related to the limited choices they are comfortable in making. Information overload is a common problem. Decision-makers normally are not required to listen to all the interests that have stake in any decision or to collect and weigh data on all possible impacts. There is virtually no empirical evidence to suggest the validity of classical formulations of problem solving in which goals are identified and ranked, all the important possible ways of reaching goals are listed, and all the important consequences of each alternative are investigated before the policy with consequences most closely matching goals is chosen (Lindblom, 1968; Dror, 1968). The decision-making strategy that Lindblom and Braybrooke (1963) call disjointed incrementalism is a better approximation of the real world. Under this descriptive model, only policies that differ incrementally from the status quo are seriously considered, and, in consequence, decision-makers focus upon a quite limited number of alternatives in making choices. The fact is that the receptivity of decision-makers is screened by a number of considerations.

Issue Context

Over time participants in a given policy area develop a particular fix or conception of the dimensions of the issues involved.

---

[1] This section is a summary of a portion of Helen Ingram, "Information Channels and Environmental Decision Making," *National Resources Journal,* **12** (1), 159–169 (1973).

Only the information related to the context in which the issue is typically viewed will be considered relevant to the decision process. It is for this reason that inputs favoring such water-related considerations as recreation, environment, and wildlife habitat were seldom considered in water resources planning when the dominant context was water development and economic growth.

Source of Information

Inputs from various publics to agency or political decision-makers are not considered equal by those who receive the input. In the basic context of agency survival, for example, input from a long-standing support group must be weighted more heavily than inputs from publics with little past or potential impact on the agency. A decision-maker cannot simply make judgments; he must concern himself with building support for his decision. He must take care of his ability to influence and attend to the consequences of choices he makes upon his future ability to influence.

Content of Information

Dexter (1963) has illustrated the fact that a congressman hears most often from those who agree with him, and that some men automatically interpret what they hear to bolster their own viewpoints. Agencies, too, seek out information supporting actions toward which they are already inclined. Agency decision-makers are particularly receptive to categories of information that justify and legitimize their decision-making process (Downs, 1965). Openness to a variety of public inputs often results in a situation of controversy where a decision-maker is pressed from opposing sides; choosing either is politically costly. In such a case, a decision-maker is likely to be more receptive to information content that places the issue in new terms amenable to settlement.

Characteristics of the Decision-Maker

The background and experience of a decision-maker often makes him more receptive to the inputs of certain disciplines and to alternatives based on certain value premises. An illustration may be cited in the water resources development field. The

ANALYTICAL FRAMEWORKS

dominance of engineers has tended to make agencies more receptive to inputs favoring construction than to inputs favoring environmental concerns. Agencies over time tend to compound the problem by selectively recruiting personnel who share the dominant characteristics of those already in the agency.

Rules and Regulations

Rules and regulations structure the formal behavior of organizations and give legitimacy to whatever information is collected and to the process by which it is collected. It is doubtful, however, if rules can build certain information into the decision-making process that would otherwise not be considered. For example, the Principles and Standards of the National Water Resources Council require that agencies seek the views of the public in the planning process. However, the rules cannot assure that compliance is more than formal, and while an agency may appear to hear various viewpoints, it may not assimilate them into water resources plans.

Timing

Decision-makers most likely will be receptive to new information during the earliest stages of the planning and decision-making process. Once the issue has been placed in a context, the decision-maker will follow routine patterns and listen to regular sources of information. Yet it is usually in the later stages that broad public inputs typically are solicited.

INFORMATION COSTS

The costs of using information ought not to be measured in money alone. Time and expertise expended and conflict endured are also costs. What follows is a listing of the potential costs that may be associated with obtaining, consuming, and acting on information.

Cost of Obtaining Information

The cost of obtaining information can be nil if it is part of the "free stream" of information available to everyone, *e.g.*, any item of news that leads the daily papers or is a subject for frequent conversation. The "opportunity cost" of collecting new information is another matter. Information will be costly to obtain if doing so requires scarce resources. Collection is often expensive in dollar terms. The diversion of skilled manpower from other tasks to collect and analyze information is another cost. Time is also a real constraint in that many of the needs of political actors are immediate whereas the derivation of benefits from public participation often requires long-term time series.

Cost of Consumption

The cost of consumption is separate from the cost of obtaining information, for not all information that is gathered by agencies is consumed. Governments annually spend millions in obtaining and publishing large volumes of information without any attempt to consider who consumes their publications, at what cost, and to what benefit. When information is packaged in professional jargon or confusing statistical tables and charts, the cost of consumption can approach infinity. New kinds of information may be outside the scope of the policy-maker's professional training, or above his capacity to comprehend. Proponents of greater public participation in the decision process must recognize the difficulty of consuming large amounts of data on public preferences. From the standpoint of the agency, there are difficulties presented both if the agency attempts to assimilate all of the inputs without some form of simplification and if it oversimplifies the inputs so that they retain little of their original meaning.

The fact that information reaches an agency is no indication that it is indeed consumed. An angry phone call may get no farther than the switchboard operator. A letter from a concerned citizen may receive a reply, but this also does not guarantee that the appropriate individual received the letter, or was even aware of the reply. Even if information should get through to the decision-making groups within an agency, it may be so watered down or distorted as to retain very little of its initial force (Rosenthal and Weis, 1966).

Cost in Value Conflict

Cost in value conflict reflects that information conflicting with a policy-maker's established values will be especially difficult to take into account because it will cause the policy-maker to alter the very premises by which he had previously considered policy. Where value conflicts are part of the cost of information, it is easier for that information to be ignored or misperceived (Rose, 1972). Because agencies typically have encouraged input from publics with values held in common with the agency, it is likely that increasing the breadth of public inputs will result in greater value conflict to agency decision-makers.

Agency doctrine plays a large part in determining receptivity to information. Rosenthal and Weis (1966) state, "Over time an organization fabricates an idealized self-image, which becomes a sort of mythological basis for the organization which explains 'what the hell we are doing.' The elements of fantasy in the view of the organization involve, usually, some distortion of reality and, therefore, prejudice the evaluation of incoming information." In his study of the Forest Service, Ashley Schiff found that research on controlled burning and the effect of vegetal cover on stream flow was heavily influenced by the doctrines that administrators found useful in promoting the agency. Research was too closely identified spiritually and structurally with "the cause" to allow impartial identification and investigation of problems of forestry management (Schiff, 1962).

The Bureau of Reclamation, as another example, has traditionally had a strong organizational image or myth of the impact of the reclamation program upon the public interest. The typical regional or district official will articulate his favorite example of how a bureau project transformed a dusty, degenerating town, with marginal farmers, poor schools, and inadequate social services, into a thriving community, supported by farmers with spending money and profit-making shopkeepers, and maintaining good educational and social facilities. It is the Bureau's belief that the reclamation program has kept people in rural areas who otherwise would long ago have moved to crowded cities. The Army Corps of Engineers official has a similar image of the river town, regularly ravaged by floods with little sense of permanency or security, in which the quality of life of residents is decidedly improved by Corps-built dams and levees.

However, the mythology of agency officials may not be in agreement with public preferences. Where a discrepancy exists, information is not likely to have much impact. For instance, trade union leaders are likely to believe that wages are low, even when indicators show that union wages are above average. Similarly, agency officials in the Bureau and the Corps are likely to believe that their programs have beneficial impacts on the public whether or not the programs engender public support.

Rosenthal and Weis have hypothesized that information is likely to be discounted in situations where value conflicts occur with established constituency relationships. An agency will tend to disregard information when it comes from individuals who are not functionally related to the organization, who are not conceived of as intended targets of agency action, or who are not regarded as legitimate critics of the agency. Agencies do not give high regard to information emanating from people who are perceived as having little status and power (Rosenthal and Weis, 1966).

The new publics that are emerging in the decision process may be both organizations generally nonsupportive of the agency or collections of more or less unorganized citizens. Incorporation of inputs from either of these sources may not serve established constituencies and may, in fact, alienate supporters. For this reason, agency officials may view the increasing role of new publics as a bother and a threat.

The accumulated costs of collecting and consuming information, along with value conflicts, make it potentially very expensive for decision-makers to feed new information into the policy-making process. There are substantial reasons not to deviate from established channels of information that have proven useful. Ordinarily, policy-makers do not face a choice between competing sources of information but rather between utilizing new information or continuing to regard what they have as satisfactory. The pressure to satisfy is always strong; as March and Simon (1958) note, there is ordinarily little or no limit to the amount of inaction an organization can undertake.

UTILITY OF NEW INFORMATION

It is only when agency officials perceive benefits from new information that override costs that they are likely to be attentive. New information may be useful in two ways: (1) it can help to justify actions that the agency is already determined to take, and (2) it can provide useful clues to agencies that are experiencing hostility in their political environments and need to establish new sources of support.

Decision-makers are particularly receptive to information justifying and legitimizing their decision-making process. Cost-benefit analysis is favored information to legislators and natural resource agencies. The ratio of benefits to costs provides a rationale for not pursuing certain projects while at the same time the economic tool is flexible enough to supply a justification to projects that have strong support. As Herbert Marshall (1965) put it, "one of the principal uses of benefit/cost analysis is to clothe politically desirable projects in the fig leaf of economic respectability."

The increase in the discount rate was at least part of the impetus for the federal agencies in the Water Resources Council to establish a task force on procedures for evaluation of water and related land resource projects. An increase of 1⅝ percent reduced the b/c ratio to less than unity for a number of projects. Without some means of analysis that extended consideration to secondary benefits, it would have been impossible to justify these projects (Jennings, 1971).

The public at large appears to be demanding concrete proof of policy results. There is a good deal of frustration with costly programs that have little effect on problems. Agencies are being asked to prove that their past actions and proposals will appreciably affect the quality of life.

Administrative agencies, like ancient societies, have a tendency to kill the bearer of bad news. In a stable situation, an agency finds little reason to reach beyond its supporting environment for adverse feedback. Yet if an agency is to survive in a changing environment, it must have some means of meeting criticism by innovating both in goals and in method. When objectives are out of phase with the aspirations of important groups in the agency environment, the agency must be prepared to take on new missions. When the methods of the agency fail to achieve its aims, there must be a vehicle for considering alternatives. An agency must have new sources of information with which to correct errors.

Resource development agencies have been subjected to a rapidly changing political environment in the past decade. The traditional agricultural support of agencies such as the Bureau of Reclamation and the Soil Conservation Service has ebbed. In place of support, these agencies have faced increasing objections from urban interests who balk at paying the bills for projects not obviously serving their needs. Environmentalists strongly criticize the adverse effects of reclamation and flood control projects upon the environment. The report of the National Water Commission describing the programs of federal water agencies as antiquated in terms of today's needs is a reflection. Resource agencies must orient themselves toward broader goals and develop methods of serving more diverse constituencies if they are to survive.

These new publics are both the potential supporters and present opponents of development projects. They must be accommodated if further resource development is to take place. For the agency with the will and capacity to innovate, full evaluations of broad public inputs can generate valuable information.

CONCLUSIONS

We are well beyond the point where there is controversy about whether new publics will be introduced into the planning process of established agencies. Any disputes over the appropriateness of change must switch their focus from "whether" to "how." The proposition developed here is that broader public inputs will be taken into account when their utility to decision-makers exceeds their costs. If the movement to introduce broad public inputs into the information upon which agency decision-makers act is to succeed, then it must be based upon an understanding of the costs and utilities of information and policy choices. Social scientists also must be receptive to information about the needs of policy-makers in order to teach them, through improved evaluation techniques, more about the needs of society.

REFERENCES

Braybrooke, D., and C. Lindblom. *A Strategy of Decision: Policy Evaluation and Social Processes* (New York: Free Press, 1963).

Dexter, L. A. "The Representative and His District," in *New Perspectives on the House of Representatives*, R. L. Peabody and N. Polsby, Eds. (Chicago: Rand McNally, 1963).

Downs, A. "Some Thoughts on Giving People Advice," *Amer. Behavioral Scientist* 10 (1), 30 (1965).

Dror, Y. *Public Policy Making Reexamined* (San Francisco: Chandler, 1968).

Ingram, H. "Information Channels and Environmental Decision Making," *Natural Resources J.* 12 (1), 150 (1973).

Ingram, H. "The Changing Decision Rules in the Politics of Water Development," *Water Resources Bull.* 8 (6), 1177 (1972).

Jennings, R. "Foreword," in *Procedures for Evaluation of Water and Related Land Resources Projects: Findings and Recommendations of the Special Task Force of the U. S. Water Resources Council*, Committee Print 92–20, 1971.

Lindblom, C. *The Policy-Making Process* (Englewood Cliffs, New Jersey: Prentice-Hall, 1968).

March, J. G., and H. A. Simon. *Organizations* (New York: John Wiley and Sons, 1958).

Marshall, H. "Politics and Efficiency in Water Development," in *Water Research*, A. V. Kneese and S. C. Smith, Eds. (Baltimore, Maryland: John Hopkins Press, 1965).

Rose, R. "The Market for Policy Indicators," in *Social Indicators and Social Policy*, Andres Shonefield and Stella Shaw, Eds. (New York: Crane-Russak Co., 1972).

Rosenthal, R. A., and R. S. Weis. "Problems of Organizational Feedback," in *Social Indicators*, Raymond A. Bauer, Ed. (Cambridge, Massachusetts: Massachusetts Institute of Technology Press, 1966).

Shiff, Ashley. *Fire and Water: Scientific Heresy in the Forest Service* (Cambridge, Massachusetts: Harvard University Press, 1962).

5. Individual Preferences and Group Choice

Nathaniel Beck

Students of public participation in water policy (or any other policy) will, at some time, wish to study the consequences of that participation. In particular, they must eventually compare an agency's actual policy choice with the policy choice that the public desires. In this chapter, we will examine the concept of public desires and group choice and show that this concept is problematic at best. We will proceed informally via examples, referring the interested reader to more exhaustive treatments of the subject by means of footnotes.

There is little difficulty with the concept of individual choice. We will assume that individuals can say which of a set of alternatives they most prefer, which they second most prefer, and so on. This ranking of alternatives by individuals will be called an (individual) preference order.[1] Can we then aggregate these individual preference orderings into a group preference ordering? This is the problem of group choice.

Obviously, there are many ways to perform this aggregation. By imposing the following four conditions (Arrow, 1965), we will rule out some of the more perverse methods of aggregation:

(1) *The Pareto Principle.* If everyone prefers A to B, society will prefer A to B.

---

[1] We will assume that these preference orders are complete and transitive. The order XYZ, for example, is complete, since either $X \geqslant Y$ or $Y \geqslant X$. It is transitive since $X \geqslant Y$ and $Y \geqslant X$ implies $X \geqslant Z$.

(2) *Independence from irrelevant alternatives.* The group choice among any set of alternatives should depend only on those alternatives.

(3) *Unrestricted domain.* The aggregation rule should work on all possible combinations of individual preferences.

(4) *Nondictatorship.* It should not be the case that whenever one individual prefers A to B, society must prefer A to B.

In addition to these conditions, we want the group preference to be transitive. (A preference is said to be transitive if, whenever A is considered to be at least as good as B, and B is considered to be at least as good as C, then A is sure to be considered at least as good as C.) Does there exist a rule meeting these requirements?

First, consider a society that must choose between two alternatives. The common way of aggregating preferences in this situation is majority rule; *i.e.*, if more than half of the people prefer A to B, society prefers A to B. Note that majority rule meets all of our conditions.[2] How well does majority rule work for more than two alternatives? Only transitivity presents problems. Let us proceed via example.

Consider a society of three people: a businessman who loves to fish, a contractor, and a landowner. Assume that this society is faced with a hydroelectric power shortage and that it can adopt one of three policies: do nothing, enlarge an already existing dam, or build a new dam. The fishing businessman most prefers enlarging the old dam, since that will yield more power without hurting his fishing. He least prefers the new dam since it threatens to destroy his favorite sport. The contractor will get most work on a new dam and least work on no dam at all, so his preferences are clear. The landowner has land that will be flooded by either dam, but enlarging the existing dam is worst for his property. The three preference orderings are summarized in Table I.

Given these individual preference orderings of the three alternatives, what is the group preference? Under majority rule, this small society prefers a new dam to an old dam (by a 2-to-1 margin, with only our businessman prefering the old dam), and society prefers no dam to a new dam (by the same 2-to-1 margin). Yet society prefers the old dam to no dam at all (by the

---

[2] Transitivity is no problem since there are only two alternatives.

Table I
Ordered Preferences of a Hypothetical Society of Three People

	Fishing Businessman	Contractor	Landowner
First choice	Old dam	New dam	No dam
Second choice	No dam	Old dam	New dam
Third choice	New dam	No dam	Old dam

same 2-to-1 margin. Thus we are in the position of having society prefer no dam to a new dam, prefer a new dam to an old dam, but yet prefer an old dam to no dam.

This is one of many cases in which majority rule leads to intransitivities. Nor should we think that this problem is limited to the method of majority rule. Arrow (1965) has shown that there is no method of aggregating preferences based on rankings that can be consistent with all four of our requisite conditions. The problem is not with majority rule but rather with the notion of societal choice itself.

Why are intransitive social preference orders so undesirable? Most obviously, the existence of intransitivities means that we cannot talk about what society most prefers. In the above example, does the miniature society most favor new dams, old dams, or no dams at all? But there are other more practical problems that intransitives give rise to.

Imagine a legislature with three members: our businessman, contractor, and landowner. Suppose that a bill has been proposed to enlarge the old dam. This bill would pass by a two-to-one vote. But suppose the landowner is clever. He moves to amend the bill to provide for building a new dam instead of enlarging the old one. Under Robert's Rules of Order, the amendment is voted on first. (That is, the bill as amended is voted against the original bill. The winner is then voted against the status quo.) Both the landowner and the businessman prefer the amendment to the original bill, so the bill is amended. But both the landowner and the businessman prefer no dam to a new dam, so the amended bill will fail when brought to a vote. Thus, by cleverly offering an amendment and thereby changing the pairing of alternatives voted upon, the landowner can get his most preferred outcome.

This problem is the direct result of an intransitivity. Had the social preference ordering been transitive, the new dam would have beaten no dam, and we would have had no problem.

But the situation is even more complex. So far we have been assuming that voters are honest, *i.e.*, they vote for the alternative they prefer. But if there are intransitivities, then there are opportunities for sophisticated voters to attain their goals by voting against their true preferences.[3] Imagine the contractor trying to decide how to vote on the proposed amendment substituting a new dam for the enlargement of the old one. Foreseeing the results of the landowner's strategy, he realizes that if he votes for the amendment, the final outcome will be no dam. He knows that it pays for him to vote against the amendment, thus defeating it. The original bill (old dam) will now pass over the amendment by a two-to-one margin, and will eventually be passed when voted against the status quo. Thus the landowner has been punished for his clever maneuver,[4] and the contractor's strategy of voting against his true preference has paid off.

Intransitivities thus lead to lack of a clear social choice, vulnerability of outcomes to maneuvering of the agenda, the dependence of outcomes on parliamentary rules, and the possibility that calculation and deceit may pay.

This lack of a clear social choice creates insoluble problems in judging whether public participation in policy-making has had any impact. Suppose, for example, that the Corps of Engineers had come into our small society and, after consulting with the citizenry, decided to build a new dam. They claim that their decision reflects "what the people want." Is there any way in which we could know that their decision represents the true social choice? The answer is, unfortunately, no. Does this leave us with no hope? Fortunately, the answer is again no.

Several avenues of escape exist. All of them are problematic, but all of them are helpful to some extent. The only avenue of escape that is closed is to search for another rule that always works. Arrow's theorem rules this route out. The best we can do is to limit the harm done by intransitivities in actual voting situations. Four types of escape from our dilemma exist: (1) technical escapes, (2) probabilistic escapes, (3) preference limitation escapes, and (4) intensity escapes.

---

[3] See Farquharson, 1969, for a discussion of sophisticated voting and its consequences.

[4] See Riker, 1965, for a real-world example of this phenomenon. Riker's example involved the defeat of a federal aid-to-education bill by exactly this method.

TECHNICAL ESCAPES

The four conditions that we previously specified as requisite to our social decision process originally seemed innocuous enough. We have already seen that they are, in fact, incompatible. One way of disposing of this dilemma is to attempt to show that the conditions are actually neither as trivial nor as necessary to our social decision process as had been assumed. That is, we can seek escapes from the dilemma by making merely *technical* changes in the four conditions.

The condition that has been most criticized (Riker and Ordeshook, 1973) is independence from irrelevant alternatives, on the grounds that it rules out taking intensities of preferences into account in the decision process. Unfortunately, these attacks are ultimately unsuccessful because they are based on a misconception of the meaning of the condition itself (Plott, 1972). Interestingly, this misconception arises from a poorly chosen example in Arrow's own work. When properly stated, all that the condition of independence from irrelevant alternatives says is that the choice from a set of alternatives should depend only on those alternatives which have no implications at all for the weighing of intensities. (We will discuss intensities in more detail later.) Thus, we cannot escape our dilemma through technical tampering with the condition of independence from irrelevant alternatives.

A more successful attack has been mounted on the condition of transitivity itself. Unfortunately, these attacks are rather obscure to those not well versed in mathematical logic, so we will simply sketch their broad outlines. All of these attacks start by asking the question, "Why do we want social preference orderings to be transitive?" Depending on the answer, analysts have attempted to find conditions that are strong enough to bring about the desired result but weak enough to be consistent with the other conditions of social choice. We will consider two answers to the question.

The first answer says that we want social preferences to be transitive so that we can guarantee that there will be a clear social choice. But there are weaker conditions than transitivity that can guarantee a social choice. Furthermore, these weaker conditions are consistent with the other conditions of social choice.

Two decision processes that meet the weaker condition are

the Pareto method (Sen, 1966) and the method of special majorities (Ferejohn and Grether, 1974). The Pareto method says that A is socially preferred to B if no individual prefers B to A. In cases where three alternatives are considered, the special majority method says that A is preferred to B, if more than two thirds of the voters (who care) prefer A to B. Both of these methods guarantee a social choice.

Unfortunately, neither method is of great practical import. Society is seldom so agreed that either the Pareto method or the method of special majority will yield a single choice. More formally, both methods will yield many alternatives that are socially indifferent, *i.e.*, where neither A nor B is preferred to the other. Thus this escape is really no escape at all.

The second answer to our question is that we wish social choice to be transitive so that the alternative which society selects will be independent of the order in which society considers the various alternatives (Plott, 1973; Ferejohn and Grether, 1975). This independence from chronological order is called "path-independence." However, even a very weak form of this condition is still highly inconsistent with the other social choice conditions. Indeed, none of the technical escapes offered by analysts to date can yield a clear social choice without violating one or more of our four conditions.

PROBABILISTIC ESCAPES

A second avenue of escape is to ask how likely an intransitivity is to occur. If intransitivities are unlikely, then we have little problem. Analysts (Niemi and Weisberg, 1968; De Meyer and Plott, 1970) have calculated the probability of an intransitivity given a random collection of preference orders. In a large group, if there are three alternatives, the probability of getting an intransitive social preference is only 0.09. But with 15 alternatives, this probability goes up to 0.61. Of course, the probability of the intransitivity involving a first-place social choice is much less than this. Thus, if we are dealing with large groups (such as the American Congress), we can declare our problem essentially solved by observing that an intransitivity is highly unlikely. Of course, the problem remains severe for decision-making in small groups such as committees.

PREFERENCE LIMITATION ESCAPES

Many of the difficulties over intransitivities that we have encountered come from our desire to find an aggregation rule that works for any possible combination of individual preferences. In fact, in many situations, many theoretically possible individual preference orderings simply will not occur. If there is agreement on a single criterion by which alternatives are ranked (although individuals differ in their preference orderings), then intransitivities will not occur.

To clarify this point, let us consider another three-person society, this time trying to decide how much to spend on a dam. Mr. Notax would like to spend as little as possible; between any two alternatives, he prefers the cheaper. Mr. Pork, on the other hand, prefers to spend as much as possible. Mr. Mod wants to spend enough to do an adequate job, but not too much. In fact, he feels that one million dollars is precisely the correct amount to spend. The further away a proposal is from one million dollars (in either direction) the less he likes it.

We can graph the proposals as in Figure 1. Moving up on the y axis means higher preference. The x axis shows the costs of

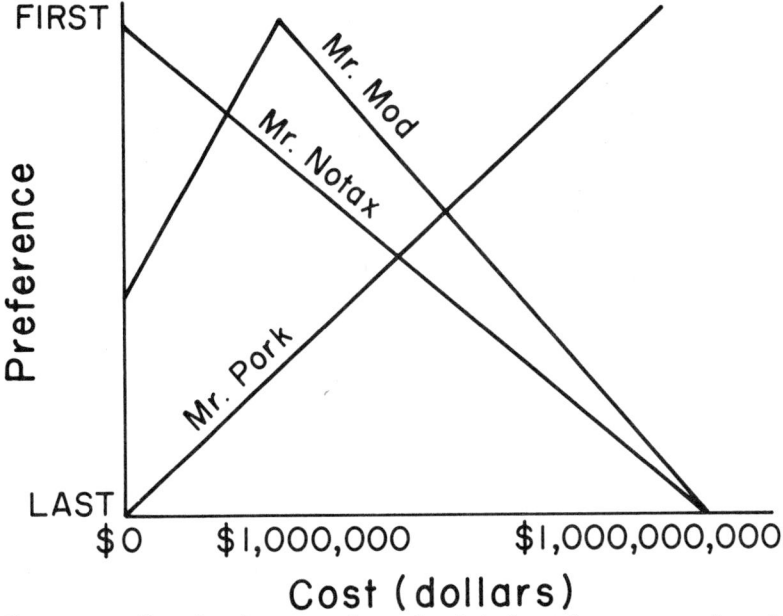

Figure 1. Graph of proposals and related preferences and costs.

various proposals. In principle, all amounts between $0 and a very large number of dollars may be graphed.

Looking at the graph, we can see that the program costing $1 million defeats any other program. It defeats programs costing less that $1 million by the votes of Mr. Mod and Mr. Pork, while it defeats programs costing more than $1 million by the votes of Mr. Mod and Mr. Notax. Note that this avoids all of the problems associated with our previous dam example. Since $1 million defeats all proposals, no one can be helped by introducing extra amendments; any proposal other than $1 million will be defeated anyway. Similarly, no one has any incentive to vote strategically against his true preferences. If Mr. Notax votes for a proposal bigger than $1 million, he can only make himself worse off. Thus, $1 million is truly a societal choice.

The preferences in Figure 1 are called single-peaked. Roughly, preferences are single-peaked if everyone evaluates policies along the same (single) dimension.[5] In this case, the dimension is money. While everyone disagreed about what is best, all agreed about which proposals are near each other and which ones differ a lot.

If preferences are single-peaked, it is easy to calculate the social choice. Arrange everyone's optimum points on the single dimension. The median optimum is then the social choice. (Everyone with optimum to the left of the median votes for the median over any point to the right, and similarly for everyone with optimum to the right of the median.) Note that this social optimum is the median and not the mean optimum. If 101 people prefer to spend no money and 100 prefer to spend $100 million, then the social choice is no spending.

How helpful is this notion of single-peakedness? If there is a natural ordering of preferences by cost, for example, then we would expect preferences to be single-peaked. On the other hand, if policies may be evaluated in different ways (by damage to land, damage to fishing, and providing jobs), then we would not

---

[5] More precisely, a set of preferences over a set of alternatives is single-peaked if there is some ordering of those alternatives so that every individual has an optimum point, and as alternatives get further away from the optimum, they move down in the preference ordering. Note that there is no ordering of the dam alternatives, so that this condition is satisfied. For any ordering of those alternatives, one person has his last choice between his first and second choice. Readers interested in pursuing single-peakedness should consult Black's (1958) exhaustive discussion of the topic.

expect preferences to be single-peaked. Thus relatively narrow questions often will yield single-peaked preferences, while the more important, broader questions generally will not.

INTENSITY ESCAPES

The fourth avenue of escape is rather different. So far we have been assuming that voters simply rank-order alternatives. But suppose they also know how strongly they hold those preferences. Can we use that information to discover a social choice? Again let us return to our original dam example.

Suppose the businessman has only a very slight preference for rebuilding the old dam over building no dam at all. Suppose also that rebuilding the old dam would provide very little profit for the contractor, so he also has only a slight preference for rebuilding the old dam over building no dam. But suppose the landowner would lose millions of dollars if the old dam is enlarged.

We still have two people preferring to enlarge the old dam rather than build none at all, so by the majority rule society prefers to enlarge the old dam rather than build none at all. But all would agree that this society would be best off if no dam were built.

In practical politics, intensities are taken into account all the time. In our example, neither the contractor nor the businessman would expend much effort to have the old dam enlarged. The landowner, on the other hand, would use all of his political resources to make sure that the dam is not enlarged. In a study of participation in water politics, Beatty (1975) has found that people who have a lot at stake in water decisions participate in the making of those decisions much more than do those who have little at stake. Thus, taking intensities into account may solve the whole problem.

For the theorist, however, intensities do pose problems of their own. A complete discussion of those problems would take us too far afield into welfare economics.[6] However, we can mention two problems.

First, taking intensities into account encourages people to exaggerate the intensity of their preferences. Had the contractor (dishonestly) screamed as loudly as the landowner, we might have thought that enlarging the old dam was the true social

---

[6] See Quirk and Saposnik, 1968, Ch. 4.

choice. But encouraging deceitfulness was one of the pitfalls we wished to avoid. Furthermore, this problem leads to a serious empirical difficulty when we attempt to measure intensities and compare them.

The second problem is an ethical one: should one person's preferences count more than another's simply because he feels more strongly? Should the landowner count more than the contractor? What if some people by nature feel more intensely about everything? How do we reconcile our desire to weigh everyone's preferences equally with our desire to allow for intensity of preferences? Obviously, we cannot resolve this problem here.[7]

At this point it would be traditional to sum up what we know about group choice. But to do so would undermine the most important point about group choice: the notion is highly problematical. Above all, we should not speak glibly about "what society wants."

REFERENCES

Arrow, *Social Choice and Individual Values*, 2nd ed. (New York: John Wiley and Sons, 1965).

Beatty, "Rational Public Participation in Water Resources Politics" unpublished manuscript, Department of Political Science, Washington State University, Pullman, Washington, 1975.

Black, *The Theory of Committees and Elections* (Cambridge, England: Cambridge University Press, 1958).

Buchanan, J., and G. Tullock. *The Calculus of Consent* (Ann Arbor, Michigan: University of Michigan Press, 1962).

Dahl, R. *A Preface to Democratic Theory* (Chicago: University of Chicago Press, 1956).

DeMeyer, F. and C. Plott. "The Probability of a Cyclical Majority," *Econometrica* 38 (2), 345 (1970).

Farquharson, R. *Theory of Voting* (New Haven, Connecticut: Yale University Press, 1969).

Ferejohn, J., and D. Grether. "On a Class of Rational Social Decision Procedures," *J. Econ. Theory*, 8 (4), 471 (1974).

Ferejohn, J., and D. Grether. "On Normative Problems of Choice," California Institute of Technology working paper No. 80, 1975.

---

[7] For good discussions of this problem, see Dahl (1956), Ch. 4, and Buchanan and Tullock (1962).

Niemi, R., and H. Weisberg. "A Mathematical Solution for the Probability of the Paradox of Voting," *Behavioral Sci.* 13 (4), 317 (1968).

Plott, C. "Ethics, Social Choice Theory and the Theory of Economics Policy," *Mathemat. Sociol.* 2 (2) 181 (1972).

Plott, C. "Path Independence, Rationality and Social Choice," *Econometrica* 41 (6), 1075 (1973).

Quirk, J., and R. Saposnik. *Introduction to General Equilibrium Theory and Welfare Economics* (New York: McGraw-Hill, 1968).

Riker, W. "Arrow's Theorem and Some Examples of the Paradox of Voting," *Mathematical Applications in Political Science*, John M. Claunch, Ed. (Dallas, Texas: Southern Methodist University Press, 1965).

Riker, W., and P. Ordeshook. *An Introduction to Positive Political Theory* (Englewood Cliffs, New Jersey: Prentice-Hall, 1973).

Sen, A. "A Possibility Theorem on Majority Decisions," *Econometrica* 34, (2), 491 (1966).

6. Measuring Political Responsiveness: A Comparison of Several Alternative Methods

Anne L. Schneider

INTRODUCTION

The question of public involvement in water resource politics turns on the problem of political responsiveness. Political responsiveness, however, is open to many definitions and many measures. Which definition and which measure are chosen will influence judgments about the need for and success of public involvement programs. The purpose of this chapter is to survey the alternative measures of political responsiveness, discuss their strengths and weaknesses, and assess their theoretical implications.

The point of view from which the discussion proceeds should be made clear. First, responsiveness is viewed here as the relationship between preferences of citizens and decisions made by government. Responsiveness is not defined nor measured in this article as a process variable involving influence, citizen articulation of preferences to leaders, communication among leader and followers or any other type of process variable. Characteristics of the political system such as competitive elections, voting turnout, legislative professionalism, and so on, may increase (or decrease) the degree of responsiveness, but they are not viewed as responsiveness, *per se*. Likewise, a high degree of communication between group and government may increase the responsiveness of the government to the group, but communication *per se* should not be included in the definition or measurement of responsiveness.

Second, responsiveness is considered to be an attribute of a government, a political system, one or more political leaders, or a policy decision made by any of these. The system-level nature of responsiveness is important because some of the methods for measuring responsiveness yield measures representing whether the government has been responsive to an *individual*, whereas others yield measures of whether the government has been responsive to a *collectivity* of individuals. Each individual in the society probably prefers that all the government decisions correspond to the decision he/she would have made if given the opportunity. On the other hand, a government or political leader cannot possibly make a decision that is responsive to each citizen in the society unless all persons hold the same preferences on the issue. If one is interested in measuring responsiveness as an attribute of the government, a political leader, or a policy decision made by a set of leaders, then an appropriate definition of responsiveness would be as follows:

> A responsive government is one that selects the policy alternative that a majority of the members of a collectivity would choose in a fair election.

This definition needs to be expanded to specify whether the members of the collectivity are permitted to vote on all possible pairs or policy alternatives or whether they are given a dichotomous choice of alternatives, or other electoral mechanisms. The point here is that governmental responsiveness is an attribute of government and should be measured by comparing a decision made by the government with one which would have been made by the collectivity. The collectivity could be the entire public or a subset of the public (such as labor unions, blacks, upper class persons, and so on).

If one is interested in studying the behavior or attitudes of individual citizens and wishes to develop a measure characterizing the degree of responsiveness as perceived by each specific individual, then a different definition of responsiveness should be used, such as:

> A government is responsive to an individual if it selects the policy alternative that the individual would have selected if given the opportunity to do so.

The purposes of the study dictate which definition will be used, but serious conceptual problems arise if one calculates an individual-level measurement of responsiveness and then simply averages these to obtain a measure of governmental responsiveness.

In the subsequent discussion, seven alternative statistical procedures—some of which have been used to measure responsiveness and some which could be used—will be reviewed. The computation of each statistic will be explained, along with possible modifications, and the theoretical implications of the statistics will be examined.

RESPONSIVENESS AS CONCURRENCE

Although Verba and Nie (1972) imply an influence dimension in their definition of responsiveness, they measure the concept in terms of the proportion of the leaders who hold the same opinion as an individual citizen. Citizens and leaders in more than 60 communities were asked to name the major political and governmental problems facing the community. Answers to the open-ended questions were coded into several categories and a responsiveness score for each individual in each community was calculated. The responsiveness score for each citizen is the proportion of the leaders who named the same topic as did the citizen. If citizen A said that taxes were the main problem and all of the leaders named taxes as one of the top three problems, then the individual's responsiveness score would be 100 percent. If half of the leaders named taxes, then the individual's score would be 50 percent.

Concurrence scores could be computed from closed questions. Suppose the citizens and leaders are asked whether more funds should be spent on sewage treatment, less funds should be spent, or expenditures should remain the same. The answers to the question could be placed on a horizontal axis, such as shown in Figure 1, and the percentage of the public and the leaders who hold each position could be placed on the vertical axis. In the example, 40 percent of the citizens and 20 percent of the leaders believe that less money should be spent on sewage treatment. Likewise, 40 percent of the citizens and 20 percent of the leaders believe that sewage treatment expenditures should remain the same. Sixty percent of the leaders believe that more should be spent, and 20 percent of the public hold this opinion.

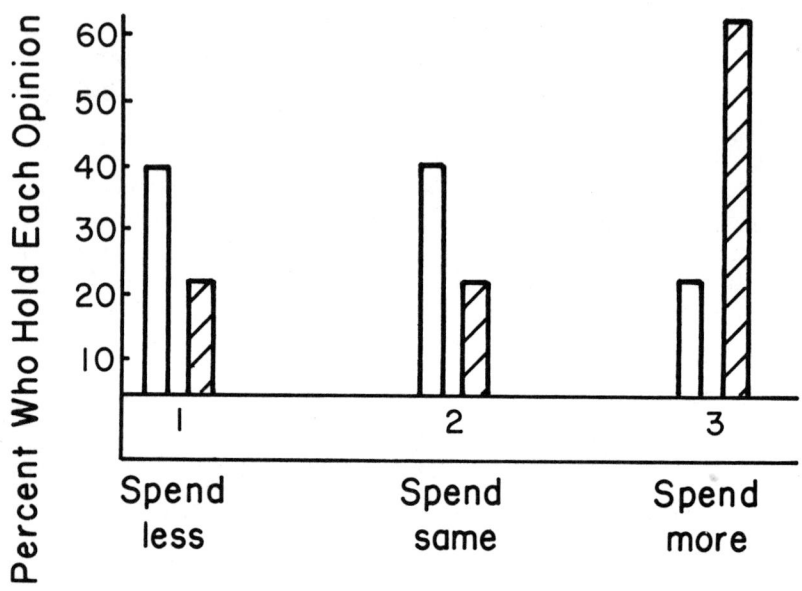

Figure 1. Distribution of citizen and leader opinions. Note: The numbers corresponding to the positions are selected arbitrarily. Shaded areas refer to leaders.

The method of computing the concurrence scores is shown in Table I. Citizens A and B have opinion score 1, citizens C and D answered that expenditures should stay the same (a score of 2), and citizen E believes that expenditures should increase (a score of 3). The numbers attached to the three positions are quite arbitrary, and do not figure in the calculation. The leaders (ten are included) divide somewhat differently. Two are at position 1, two at position 2, and six at position 3. The responsiveness score of an individual is equal to the percentage of the leaders who share his opinion. Thus, the scores for individuals A through D are 20 percent for each. Individual E would have a concurrence score of 60 percent.

Verba and Nie computed the concurrence score for the community by summing the scores of the individuals and obtaining the mean. In the example, the average concurrence is 28 percent. This number is interpreted to mean that, on the average, 28 percent of the leaders hold the same position as the citizens.

A concurrence score for a policy decision made by the ten leaders could be calculated as shown in the last columns of Table I. In the example, each citizen's concurrence score would be zero if the decision is not at the same policy position he preferred, and would be 1.00 if the decision is the one he preferred. The mean for all citizens represents the percentage of citizens who held the same position as the one reflected in the policy decision.

Table I
Computation of Concurrence Scores

Citizen	*Multiple Leaders*			*Collective Decision*	
	Citizen Position	Number of Leaders at Position	Percentage Leaders and C Score	Decision at Position	Decision C Score
A	1	2	20%	3	0
B	1	2[a]	20	3	0
C	2	2	20	3	0
D	2	2[a]	20	3	0
E	3	6	60	3	1.0
	N = 5	N = 10	$\overline{X} = 140/5$		$\overline{X} = 1.0/5$
C score for community = 28 percent					

[a]These are the same two leaders used for another citizen and are not counted twice when computing the total number of leaders. There are 10 leaders in the example.

A concurrence score such as the one developed by Verba and Nie provides a measure of responsiveness for each individual in relation to a group of leaders or a collective decision. The concurrence scores range from zero (no leader agrees with the citizen's position) to 1.00 (all leaders agree with the citizen's position).

The formula for the concurrence index is as follows (Verba and Nie):

$$C_{j'} = \frac{\Sigma L_j}{N_L}$$

where:
   C_j = an individual whose position is j
   ΣL_j = the sum of the leaders whose position is j
   N_L = the total number of leaders

DISCUSSION

The concurrence measure is an appropriate statistic to use for obtaining a responsiveness score for an individual. The measure pertains to the proportion of the leaders who are in agreement with the citizen, and implies that an individual will view the government as more responsive to him if a greater proportion of the leaders agree with his positions on the issues.

The major problem with using the concurrence index to obtain individual-level scores is that it does not take into account the "distance" between the position preferred by the citizen and the position preferred by the leaders when preferences have been measured on an ordinal or interval scale. Suppose citizen A prefers that the government spend less money on irrigation development. The concurrence index will give the individual a responsiveness score of 1.0 if the government spends less, but will give him a score of zero if the government spends the same amount or if the government spends more. A more appropriate statistic for ordinal or interval data would make some differentiation concerning the degree of responsiveness, because the individual probably would be more satisfied with the same level of expenditures than he would be if the government increased expenditures.

The mean value of individual concurrence scores should not be used to characterize the degree of governmental responsiveness to the community. There are several reasons for this. First, the value of the concurrence scores varies with the number of categories used when coding the questions asked of citizens and leaders. Using the data in Table I as an example, suppose the question contained five categories of responses instead of three (spend much more, some more, same, some less, much less). With five possible categories of responses, it is less likely that leaders will adopt exactly the same position as the citizen, and the concurrence scores will be smaller. Questions with small numbers of responses will automatically bias the scores upward, and questions with large numbers of responses will bias the scores downward. To use the concurrence index for computing composite scores across more than one question, each question must have the same number of response categories. And, if one community is to be compared to another, the responses by individuals to open-ended questions must be coded into the same number of categories in each community.

The ability of a political system to be "responsive" (as measured by the concurrence index) is to a great extent *beyond the control of the government*. Responsive political behavior by the leaders would depend not only on the leaders, but on the homogeneity of preferences in the community. Concurrence scores for a political unit such as a state or city will be positively related to the homogeneity of citizen preferences because the maximum score cannot exceed the largest percentage grouping of citizens at one position on an opinion scale. For example, suppose a sample of persons who live in a particular city are asked whether they approve or disapprove of a flood control project. If all the citizens approve the project and all the leaders approve of it, the concurrence score for the community is 100 percent. But if half the citizens approve and half disapprove, the highest concurrence score would be 50 percent, no matter which position the leaders took. As another example, suppose a question contained five categories of responses, and the citizens were divided equally among the five categories so that 20 percent is the largest plurality at any one position. No matter what position the leaders took, the maximum responsiveness score is 20 percent.

As a correction, one could divide the concurrence score by the maximum possible score, given the distribution of preferences. The resulting value (C') represents the proportion of persons to whom the government was responsive as a percentage of those it would have been possible to satisfy with the best decision.

Theoretical Implications

Leaders who wish to obtain a higher level of responsiveness, as measured by the concurrence index, should select the policy alternative that is favored by a larger proportion of the electorate. This position will have a higher concurrence score than any other position the leaders could take. In terms of democratic theory, the decision rule that is implied could be stated as follows:

> Decision Rule for Concurrence (C): The more responsive decision is the one a plurality of citizens would choose in an election that had one round of voting and several alternatives. The decision is more responsive if the plurality is greater, and it can reach a maximum only when the citizen vote is unanimous.

It should be pointed out that when a plurality of citizens prefer, for example, that the government concentrate its efforts on water quality, this does not mean that a majority of citizens would select that policy area if water quality were paired against every other possible policy. An example should illustrate the difference. Five citizens rank the policies in which they think the government should place its greatest efforts as shown below:

Ranks

Citizen	First	Second	Third
A	Crime	Education	Transportation
B	Crime	Education	Jobs
C	Education	Transportation	Water
D	Jobs	Education	Racial Equality
E	Transportation	Education	Jobs

If leaders, in order to be responsive, select the policy area with a plurality of votes in an election in which citizens voted their first preference among the alternatives listed above, crime would receive 40 percent of the vote, would win the election, and would be judged the most responsive policy choice for the leaders (with a score of 40 percent or, using C', a score of 100 percent). However, if the election were constructed so that citizens voted between pairs of issues and crime were paired with education, education would receive more votes than crime, since citizens C, D, and E would vote for education rather than crime. And, regardless of which pair is voted on first, if citizens could continue to vote for several "rounds" in the election, education would eventually be chosen by a majority vote as the policy area for major governmental efforts.[1] The implication is that the concurrence index (C or C') would judge a government that decided to emphasize crime prevention as more responsive than one emphasizing education, even though the citizens would choose education if given the opportunity to do so.

RESPONSIVENESS AS A "MATCH" BETWEEN POLICY AND PREFERENCES

Frank Munger (1969), Hedlund and Friesma (1972), Shaffer and Weber (1975), and others conceptualized responsiveness

---

[1] This assumes that Arrow's paradox will not occur, and that there will be one alternative which can defeat all the others in a head-to-head vote (a condorcet winner).

as a "match" between a policy position, and the dominant preference of the public. In Munger's formulation, the policy positions taken by the states were dichotomized so that a state had either adopted a policy (such as shorelines protection law) or had not adopted the policy. The public preferences in each state were estimated from questions on an AIPO poll concerning whether the citizen would approve or disapprove of the policy. If the state had adopted a policy such as shorelines protection law, and a majority of persons in the state approved of shorelines protection law, then the responsiveness score for the state would be 1.0. If the dominant preferences of the public were different than the policy position, the state's score would be zero. Similarly, Hedlund and Friesma conceptualized responsiveness for legislators by whether the legislator voted in accordance with dominant preferences in the constituency on referendum issues. If the legislator voted with a majority, the responsiveness score was 1.0. If not, the score was zero.

This approach to measuring responsiveness assumes that a decision is a responsive one if it matches the preferences of a majority of persons when the leaders and citizens have selected from between two alternatives. A decision by a state, county, or city government either *is* responsive or is *not* responsive.

Weber and Shaffer conceptualized the term in a slightly different way, and used a variant of the matching procedure to measure responsiveness. Their conceptualization was that if the government's policy is approved by 50 percent or more of the citizens, then the policy is responsive to them, and is equally responsive regardless of whether the percentage of persons who approve the policy is 51 percent, 70 percent, or 100 percent. The scores would be 1.0. On the other hand, if the state adopts a policy and 51 percent disapprove, they do not consider the state to be as unresponsive as if 90 percent disapproved.

Computation

The hypothetical data in Table II illustrate the responsiveness scores that would be given to the government of each community, in several situations, by the concurrence index (C), the matching index (X), the Weber Shaffer revision of the matching procedure (X'), and the suggested modification of the concurrence index (C'). The illustration presumes that policies and preferences are each dichotomized so that only two positions could be

Table II
Comparing Three Measures of Responsiveness

Community	Policy Position of Community's Government	Percentage of Public Favoring Position 1	X ("Matching")	X' ("Weber's Matching")	C (Concurrence)	C' (Modified Concurrence)
A	1	100	1.0	1.0	1.00	1.00
B	1	75	1.0	1.0	0.75	1.00
C	1	51	1.0	1.0	0.51	1.00
D	1	50	—	1.0	0.50	1.00
E	1	49	0	0.98[a]	0.49[b]	0.98[c]
F	1	40	0	0.80	0.40	0.66
G	1	30	0	0.60	0.30	0.42
H	1	10	0	0.20	0.10	0.11
I	1	0	0	0	0	0

[a] X' is a transformation of the percentages to reduce skewness in the scale. If the percentage is below 50 percent, the value is multiplied by 2.

[b] C is equal to the percentage who favor the policy.

[c] C' is found by dividing the percentage favoring the government's position by the percentage who oppose if the government's position is not favored by a majority. Or, to put it another way, the percentage who agree with the government's position is divided by the highest percentage at any one position.

taken on the issue. In the example, all of the governments have taken position 1.

All three methods yield the same score for the government that adopts position 1, and in which all of the citizens agree with that position. If 75 percent agree with position 1, however, the matching procedures (X and X') and C' give a score of 1.0, whereas the concurrence index (C) would be 0.75. If 49 percent of the public agree with position 1, the responsiveness scores would be zero, 0.98, 0.49, and 0.98.

Discussion

The matching procedures (or C') are suitable for measuring responsiveness when the best data available pertain only to dichotomized preferences and policies (such as comparing legislative roll call votes with constituency votes on a referendum issue).

One problem in using the Munger type of matching procedure (scores of 1.0 or zero) is that the information concerning constituency preferences needs to be very precise, since a difference between 51 percent and 49 percent favoring the policy will change a government's score from 1.0 to zero. If survey data are used, or if opinions are simulated, any community with a very narrow division of opinion would be difficult to classify, since the margin of error would be greater than 2 percent. If votes on referendums are used to estimate citizen preferences, then there is little error in the votes themselves, but the nonvoting citizens are omitted from consideration. In a study using votes on referendum, where only 30 percent or 40 percent of the public cast a vote, there is a serious question as to whether the votes themselves should be considered a reflection of *community* preferences. And, if the vote is not an accurate indication of community preferences, the responsiveness scores do not measure responsiveness to the community.

A major limitation to all these approaches is that none takes advantage of the ordinal or interval characteristics of some types of data. Responsiveness is viewed as a percentage problem: What percent of the leaders agree with an average citizen? What percent of the citizens agree with a leader (or a policy)? When interval level or ordinal data are available, some consideration should be given to the distance between the citizen's position and the actual policy. To illustrate the distinction, consider the situation depicted in Figure 2. In this hypothetical community, half the citizens are willing to vote for a city bond issue that would allocate $13 million to build a new water treatment plant. Half the citizens do not want to spend any money at all on a new water treatment plant. The city must decide whether to place the $13 million plant on the next budget election, to leave it off, or to place an issue for something less than $13 million on the next ballot. What is the most responsive decision? The concurrence index would compute a responsiveness score of 50 percent if the city selects position 1 or position 5, but would measure the responsiveness as zero if the city decides to put a $7.5 million plant on the ballot (no citizens preferred that position). The matching procedure (X) would not be able to calculate a responsiveness score. Weber and Shaffer's index (X'), as well as C', would give the city a score of 1.0 regardless of whether they selected position 1 or position 5. The score would be zero if they decided on a $7.5 million plant.

The fundamental question posed from the data is this: Is it more responsive to give half the people exactly what they want or to give all the people half of what they want?

Theoretical Implications

The matching procedures imply a somewhat different decision rule than the one which underlies the concurrence index. First,

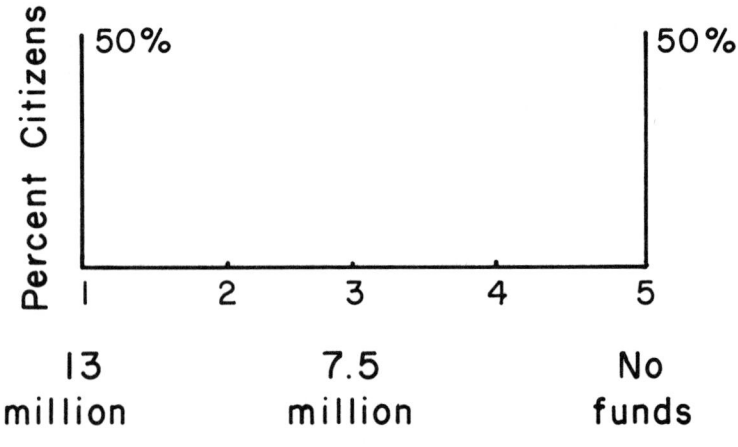

Figure 2. Distance measures.

it should be noted that there are only two policy choices, and the two are paired against each other. In contrast, the concurrence scores as they have been used in actual research summarize responsiveness across a variety of topics. If each policy area were paired against another policy, then the concurrence method would be similar to the matching procedures and, if the statistic C' were used, the scores would be relatively comparable. The decision rule underlying the matching procedures, when used on dichotomous alternatives, could be stated as follows:

> Decision Rule X: A responsive decision is one a majority of citizens would choose in an election with one round of voting and a dichotomous choice of alternatives. An unresponsive decision is one that would not be approved by majority vote, and there are no gradations of responsiveness.

> Decision Rule X': A responsive decision is one a majority of citizens would choose in an election with one round of voting and a dichotomous choice of alternatives. Responsiveness scores for decisions made by the government that do not have majority support decline as a function of the proportion of the citizens who favor the decision.

MEASURING RESPONSIVENESS AS DISTANCE

Many procedures are available to apply to the problem of measuring the similarities and differences between an individual who holds opinions i . . . j, and some other individual or group of individuals (such as leaders) who hold opinions i . . . j. One procedure, developed by Cronbach and Gleser (1953), is to compute the distance between them on one or more variates. The statistic, called D^2, is applied here to the problem of measuring responsiveness for several citizens in relation to several policies adopted by the government.

Computation

Suppose the citizens are given a series of questions concerning whether they approve of greater or lower expenditures on a number of policy areas. Suppose the actual policy outcomes are determined and categorized into five groups corresponding (by assumption) to the responses available to the citizen.

In Table III, the outcomes of five expenditure decisions are

Table III
Similarity of Preference and Policy Five Policy Expenditure Items

	a	b	c	d	e
Outcome of Decision	2	3	4	2	1
Person 1	1	2	2	1	1
Person 2	4	5	4	3	5
Person 3	5	5	1	4	5

Person 1 with Outcome	D²
1 − 2 = −1	1
2 − 3 = −1	1
2 − 4 = −2	4
1 − 2 = −1	1
1 − 1 = 0	0
	D² = 7

DI = 1 − (7/80) = 0.93

Person 2 with Outcome	D²
4 − 2 = 2	4
5 − 3 = 2	4
4 − 4 = 0	0
3 − 2 = 1	1
5 − 1 = 4	16
	D² = 25

DI = 1 − (25/80) = 0.67

Person 3 with Outcome	D²
5 − 2 = 3	9
5 − 3 = 2	4
1 − 4 = −3	9
4 − 2 = 2	4
5 − 1 = 4	16
	D² = 42

DI = 1 − (42/80) = 0.48

$$D^2 = \sum_{i=1} (C_{jn} - D_j)^2$$

$$DI = 1 - \frac{\sum_{i=1} (C_j - D_j)^2}{\text{Max} (C_j - D_j)^2}$$

where:
C_j = Citizen's position on issue one
D_j = Decision on issue one

in the first row. The score of 1 indicates much lower expenditures, 5 indicates much greater expenditures, 4 indicates some greater, 3 represents the same, and 2 means somewhat lower expenditures. Each individual's preference score is subtracted from each policy outcome score, and squared as shown in the area below the table. The sum of the squared deviations for the first person with the outcome is the D^2 value for that person.

One problem with the Cronbach and Gleser statistic D^2 is that it varies with the number of items used, and with the number of possible responses. This variance can be removed by computing the maximum value of D^2 for any given number of items and range of possible responses. In the example above, the maximum distance on any item is four (5–1), and since there are five items, the maximum value of D^2 is 80 ($4^2 \times 5$). D^2 for any given person could be divided by the maximum. With this correction, the scores would range from zero (no difference between the citizen and the policies) to 1.0 (the greatest possible distance). If the scores are then subtracted from 1.0, the index is reversed and the higher scores represent greater responsiveness. Values of this type (called DI) for each of the three individuals in Table III have been computed according to the formula shown.

A measurement of the responsiveness of a decision, or series of decisions, to the public could be obtained by computing the distance between the decision and each individual's position. In Table III this would be done by computing scores down the columns instead of across the rows. The sum of the distances squared, divided by the maximum possible distance, represents the responsiveness of the decision, and the responsiveness of the government, to the public in relation to that decision. By pooling the five decisions, a composite score of governmental responsiveness could be computed. Thus, the D^2 statistic, or the modification suggested here, *DI*, can be used to generate responsiveness scores for an individual in terms of how much distance the individual could be expected to perceive between his own opinion and that of a leader or decision made by a group of leaders. In addition, D^2 or *DI* can be used to measure the responsiveness of the government to the public.

Discussion

The major advantage of this procedure over the concurrence indices for measuring individual-level responsiveness is that it permits a decision that is closer to an individual's preference to be considered more responsive than a decision more removed from his preferences. The implied definition of responsiveness, at the individual level, is that an individual will judge the responsiveness of the decision not in terms of whether the alternative chosen is the one the individual prefers, but in terms of how close the decision lies to his own preferred position. To use this or any other type of "distance" measure, one must have data that is at least ordinal-level.

The use of D^2 or DI to measure the extent of governmental responsiveness to the public shares a common problem with the concurrence index: the decision chosen cannot possibly be maximally responsive unless all the citizens share the same point of view on the issue. The only way to obtain zero distances is for every citizen to have the same opinion and for the leaders to select that position as the chosen policy alternative. The problem can be corrected in the same way as for the concurrence index, however. If the resulting score is divided by the most responsive decision that *could have been made*, then the resulting scores represent whether the leaders selected the best alternative from among those available (score of 1.0) or whether they selected a suboptimal alternative.

Theoretical Implications

Presuming that leaders wish to be responsive, what position should they select in order to achieve the highest possible responsiveness score, given the distribution of preferences and the D^2 or DI method of measuring responsiveness? The position that would always receive the highest responsiveness score is at the mean of the citizens' preferences. The decision rule could be defined as:

> Decision Rule D^2 or DI: The more responsive decision is the one that minimizes the squared deviations between the decision and the preference of each individual. Maximum responsiveness can be achieved only if the citizens unanimously support one position.

The implications of defining the most responsive decision as the mean of the distribution of citizen preferences will be discussed in the next section.

RESPONSIVENESS AS OPINION

Another statistic that has been used to measure the responsiveness of government policy decisions to the public is an index of opinion-policy congruity (Schneider, 1973). This statistic (M) was developed explicitly to measure the responsiveness of *government* rather than responsiveness as perceived by the citizens.

Computation

To compute the value of M for a government one must locate the median preference of the constituents and the policy decision made by the government on an ordinal or interval-level opinion scale. The distance between the policy score and the median opinion score is the absolute value of the difference. This value is subtracted from 1.0 to produce the responsiveness score:

$$M = 1.0 - [P - E]$$

where:

P = policy position of the government
E = median of constituents opinion distribution

The statistic can be generalized to avoid problems of arbitrarily assigned values to the policy positions and to insure comparable scores for different policy areas by standardizing it (in order to pool questions) or by computing the value as a proportion of the maximum distance between the median and the poorest policy choice:

$$M' = 1.0 - \frac{[P - E]}{\text{Max}\,[P - E]}$$

The computational procedure for M' is illustrated with hypothetical data in Table IV, for a single state in which 20 percent of the constituents are located at position 1 on a five-point scale, 10 percent are at positions 2, 3, and 5 (each), and 50 percent are at position 4. If the state selects a policy alternative located at position 1, its responsiveness score (M') would be zero, since this is the least responsive decision that could be made, given the distribution of preferences. If the state chooses position 2, its score is 0.44, and if it selected either position 3 or 5 (which lie on either side of the best decision) the responsiveness score would be 0.77. At the median (position 4) the responsiveness score is 1.0. It does not matter what percentage of the citizens are at position 1. As long as position 4 is the median, the score for a decision at position 1 would be zero.

Table IV
Congruity Sources

Position on 5-point Scale	Percentage of Citizens	Decision Position	Median	[P−E]	$\dfrac{[P-E]}{Max\,[P-E]}$	M'
1	20	1	4	3	1.00	0
2	10	2	4	2	0.66	0.44
3	10	3	4	1	0.33	0.77
4	50	4	4	0	0	1.00
5	10	5	4	1	0.33	0.77

Median = Position 4
Max [P−E] = [4−1] = 3

DISCUSSION

The rationale underlying the use of this statistic is that a responsive government should select the policy alternative the citizens would select by a majority decision if they were allowed to vote on all possible alternatives. A government that is responsive to the public is the one that would make the same decisions as the citizens. The degree of nonresponsiveness depends on the amount of distance between the policy selected by the government and the one the citizens would have selected if they had been given the opportunity to do so.

The statistics M and M' are similar to D^2 in that one must assume each person's preference ordering is single-peaked and declines monotonically from the peak on the scale that is used to measure preferences. If a citizen's first choice for the policy is at position 1, then his second choice is position 2, and so on, with his fifth preference being position 5. Or, if a citizen's first choice is position 3, then he is indifferent between positions 4 and 2, but prefers either of those to positions 5 and 1. If this assumption is correct and if all citizens vote, the median position is the one that would win by a majority decision over any other position.

The distribution of preferences in Figure 3 represents a hypo-

ANALYTICAL FRAMEWORKS 105

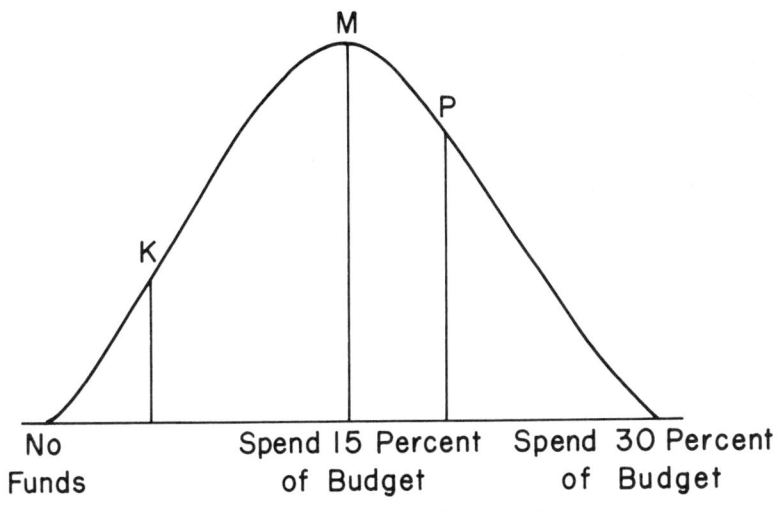

Figure 3. The median position.

thetical community's opinions on the proportion of the budget that should be allocated to some particular public service area (such as domestic water supply). Most citizens prefer that the government allocate about 15 percent of the budget to water supply. The lowest extreme is to allocate no funds to this service area, and the highest amount preferred is 30 percent. What policy should the government adopt if it is to select the most responsive position? Defining responsiveness as the policy the citizens would choose, the government should select the median position, (*M*) in Figure 3. Suppose that the citizens were asked to vote on whether the policy should be *M* or *P*. All persons to the right of *P* (about 15 percent) would vote for *P*, and half of those between *M* and *P*, who are closer to *P*, would vote for *P* (about 15 percent). All others would vote for *M*, and position *M* would receive more votes than position *P*. The median position would defeat any other position on the continuum if everyone voted or if nonvoting is randomly distributed.

Consider what would happen if the government presented only two alternatives to the citizens: alternative *P* and alternative *K*. Position *P* would receive the votes of all persons whose preferences are closer to *P* than to *K*, and would win with a sizeable majority even though it is not the most responsive decision.

106 WATER POLITICS AND PUBLIC INVOLVEMENT

Only if the public is allowed to vote on all possible pairs of decisions will the most responsive one be selected because many positions could obtain a majority vote when paired against positions near either tail of the distribution. This conceptualization of responsiveness, and the statistics accompanying it, produce a more precise measure of responsiveness than the matching procedures in which the government is considered to be responsive if the policy chosen receives majority support when paired against only one other alternative.

Theoretical Implications

One major theoretical distinction between use of the statistic M and D^2 is that the latter would define the most responsive position as the mean of the citizens' preferences rather than the median. The difference between the mean and the median relevant to this exercise is that the mean is more sensitive to extreme scores than is the median.

On the scale shown in Figure 4, the median is considerably to the right of the mean, and if the median were considered the most responsive policy position, a rather conservative policy would be selected. If the mean is defined as the more responsive position, a moderate policy would be best. To define the most responsive policy position as the mean of the opinion distribution gives greater weight to a small proportion of persons holding extreme opinions. When opinion distributions are not symmetric (as those in Figure 4 are not), the mean preference could be

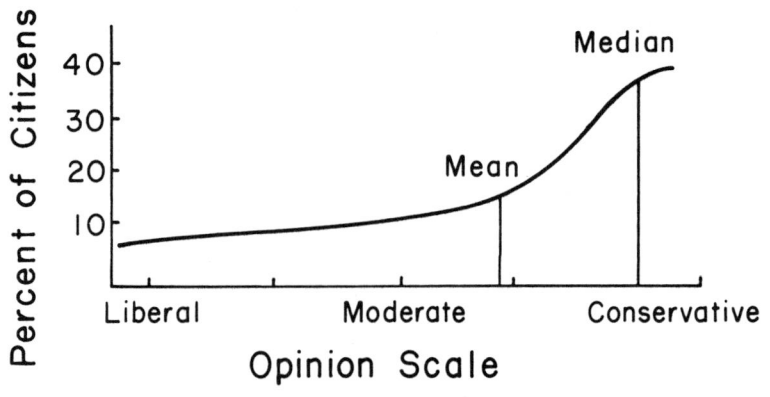

Figure 4. The mean and the median.

considered more responsive than the median if we wish to believe that persons with extreme opinions care more about the issue, and if we wish to allow persons who care more about the issue to have a greater weight in determining the decision. If this is done, however, there is no mathematically precise way of stating the decision rule being used.

The decision rule for the statistic M or M' can be stated as:

> Decision Rule M and M': The most responsive decision is the one a majority of citizens would choose in an election in which each citizen voted and in which successive votes on all pairs of alternatives are allowed until the optimal decision is determined. Responsiveness scores decline as a function of the deviations between the actual decision and the most responsive one.

Measuring responsiveness as the distance between the median and the actual policy has some appealing characteristics. First, it is identified with a precise decision rule concerning an *aggregate* of persons, and represents the difference between what the leaders actually did and what they should have done to maximize responsiveness. Thus, the measure is particularly appropriate in studies that wish to explain responsiveness by characteristics of the political process which might influence leaders or by characteristics of leaders. The score does not vary automatically with the homogeneity of citizen preferences. Therefore (in contrast to the concurrence scores), the amount of responsiveness is entirely controlled by the leaders.

On the other hand, the responsiveness score calculated in this fashion should not be used as a measure of citizen satisfaction with the policy position selected by the leaders. Suppose the distribution of opinions is bimodal, with half the citizens supporting the highest level of expenditures and half supporting the smallest level. The median is still at the center of the distribution, since that position would defeat all others in an election (assuming that everyone votes, or that nonvoting is random). However, no citizen would be particularly pleased with the outcome, since the median is relatively distant from all preferences. Responsiveness scores calculated in this manner are not very useful in studying whether citizens to whom the system is unresponsive are more or less apt to vote in elections. If one wishes to correlate citizen perceptions of responsiveness with other attitudes or behaviors, then responsiveness should be measured for each individual rather than for the aggregate of individuals.

Cochran's D^2 or the concurrence index would be more appropriate. The measure M' can be computed only when the possible policy positions are at least ordinal in nature, and numerous enough to compute a median position.

RESPONSIVENESS AS COVARIANCE OF CITIZEN OPINION AND POLICIES

Some research involves a comparison among independent political units such as cities, counties, and states, and each unit can be characterized in terms of citizen opinion and the policy alternative selected by the leader(s). In studies with large samples in several independent units, regression-correlation analysis is one of the alternative procedures that could be used to measure responsiveness. Miller and Stokes (1963), for example, concluded that congressmen are more responsive to their constituents on civil rights policy than on foreign policy or welfare policy. This conclusion was reached because the correlation coefficient (r) between constituency opinion and congressmen's votes on civil rights issues was higher than for the other policy areas.

Discussion

The data from four hypothetical states indicating the proportion of the budget that the citizens prefer to have allocated to water programs and the amount the state has actually allocated to water are presented in Table V. The spending patterns of the

Table V
Covariance

State	Citizen Opinion[a]	State Policy	$Y = a + bX$
A	5%	10%	$a = 0.05$
B	10%	15%	$b = 1.0$
C	15%	20%	$r = 1.0$
D	20%	25%	

[a]Proportion of budget citizens prefer the state allocate to water. This figure could be the median preference or mean preference.

states covary with preferences, but are 5 percent greater than what the public prefers. The intercept (alpha) for these data represents the average expenditure when the public prefers zero spending. The 1.0 correlation coefficient and regression coefficient indicate a perfect covariance.

If the correlation coefficient or standardized regression coefficient is used as the indicator of responsiveness, one might wonder why perfect responsiveness is found for the data in Table V when, in fact, each state is "wrong" by 5 percent. This statistic does not require a perfect "match" of opinion with policy. Rather, if citizens in state A are "X units" above average in terms of their opinions, then the policy in that state should be "X units" above the average state. The implication of measuring responsiveness with correlation-regression analysis is that the responsive leader (or policy) is determined by comparing leaders with other leaders and citizens with other citizens. If citizens prefer a liberal policy, the leaders do not have to adopt liberal policies in order to be responsive. Rather, the leaders only need to be more liberal than other leaders. Suppose all the leaders are conservative, and all the citizens are on the liberal side of a continuum. If the leaders from the more liberal constituencies are less conservative than their colleagues, a regression analysis could reveal a "responsive" system.

This type of problem would seem to argue against the use of regression-correlation analysis, since several of the other procedures already discussed are based on a conceptualization of responsiveness that is intuitively more appealing. On the other hand, the data available to characterize citizen opinion often are far less precise than those in the previous example. The survey instrument may only ask whether citizens prefer that the government spend more, the same, or less on water or education. If the government spends $5 million less and the citizens' preference was to spend more, how is one to compute the "distance" between these? The actual expenditures could be coded into three categories corresponding to the question asked of the citizens. Or, the citizen responses could be coded with dollar values by characterizing "spend more" as the average increase in expenditures for states that increased spending, or by using some other arbitrarily selected coding rule.

A decision rule corresponding (roughly) to this approach might be stated as:

Decision Rule (r): A more responsive decision is one that deviates from an average decision in other governmental units in direct relation to how the constituency opinions deviate from the opinions of constituents in other governmental units.

RESPONSIVENESS AS REPRESENTATION

An individual citizen probably judges the responsiveness of his/her political system from a private rather than a collective perspective. That is, the individual would prefer that the government select policy alternatives that the individual would select if he/she could make the decision alone. A leader, group of leaders, or outside observer are more apt to judge the responsiveness of the system in accordance with whether the government selected the most responsive decision available to it. Another criterion that might be used by leaders or outside observers is to judge the responsiveness in terms of whether the distribution of preferences among the leaders corresponds to the distribution of preferences among the citizens. This characteristic of a political system is usually referred to as the representativeness of the government.

Measurement

The problem of measuring representation is similar to the problem of measuring the degree of equality, or inequality. That is, what proportion of the citizens are represented by what proportion of the leaders? Viewed in this manner, the desired measurement would be the degree of under- and overrepresentation of particular preferences. One method is to compute the cumulative percentages of citizens holding specified policy positions and of leaders holding the same positions.

A distribution of preferences for leaders and citizens is shown in Figure 5 on an issue that has five possible positions. As shown by comparing the shaded with the unshaded areas, the citizens holding opinions at position A are greatly overrepresented by leaders (5 percent of the citizens and 30 percent of the leaders hold this position). Citizens at position B are also overrepresented in that 20 percent of the leaders hold that opinion, but are representative of only 10 percent of the citizens. In order to calculate a summary statistic representing the extent of unequal representation, the percentages can be converted to cumu-

[Bar chart showing percentages at positions A through E]

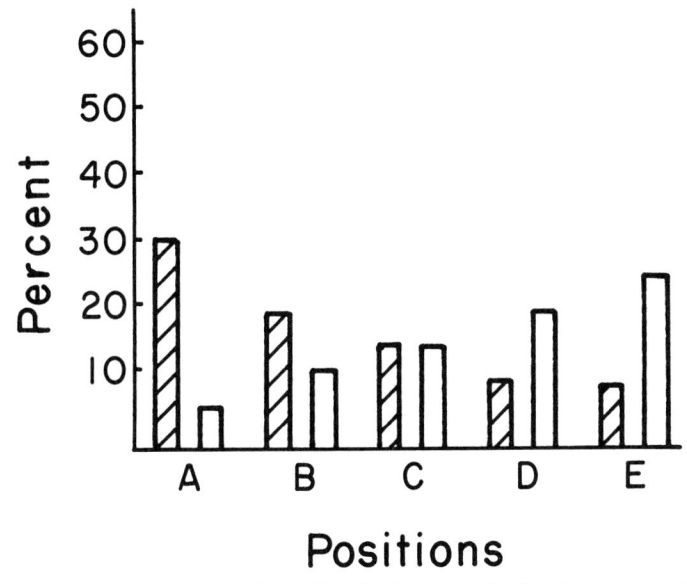

Figure 5. Representation. Shaded areas indicate percentage of leaders. Unshaded are the percentage of citizens at the position.

lative percentages as shown in Table VI. The cumulative percentages are then plotted as in Figure 6. A curve of this type, based on cumulative percentages, is called a Lorenz curve (Alker, 1965). The information in Figure 6 is interpreted with statements such as "30 percent of the citizens are represented by 5 percent of the leaders; 50 percent of the people are represented by 15 percent of the leaders; and so on." If representation were distributed equally, 10 percent of the people would be represented by 10 percent of the leaders, 20 percent by 20 percent, and so on. This is indicated by the straight line of perfect equality in Figure 6.

In order to draw a diagram of this type and compute statistics from it, one must begin the cumulative distribution computations with the most disadvantaged group of citizens and proceed to the most advantaged, even if this means rearranging some of the positions on the scale.

In the example, the slope of the line reaches 1.0 for citizens who hold position C. Thus, 30 percent of the citizens are overrepresented in the example and 70 percent are underrepresented.

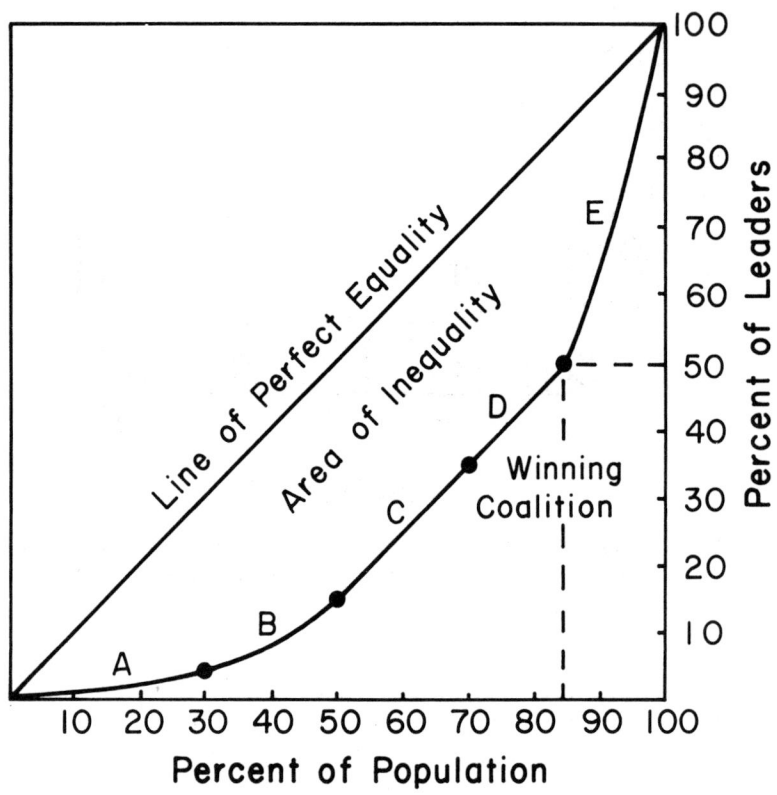

Figure 6. Lorenz curve.

Another interesting statistic that can be determined from the diagram is the percentage of the citizens who hold a winning majority in the legislature. For the hypothetical data used in Figure 6, 20 percent of the citizens are represented by enough legislators (50 percent) to control the decision-making process. In addition, the slope of each segment of the Lorenz curve can be calculated by dividing the values on the horizontal into those on the vertical axis. The results are shown in Table VI, and indicate that persons who hold position A are underrepresented with a score of 0.167, whereas those at position E are represented by 2.5 times as many legislators as would be expected if all persons were equally represented.

ANALYTICAL FRAMEWORKS 113

Table VI
Cumulative Percentages

Position	Percentage Leaders	Percentage Citizens	Cumulative Percentage Leaders	Cumulative Percentage Citizens	Slope of Line in Figure 5
A	5	30	5	30	0.167
B	10	20	15	50	0.5
C	20	20	35	70	1.0
D	30	15	65	85	2.0
E	35	15	100	100	2.5

A statistic summarizing the entire distribution is the Gini coefficient, which is a measure of the area of inequality as a proportion of the maximum area of inequality.

Discussion and Implications

Underlying the use of these statistics to measure responsiveness is the idea that each group of citizens who share a common preference should be represented by a proportional group of leaders. The decision rule could be stated this way:

> Decision Rule (Lorenz curve): A responsive political system is one in which the preferences of each citizen or group of citizens are shared by a proportion of leaders equal to the citizen's or group's proportion in the total population.

The statistics computed from the Lorenz curve do not take into consideration how far away from the citizen's preference the leaders are, and therefore do not take advantage of ordinal or interval-level opinion scales. The leaders' preferences must exactly match those of the citizen before the leader is considered responsive. And, as suggested above, citizens probably do not judge the responsiveness of the system in terms of whether their opinions are proportionately represented among the leaders. Although it is possible that some persons might take such an objective view, it is more likely that individuals prefer to have a maximum (not a proportionate) amount of representation. The concurrence index uses the latter perspective in that the responsiveness score depends on what percentage of the leaders agree with the citizen, not on whether a proportionate number of leaders agree with a group of citizens. On the other hand, the argument has been made several times in this chapter that the responsiveness of the *government* to the *public* should not be evaluated from the viewpoint of each citizen, taken one at a time, because the resulting scores do not indicate whether the political leaders selected the most responsive alternative available to them.

CONCLUSION

The statistics discussed here are certainly not the only ones that could be used to measure those aspects of responsiveness concerning the similarity between preferences of leaders and followers. Any statistic chosen, however, implies a particular definition of responsiveness, and some definitions are more appropriate than others given the context of the research.

The measurements pertain mainly to developing scores for individuals in relation to one decision or one leader for the government in relation to one decision. Although most of the measures can be used to calculate overall responsiveness scores for the government (or individuals) on a variety of decisions, there are several conceptual problems involved in aggregating the scores for each decision into a composite index.

ACKNOWLEDGMENTS

Comments on an earlier draft of this chapter from Robyn Dawes, Lita Furby, Harmon Zeigler, Harvey Tucker, and Peter Schneider were most helpful.

REFERENCES

Alker, H. R., Jr. *Mathematics and Politics* (New York: Macmillan, 1965).
Cronbach, L. J., and G. C. Gleser. "Assessing Similarity Between Profiles," *Psychological Bull.* 50 (6), 456 (1953).
Hedlund, R. D., and H. P. Friesma. "Representatives' Perceptions of Constituency Opinion," *J. Politics*, 34 (3), 730 (1972).
Miller, W. E., and D. E. Stokes. "Constituency Influence in Congress," *Amer. Pol. Sci. Rev.* 57 (1) 45, (1963).
Munger, F. J. "Opinions, Elections, Parties and Policies," paper prepared for the 1969 American Political Science Association meetings, New York, September, 1969.
Schneider, A. L. "Public Opinion, Political Processes and Wel-

fare Allocation Policy in the American States," unpublished doctoral dissertation, Indiana University, Bloomington, Indiana, 1973.

Shaffer, W. R., and R. E. Weber. "Political Responsiveness in the American States," Sage Professional Papers, Series on Public Administration (forthcoming).

Verba, S., and N. H. Nie. *Participation in America* (New York: Harper and Row, 1972).

Part III

Participation Patterns and Evaluation

About the Contributors

John C. Hendee is Recreation Research Project Leader for the U.S. Forest Service, Pacific Northwest Forest and Range Experiment Station, and Affiliate, Associate Professor of Forest Resources, University of Washington. He has authored many articles derived from his research on outdoor recreation, wilderness, wildlife, and public involvement. In 1974 he received an American Motors "Conservationist of the Year" award for his work in "applying social research methods to help solve people-problems in resource management." Dr. Hendee recently led a task force review of Forest Service public involvement and, as a member of an international committee, helped write a new North American Wildlife policy. Dr. Hendee received his PhD from the University of Washington.

Robert C. Lucas is Project Leader for Wilderness Management Research for the United States Forest Service, Intermountain Forest and Range Experiment Station in Missoula, Montana. He is also a faculty affiliate in both the geography and forestry departments at the University of Montana. His research and publications have focused on visitor use of wilderness, particularly resource perceptions and spatial behavior as related to wilderness management. His PhD is from the University of Minnesota, where he also taught from 1960 to 1967.

Robert H. Tracy is Director of Resource Management for the Alaska Region of the U.S. Forest Service in Juneau, Alaska. He has a BS in Forest Management from Colorado State University. He has had a variety of assignments in the National Forest System in Alaska, California, Idaho, Washington, and Oregon, including District Ranger, Deputy Forest Supervisor, Forest Supervisor, and staff assignments in timber management, watershed management, and fire control. As Supervisor of the Targhee National Forest in Idaho he was directly involved in the Forest Service Roadless Area Review conducted to identify wilderness study areas on National Forest lands throughout the United States. While still assigned to the Targhee he served on a nationwide Forest Service task force assigned to review and evaluate forest service experiences and techniques in public involvement. He has been in his present assignment in Alaska since 1973.

Tony M. Staed is the National Coordinator of the U.S. Forest Service's Inform and Involve Program on public involvement in Washington, D.C. His responsibilities include the implementation and coordination of public involvement processes nationwide on such efforts as the recent Environmental Program for the Future and the Forest and Rangeland Renewable Resources Planning Act. His primary professional interests are centered on the integration of public thinking into the Forest Service's decision-making processes.

Roger N. Clark is a research social scientist at the Recreation Research Project of the U.S. Forest Service in Seattle, Washington. He received his BS and PhD in forestry at the University of Washington. His graduate studies focused on the application of social research methods to the study of human behavior in the natural resource area. His research has focused on depreciative behavior in outdoor recreation settings, citizen participation in resource decision-making, and social aspects of hunting and high mountain lake fishing. Current work includes investigations of dispersed recreation and a continuing look at ways to control depreciative behaviors.

George H. Stankey is a research social scientist at the Wilderness Management Research Project of the U.S. Forest Service in Missoula, Montana. He received his BS and MS degrees in geography from Oregon State University, and his PhD, also in geography, from Michigan State University. His work has focused on social aspects of wilderness carrying capacity, citizen participation in resource dicision-making, and other problems on the man-natural resource interface. He has published a number of papers on these topics. Current research includes continuing investigations of how users define capacity of wilderness and other dispersed settings and how management can protect and enhance visitor experiences.

Ronald A. Yarnell, while employed by the U.S. Forest Service, participated in Codinvolve analyses of public involvement.

Kathleen M. Beatty is a graduate student in the department of Political Science, Washington State University, in which she is a graduate teaching assistant. She earned her MA at Tufts University. Previously she worked for the Southwest Center for Urban Research and the Institute for Urban Studies. Her current research interests are in the general area of public policy formation, with special emphasis on environmental politics.

Douglas D. Rose is Associate Professor of Political Science at Tulane University. He earned his PhD at the University of Minnesota, and also has taught at the University of California at Berkeley. Specializing in the analysis of public policy formation, he has contributed to several books and journals, including *The American Political Science Review*. His current research interest is the impact of personal values on political preferences.

Daniel A. Mazmanian is Assistant Professor of Political Science at Pomona College. He received his PhD from Washington University, St. Louis. Previously he was a research associate in the Brookings Institution Governmental Studies program. He is the author of several papers, and the book, *Third Parties in Presidential Elections*. Currently he is involved in an ongoing study of public participation in the programs of the Army Corps of Engineers.

Jeanne Nienaber is Assistant Professor of Political Science at the University of Arizona. She received her PhD in 1973 from the University of California, Berkeley, and has worked in the field of environmental policy for several years. Professor Nienaber spent the academic year 1973–74 as Resident Scholar to the Board of Engineers, Corps of Engineers, in Washington, D.C., before joining the faculty at the University of Arizona. She is coauthor with Aaron Wildavsky of *The Budgeting and Evaluation of Federal Recreation Programs or, Money Doesn't Grow on Trees*.

Part III
Participation Patterns and Evaluation

The examination of public involvement cannot be confined to theory and methodology. To be useful to scholars and practitioners, theory and method must confront and interpret various aspects of water resource politics. Part III provides examples of that interaction between politics on the one hand and theory and method on the other. It begins with descriptions of public involvement techniques. Then, two chapters examine the foundations of public participation in water politics and public water policy preferences. The remainder of the chapters evaluate public participation programs.

John C. Hendee, *et al.*, in Chapter 7, present an analysis of the different methods for acquiring public input in natural resource policy. Hendee's analysis is based on experience with the U.S. Forest Service, but the results are just as relevant to water resources. Hendee identifies the policy processes at which public involvement can be important. He then describes each technique for public input in terms of its strengths and its weaknesses, and provides guidelines for its use. Hendee then interprets the use of public input techniques in terms of their success as stimuli to public involvement.

Clark, Hendee, and Stankey (Chapter 8) describe Codinvolve, a specially adapted content-analysis system developed to summarize large amounts of complex public input. The system has been utilized in a variety of land-management issues involving thousands of citizen responses. A case study is presented describing the application of Codinvolve, its flexibility, advantages and disadvantages. Reactions to Codinvolve from both resource managers and the public are described.

Pierce, Beatty, and Doerksen (Chapter 9) assess the degree to which the characteristics of individuals who participate in water resource politics fit a rational behavior framework. If individuals who participate in water resource politics are motivated by rational concerns, then public involvement programs must provide appropriate incentives to participation. The authors conclude that present participation can be explained within a rational framework. Thus, public involvement programs must demonstrate to individuals that involvement will have some impact on policies that affect their interests. If benefits are not seen as forthcoming, the rational participant will ignore the public involvement program, and the purpose of the program will not be met.

Douglas Rose, in Chapter 10, assesses the meaning of public opinion on water policy. He focuses on the extent to which public preferences about water policy are founded in personal values, water resource use, and identifications with water-relevant groups. The relationships are important to policy-makers concerned with representing and interpreting public sentiment about water resource issues. Public officials can be more responsive to public preferences and can design public involvement programs more efficiently by understanding the sources of public preferences and variations in those preferences. Rose finds, for example, that there is general agreement among the public as to water policy priorities. But, within that general agreement, water policy preferences are linked to personal values, water uses, and group identifications consistent with the preferences.

Daniel Mazmanian, in Chapter 11, evaluates the success of a set of public participation programs employed by the Army Corps of Engineers. The Corps had assumed that open planning would increase public satisfaction with the Corps' water resource proposals. Mazmanian found that the public participants supported the Corps for its open process, but that support had no substantial impact on the evaluation of Corps proposals. Thus, he concludes, in the short run planners should not see public participation processes as mechanisms by which to alter participant attitudes. The Corps' purpose failed because the Corps uncritically accepted the "participation thesis' and because many participants began with attitudes negative to the proposal. In the long run, however, public involvement programs may generate the intended support for the Corps. That is, public involvement programs may not alter specific public attitudes but may form an environment more favorable or receptive to future Corps proposals. The lesson for planners is to take a long-range view, and not to dispense with public involvement because of early indications of failure.

In Chapter 12, Mazmanian and Jeanne Nienaber evaluate public participation in the Army Corps of Engineers from two perspectives: that of social choice theory to explain individual participation, and that of organizational theory to explain bureaucratic response. They examine the Corps' decision to open its planning process and the impact of that change on the kinds of people participating and the behavior of the Corps itself. They conclude that the results are mixed. Generally, agency personnel found some benefits from the participation, but on the whole the costs outweighed them. For the public, the participation program stimulated the involvement of person's previously uninvolved, thereby partially overcoming the "freerider" problem.

Pierce and Doerksen, in Chapter 13, evaluate several aspects of one public involvement program: the citizen advisory committees of the Washington State Water Program. The central concern is the impact on the committee's representativeness and perceptions of public officials' responsiveness to the method by which the CAC members were recruited. The chapter concludes that as the openness of the recruitment process increases the representativeness of the CAC *vis-à-vis* its public decreases, and the perception of officials' responsiveness decreases.

7. Methods for Acquiring Public Input

John C. Hendee, Robert C. Lucas, Robert H. Tracy,
Tony Staed, Roger N. Clark,
George H. Stankey and Ronald A. Yarnell

BACKGROUND

During the fall of 1971, the Forest Service entered the public participation stage of its Roadless Area review, one of the most extensive land-resource evaluations, and probably the most widespread public involvement effort ever attempted by a federal agency. From November, 1971, to May, 1972, more than 300 public meetings and many other public involvement activities were held across the nation to solicit citizen views about which of the nearly 1600 blocks of undeveloped National Forest land should be studied for possible classification as Wilderness.

During this intensive public participation effort, several National Forests and regions sought technical help from Forest Service Research, universities, and consultants. Their problems spanned the full range of public involvement activities.

During February, 1972, there was a meeting of Forest Service Recreation Research project leaders and key scientists in Phoenix. Because of their people-research orientation and social science training, many of these recreation researchers had already been asked for help and advice in the public involvement phase of the Roadless Area review and other land use planning issues. At Phoenix there was considerable discussion about how to respond to those requests. Out of this discussion emerged a study to review Forest Service experiences in public involvement to identify techniques and procedures that had been found effective under various conditions. This inventory and critique of public participation methods is based on information collected using a 20-page open-ended questionnaire and follow-up interviews with officials from 27 National Forests across the country, and each of the 9 Forest Service regional offices. All of these officials had recent experiences in major public involvement efforts. Although the study was oriented specifically to the Forest Service, it is anticipated that the findings are broadly applicable to other resource agencies.

PUBLIC INPUT COLLECTION TECHNIQUES

The actual acquiring of citizen inputs to aid in resource decision-making must be viewed as part of a broader set of public involvement tasks. The following framework identifies five interrelated public involvement processes, only one of which is devoted exclusively to the collection of citizen input.[1]

(1) *Issue Definition:* The process or stage in resource planning where managers, working within legal, fiscal, political, resource capability and environmental constraints, identify a range of feasible alternatives for comment by the public.

(2) *Public input collection:* Activities including efforts to inform the public and solicit and record their views about resource allocation and management issues or alternatives.

(3) *Public input analysis:* The summary and display of the number, content, and nature of public input about alternatives.

(4) *Public input evaluation:* The subjective interpretation or weighing of the importance of various kinds of public input, and its integration with other factors relative to a decision or recommendation.

(5) *Decision implementation:* All activity such as providing feedback to the public, facilitating review when necessary and taking whatever steps are required to translate a decision into a program of action.

It is important to view any public participation technique or method as fitting in a broader, interrelated framework. For ex-

---

[1] This framework is described in another chapter and in Hendee *et al.* (1973); Hendee (1974); and Hendee *et al.* (1974).

ample, the methods used to collect public input are affected by the way in which the issue has been defined, and the form and manner in which input is collected affects the way in which it can be analyzed and evaluated (Hendee et al., 1973; Hendee 1974; Hendee, Clark, and Stankey, 1974).

Collection of input requires effort to inform the public about issues and alternatives so they can react in meaningful ways. It also includes efforts to solicit and record citizens' views about what courses of action they prefer. A wide range of public input collection techniques are available and may be used. Advisory boards, ad hoc committees, public meetings, contacts with key opinion leaders, professional contacts, workshops, letters, editorials, opinion polls, petitions, and surveys all are possible sources of public views. There is not a single "best way" to obtain public input. The appropriateness of each technique that might be used will vary with the issue and with local and regional conditions. To best serve decision-making purposes, a balanced program of collection activities is needed. The objective is to collect a broad range of views, ideally from all who are interested or affected and, practically, from as many of them as possible. Every technique has strengths and weaknesses and only a combination can do an adequate job; a tailor-made approach is needed for each land use issue.

The study of Forest Service public involvement found that 14 different collection techniques had been used (see Table I). Following is a description of each input collection technique used, an evaluation of its specific strengths and weaknesses, and recommended guidelines for its use.[2]

Public Meetings

Public meetings are sessions open to the general public at which most of the interaction takes place between an audience and the persons conducting the meeting. It may include formal statements, focus on questions and answers, or be just a listening session. By contrast, workshops divide the audience into smaller

---

[2] Guidelines and critiques of input collection methods also appear in U.S. Forest Service (1974); Heberlein (1975) and T. A. Heberlein. "Some Observations on Alternative Mechanisms for Public Involvement: The Hearing, Public Opinion Poll, The Workshop and Quasi Experiment," *Natural Resources Journal*, forthcoming.

Table I
Use of Public Input Collection Techniques by the
Forest Service Units Studied[a]

Collection Technique	Percentage of Units Which Used Technique
Public meetings	87
Field trips	13
Presentation to groups	26
Workshops	3
Ad hoc committees	11
Advisory groups	13
Key contacts	68
Direct mail	1
Questionnaire response forms	3
Agency reports	25
Day-to-day contacts	11
Mailing lists	46
Interviews	1
Mass media	63

[a]Hendee et al., 1973.

groups, and most interaction takes place within these groups. Sometimes meetings are held with special-interest groups and the discussion and interaction may share many of the same characteristics as public meetings, except that the representation of views is different than with a cross section of the public.

Public meetings were by far the most commonly used input collection technique. Table I shows that public meetings were almost universally used in the issues studied. When public meetings were used, there usually were several of them.

Strengths

A public meeting probably facilitates presenting large amounts of information. A wide variety of media can be used—slides, movies, maps with overlays, scale models, videotapes, lectures, handouts, and so on. The information flow can be flexible and two-way; audience questions can suggest which items to clarify, to emphasize or to touch lightly. This flexible, varied-communication capability is the main strength of public meetings.

At public meetings citizens may learn from one another because ideas are exchanged. Attendance at meetings is also one measure of local interest in an issue.

The open, public forum offered by meetings has some value in and of itself. The input is highly visible, and this contributes to credibility. One forest supervisor said, "Public meetings are needed, regardless of their relatively low value. The exposure of Forest Service people to the public tends to build public confidence. Meetings are visible evidence that the public has had a chance to have its say."

Sometimes it is important and helpful for resource managers to sense the emotional intensity with which people hold ideas. Personal contact transmits emotion more effectively than mail or other impersonal means of input. Many officers said this was one of the main benefits of public meetings. As one commented, "You've got to see the interest groups in action to sense the intensity of their belief and commitment."

Weaknesses

Public meetings are difficult to conduct. They are costly, time-consuming, and an unskilled chairman can lose control of the session. Tempers can flare on all sides. And there is an ever present danger that public meetings can be equated with public involvement whereas they are but one technique for acquiring input.

A speaker can "grandstand" to try to sway the audience, to inflame emotions or to convince those he represents that he is doing his job. On the other hand, many people find it hard to speak up in meetings because they are shy or lack confidence in their speaking ability. At most meetings, a majority of those attending do not speak.

Unpopular viewpoints may be suppressed because input is exposed to everyone at the meeting. This is particularly a problem in smaller, closely knit communities, and in one-industry towns. One forest supervisor cited several examples of individuals who said one thing in a meeting and something quite different in writing. He also reported that several who voiced opinions at a meeting later told him they never would do so again because of repercussions. A few cases were cited where people who spoke lost their jobs as a consequence.

Sometimes people suppress their true feelings to avoid hurting others. There was one example in which a vocal minority dominated the public meeting while the majority sat in silence. In this small community, people apparently were unwilling to offend their neighbors in public, but later poured out their opposition in the privacy of letters.

Meetings make demands on the public's time. Usually a person spends an entire evening to make a brief comment. So the danger of over-working the public may be greater where public meetings are common. Fewer people may make inputs, and representation may suffer. Distance is a barrier to nonlocal input, and scheduling is a difficult decision even for local input. People must come when and where the meeting is scheduled. By contrast, they can write a letter at their convenience.

Finally, meetings can intensify preexisting polarization. Each group can "egg on" the other and reopen wounds, thus making any final decision harder to accept.

Guidelines for Use

Public meetings should not be used automatically, but only in cases where many or most of the following apply:

(a) The public seems to want a visible public-involvement session, and interest is high enough to indicate a reasonable turnout.
(b) The issue is controversial. This suggests some sort of public gathering is needed as one collection technique, but workshops (see below) may be better if interaction within the public seems desirable.
(c) The need for information is great and lends itself to effective presentation to a group.
(d) The issue and community are such that they are not likely to cause some public input to be suppressed or distorted. If suppression or distortion of input seems likely but, for other reasons, a meeting still seems necessary, it is absolutely essential to provide other, alternative ways of making confidential input. (This should be done in almost all cases anyway.)

Conducting a public meeting calls for special skills and personality traits, and not everyone can do it well. People who are not suited for the job should not be put on the spot regardless of their position in the organization.

Workshops

The workshop technique is one in which participants (who may be invited individually or attend in response to an open public invitation) are divided into small, mixed-interest groups, and asked to address an issue and recommend a decision. This technique has had very limited application to date, although its use appears to be increasing. Of the workshops reported, attendance ranged from 100 to nearly 1,000.

Strengths

Workshops appear to win more complete and enthusiastic public participation than any of the other techniques. Workshops usually interest participants because they can do something other than sit and listen. A workshop provides an action focus for energy, interest, and creative abilities.

This technique provides an excellent opportunity for those with opposing viewpoints to establish a dialogue, whether or not they reach agreement. There is at least some indication that persons with opposing views may experience some innoculation of their views and attempt to reach a compromise. People get acquainted with others who hold different views, often for the first time. The technique may, in fact, be effective in determining acceptable trade-offs between interests. Workshops provide a fair opportunity to describe issues and alternatives and to correct misconceptions. In particular, the public can become more aware of constraints and begin to appreciate the complexities of resource decision-making.

Weaknesses

Workshops are costly and time-consuming for the agency and demanding of the public's time. If the approach is overworked, it may tend to weed out participation by all but the most avid individuals and interest groups. This can result in biased input, excluding persons who do not have the time or interest to participate fully.

The workshop can be "stacked" by a special-interest group, thereby throwing a bias into the results. The same persons can appear repeatedly at a series of workshops. Further bias will be introduced in favor of local input because of the difficulty of securing regional and national participation.

By asking each workshop group to produce a compromise recommendation, the full range of conflicting ideas may be obscured, although this can be minimized by providing for minority reports.

Guidelines for Use

The workshop method should be chosen under the same general conditions as a public meeting, especially when group interaction seems more appropriate than individual statements. A workshop is not a substitute for question-and-answer-type meetings that usually would precede any public input. The group interaction may be especially useful where it is apparent that more than two viewpoints are held and where opinion is not yet supporting one position. Workshops would be open meetings to avoid bias or any suggestion of "deck-stacking."

Workshop groups should not be forced into a single group recommendation; minority reports should be permitted. Excessive pressure to "kiss and make up" could backfire. Persons should not feel they have been manipulated into modifying their views or kept from submitting their personal opinions.

Ad Hoc Committees or Temporary Working Groups

Ad hoc committees are temporary, structured committees (selected either by the agency or by interest groups in response to an agency invitation) that address themselves to a specific issue and recommend decisions. When the issue is resolved, the ad hoc committee is dissolved. Ad hoc committees were used by approximately ten percent of the Forest Service units studied.

Strengths

Strengths of this technique may be summarized as follows: capable, interested committee members can be selected; there is ample opportunity to inform the committee, thus avoiding misconceptions that might lead to faulty recommendations; a properly structured committee can reflect general public opinion; sound, supportable recommendations usually are obtained; the public is likely to support the committee's decision; and, the credibility of subsequent decisions may be enhanced if they follow the recommendations of a representative ad hoc committee.

Weaknesses

The new Public Law 92–463, Federal Advisory Committee Act, seriously complicates the use of this approach by federal agencies. Committees having fixed membership selected by a federal official, created for purposes of providing advice, having an organizational structure and holding periodic meetings, would normally be subject to terms of the Act.

Requirements of the Act include filing of charter, meeting announcements, and minutes in the Federal Register; justification statements for the Office of Management and Budget; public announcements of meetings, and filing of annual reports. Requirements of the Act are so cumbersome that they preclude use of this technique for most issues.

There is very real danger that selection of committee members can introduce bias that does not represent the entire range of public interests. Several officers stressed this problem. If one-time, informal working groups are used, the danger of bias seems even greater. Allowing interest groups to choose their own representatives can help credibility, but probably increases the risk of bias.

Guidelines for Use

In selecting members, a full range of interests must be represented, as a biased group can give dangerously misleading advice. It is desirable to include some nonlocal people. Through such means as news media, the public should be informed of the ad hoc committee's activities and progress.

Finally, there always should be opportunities for nonmembers to voice their views. Including them protects the decision-makers from accepting bad advice unknowingly. Letters, public meetings, or both would be appropriate.

Advisory Groups

Advisory groups include the traditional, formal, standing committees such as Forest Grazing Boards and Forest, Regional, and National Multiple-Use Advisory Committees. They are structured committees, normally selected by the forest supervisor, regional forester, or chief. Traditionally they have formal charters and by-laws. Also traditional, multiple-use advisory groups are selected to represent a cross section of interests.

Strengths

The agency can deliberately select capable, concerned people representing a broad spectrum of interests. An advisory group provides a good opportunity for the line officer to develop a strong, one-to-one relationship with each individual committee member. These individual relationships may prove more useful than the committee itself.

If properly structured, an advisory group can function as a sounding board reflecting general public opinion, at least for the local public. The group can help the agency evaluate public input. Its greatest strength may be that the committee is an effective means of dispensing accurate and full information to the public.

Weaknesses

Selection of committee members can introduce bias not representative of the public. Given the multitude of viewpoints in society, it is very difficult to represent them all on a committee, and skillful use of a committee by administrators is difficult (Campion, 1972). Advisory committees are immediately suspect by some. Often in the past, such groups have not adequately reflected the full range of interests. Their representativeness and credibility must be clearly established, or use of advisory committees can backfire.

Membership tends to become permanent because of reluctance to tell members their services are no longer desired. There is danger that deadwood will build up and render the committee ineffective.

Public Law 92–463, Federal Advisory Committee Act, imposes upon Advisory committees the same complications cited for ad hoc committees. In particular, the disclosure requirements of the law may inhibit member contributions.

Key Contacts

By "key contacts" is meant seeking input from such opinion leaders as local political figures, congressmen, active members of organized groups, and respected businessmen and citizens. The emphasis is on gathering their opinions, not on asking them to endorse or support an agency position. Next to public meetings, key contacts have been the most common source of public involvement among the Forest Service units studied.

Strengths

Input can be obtained from informed, influential people, who often can indicate community opinion. Key people can inform others about issues and stimulate input. The involvement of key people can contribute to public understanding and acceptance of decisions. Input can be obtained in person, one-on-one, in depth, and detail. Unlike some of the group situations cited above, it is possible to contact key people outside the local area by telephone or other means.

Weaknesses

It is easy to introduce bias in selecting contacts. The practice has received a bad reputation in many circles because of this, and several forest officers expressed concern about the danger of a forest officer's key-contact list growing to reflect his biases. Most key-contact lists presently in use reflect local interests.

The general public can feel bypassed and may resent decisions that seem to have been worked out with the "big shots." Finally, if input is oral, based on personal discussion with the key person, it may be difficult to document for analysis.

Guidelines for Use

Contacts must reflect fairly representative and differing viewpoints, not just those of comfortable, old friends. Input from contacts should be summarized in writing immediately afterward and be filed for analysis. If used in decision-making, this input must be available for review by other members of the public. Although this may inhibit some contacts, it seems necessary both by law and to avoid public suspicion of dealing behind closed doors.

Direct Mail

Direct mail technique consists of sending information on an issue to as many potentially affected people as possible, and requesting input, usually a letter, in return.

Only a few examples of this technique were discovered in the study. One example was found in the Chugach National Forest in Alaska. Information was mailed to everyone listed in the local telephone directory, requesting letters in reply. The issue was a proposed closure of an area to all-terrain vehicles. Vehicle-users had dominated an earlier public meeting. But a mailing produced a size-return that overwhelmingly supported closure.

Strengths

Most people in the area covered are alerted to their chance to become involved. Individual input is not exposed to the public, so there is no pressure to conform or to express a particular view. Citizens can respond at their leisure, avoiding scheduling problems. The resulting input is easy to analyze; it is written and usually focuses on the issue. An appropriate mailing list, however, can be difficult to develop. The number of potentially interested people can be very large, making a comprehensive mailing job even more formidable.

Weaknesses

If some interested people are left off the mailing list, and other steps to inform the public are not made, resentment is likely to occur. Many uninterested people usually are contacted in the effort to reach interested ones. Where a great deal of information is needed, preparing and mailing it becomes disproportionately expensive and burdensome.

Guidelines for Use

Direct mail should be considered for issues that can be explained adequately in a concise way, and that affect a fairly small, readily-defined number of people. Its use is especially appropriate where privacy seems desirable. Direct mail is useful in small towns and rural areas where a mailing list does not present an insurmountable hurdle and where it may be difficult to get frank input unless privacy can be assured.

Press releases and other types of announcements inviting citizen involvement should be used as a supplementary means to reach those interested people whom the mailing might miss.

Soliciting Written Input

This technique refers to encouraging people to submit their comments in writing, after they have been informed through the mass media, personal contact, mailings, meetings, or in any other way. Individuals and organizations usually are asked to write letters. Most units studied indicated that soliciting written input was one of the more efficient collection techniques.

Strengths

Proper publicity can stimulate a great number of individual responses. Nonlocal people can participate, assuming that they are informed. The burden on the public in terms of time and travel is minimal, and there are no scheduling conflicts.

Writing affords privacy for people who prefer to not be conspicuously identified with their position. However, the content of written input is public information. We were told that some special interests objected when their input was shown to other citizens. It is easy to say, "If they won't stand behind their position publicly, they shouldn t say it," especially when the input comes from a company or organization. But it is equally easy to agree that it is fair to shield an individual who might be subject to retaliation. Numbering letters and covering up names and addresses would make the *content* available to any interested citizen while preserving anonymity.

This technique offers advantages in analysis as well. Comparatively little agency time, effort, and special skill is needed to stimulate written comments. The input is much easier to analyze using systematic techniques such as Codinvolve, yet the public can express values in its own language (Clark, Stankey, and Hendee, 1974).

Weaknesses

Writing usually does not give people a chance to see how others feel, and to change their position as a consequence. However, this is not an insurmountable problem. All input occasionally has been printed up and distributed to everyone who contributed. In other cases, respondents were invited to read through the collected letters.

When people write their input, communication tends to be one-way. That is, it is more difficult for the agency to reply, answer a question, or correct a misimpression than it is in a meeting.

Guidelines for Use

A variety of means should be employed to inform the public

about the issue and to alert them to the opportunity for writing input. Mass media, mailing lists, personal contact with key people, public meetings and workshops are helpful. In soliciting written input, it should be made clear what sort of input on what aspect of the issue is needed.

Questionnaires, Surveys, and Response Forms

Questionnaires are printed instruments asking the same questions of each respondent. Questionnaire items can be open-ended or feature-fixed alternative responses. The citizen marks those that reflect his views. Questionnaires are used in three ways. They can be given informally to interested persons to inform them, focus their attention and facilitate their response. They may be used in a formal study of opinion, in which case they are sent only to a random sample of the public. They can be attached as tear sheet response forms to brochures describing the issue and soliciting input.

Three cases of informal questionnaire use were found in the study of Forest Service public involvement. Recently, since completion of the roadless area review, the use of tear sheet response forms has been used many times with good results. A brochure is used to explain the issue and a tear sheet response form on the back provides, usually, for a combination of fixed and open-ended response. For example, the response form might ask respondents to indicate their favored land use alternative and tell why they feel that way.

Strengths

Questionnaires provide input that is easy to analyze. Multiple-choice answers can be classified and coded to simplify analysis, although it is difficult to determine what the results mean if words have been put in people's mouths. Questionnaire respondents do not ramble; they comment on the topic. They encourage a large input. People fill out a questionnaire who would not write a letter or speak in a meeting. Distance and rigid scheduling are not problems, making it easier to tap nonlocal opinion.

Weaknesses

Questionnaire design is a *very* specialized skill (Potter et al., 1972); amateur efforts can severely bias input. The scientifically designed sample required for a formal survey is difficult to construct and costly, and sampling lists often are unavailable. Sampling requires special skills which are in short supply.

Also the informal distribution of questionnaires can produce biased results. This, however, is no more likely to occur with a questionnaire than with any other collection technique not based on a sample. Interest in questionnaires is often prompted by desire to get input representative of the entire public. That is not achieved merely by using this tool. A small proportion of the general population is likely to respond, which limits the ability to generalize from the findings to the general population. Finally, the sharp focusing of questions or use of structured response forms can discourage valuable supplementary comments by respondents and can thus restrict input.

Reports from Other Agencies or Organizations

Reports, data compilations and the official positions or opinions of other governmental agencies, conservation groups, or industry associations are included under this heading. This is not a technique that was used systematically and consistently by the Forest Service units studied.

The input reflects expert knowledge from a relevant, affected group or interest and may be used to obtain new, detailed information.

On the negative side, views expressed can be narrow and specialized, and not reflect the view of a majority of members of an organization or agency. The opinions from other agencies may reflect the agencies' ambition and objectives.

Day-to-Day Public Contacts

Perhaps this activity should not be considered as a separate technique since it takes place without respect to issues and regardless of what other techniques are used. It consists of informally disseminating information and collecting opinions through normal and continuing business and personal associations.

Strengths

Because it is nonstructured, it encourages free expression of opinion. It can help, therefore, establish rapport and confidence between the public and the agency by allowing for careful explanation and complete understanding of issues and providing the opportunity for quick responses. It may help to "feel the public pulse" so that we can anticipate reactions from more formal techniques. Also, it provides an opportunity to encourage more formal public participation. Good administrators, like politicians, routinely carry out day-to-day public contacts.

Weaknesses

It reaches a very limited public, primarily local, and tends to be biased in other ways because it most often comes from those we agree with or from a few outspoken individuals. Its informality increases the likelihood that it will not be documented.

Mass Media

By definition, the mass media (newspaper, magazines, radio, television) can help to inform the public of the issue, to solicit public input, and to provide channels for feedback to the public concerning decisions. Mass media were used often by the Forest Service units studied.

Most Forest Service officials felt that local newspapers generally gave the Forest Service good coverage on public-involvement issues, including occasional front-page stories or editorial review. In urban areas, however, newspaper coverage was less complete.

Radio and television air time in small and medium-sized markets was always extended to Forest Service officials when they asked for it. But in areas of larger population, competition was great for air time. When television and radio were used, Forest Service officials felt it was an extremely valuable medium for explaining the issue and securing public involvement. Interviews, announcements, news items, talk shows, and editorials afforded the Forest Service access to television and radio time.

The strength of the mass media is the ability to reach a large segment of the population, and to present a large amount of information in an interesting, attractive way.

There are weaknesses as well. Real skill is needed to use the media well. An amateurish job may be worse than not trying at all. The message may, in some cases, be distorted or oversimplified by reporters who do not fully understand the issue or by the limited time or space available for the story. Finally, in urban areas there is much competition for prime time and front-page space.

CONCLUSIONS AND RECOMMENDATIONS

The review of Forest Service public involvement led to several conclusions and recommendations concerning public input collection that seem applicable to all public resource agencies.

Many Forest Service officers expressed disappointment at the relatively small number of people who contributed input in public-involvement efforts. There were some real flops, such as a meeting in an eastern metropolis that only four people attended, and other sessions where most of the audience consisted of Forest Service people. The Roadless Area review, which appeared to be of broad interest, stimulated input from only about one person in a thousand. In California, sometimes regarded as a hotbed of conservation concern, less than 5,000 responses were received, about one for every 4,000 citizens in the State.

Our observations and interviews indicated that locally run, decentralized public involvement efforts produced more public input than centrally directed programs. A number of factors are probably at work: local credibility, personal contacts, proximity to the area in question, proportionately greater interest of smaller communities (partly because the impact is more apparent), and others.

There was a feeling expressed by forest officers that the input came overwhelmingly from special interests rather than the "general public." But specific analysis of input in several cases indicates that less input came from organized groups than the decision-makers had expected, and a broader range of views surfaced than was anticipated. However, even the private citizens who responded usually had a personal interest in the issue. Many forest officers asked, "How can we get the silent majority to speak up?"

Is the desire for full public representation feasible or unrealistic? We suggest the following perspective.

Resource managers should strive for public involvement as extensive as possible. This requires attention to the whole involvement process, but especially to publicity and to providing a variety of means for input by using several input techniques. But agencies should recognize that even with extensive publicity and many alternate convenient ways for the public to participate, only a small minority (primarily made up of those who will be most directly affected) will provide input. This is true of public participation in all types of problems, not just those of natural resources, and should not cause disappointment. For example, many people affected by a proposed housing development will attend a zoning hearing; those who live across town won't. The "silent majority" (assuming publicity has been adequate to make them aware of the issue and its possible consequences) may be speaking by their silence. They are saying, "No opinion," "I don't think it affects me," "I don't care," "I'll pass," or "Somebody else can have my proxy."

In our complex pluralistic society, citizens are likely to remain passive on well over 90 percent of their opportunities for public involvement. To the extent the "silent majority" has ideas about issues, they are probably just as diverse as those that are expressed. It is a mistake to think there is one opinion held by the entire "silent majority."

It is unrealistic to expect many inputs from people who do not have a special interest and are not directly affected. The agency has a responsiblity to protect public values—but anything that smells of "hiding behind the silent majority" is dangerous and threatens the public involvement effort. It is more important to see that all directly affected interests have made their views known. And if they have not, their views should be solicited.

Local, Regional, and National Input

All Forest Service officers interviewed agreed that their public involvement efforts stimulated overwhelmingly local input, a little regional input and virtually no national input. Most of them thought this was undesirable. The usual remark was, "After all, these are *National* forests."

This is a complex issue. First, it must be recognized that a considerable amount of national input is available through Congress, the White House, executive departments and lobbyists, as well as from the Washington office of the Forest Service, particularly on broad issues affecting many National Forests. The same is true of public involvement by other federal agencies.

Second, resource issues vary in their inherent scope of interest. For example, a specific road closure may be of interest to few citizens beyond the local area. Even most issues that stimulate national interests have a core area of higher interest. Managers must exercise judgment in seeing that all who are interested in or affected by a pending decision have been informed, and that relevant general publics are notified as well.

How large an area should be covered in publicity efforts? (*Every* issue cannot be publicized nationwide.) There often will be a few people from outside the area who have a special interest —dude-ranch guests, outfitter customers, nonresident hunters, stockholders of timber or mining firms, long-time recreationists. Often it is impossible to identify them. Whenever possible, they should be notified of any issue that may affect them. The Forest Service should act directly to assure that newspaper editors are offered both the backgound and the day-to-day information they need.

Managers should recognize that it is usually impossible to achieve "demographic representativeness" from their public involvement efforts, that is, input representative of the age, sex, occupation, education and racial composition of the community. However, they are obliged to achieve "interest representativeness"—input representing all segments of the public who are directly interested or affected. Both demographic and interest representativeness are important guiding concepts. The former serves as a generally unattainable goal, but one to strive for; the latter serves as a criteria against which public input collective efforts must be judged.

ACKNOWLEDGMENTS

Much of this material originally appeared as "Collecting Public Inputs: Techniques, Issues and Experience" in *Public Involvement and the Forest Service: Experience Effectiveness and Suggested Direction* by John C. Hendee, Robert C. Lucas, Robert H. Tracy, Tony Staed, Roger N. Clark, George H. Stankey and Ronald A. Yarnell (Washington, D.C.: U.S. Forest Service, NTIS Accession No. PB 234 244/AS, 1973) Chapter III, pp. 41–81.

REFERENCES

Campion, T. B. "Public Involvement in Decision-Making in the Shoshone National Forest," Masters Thesis, University of Colorado, Boulder, Colorado (1972).

Clark, R. N., G. H. Stankey, and J. C. Hendee. "An Introduction to CODINVOLVE: A System for Analyzing, Storing, and Retrieving Public Input to Resource Decisions," USDA Forest Service Research Note PNW–223 (1974).

Heberlein, T. A. "Principles of Public Involvement for National Park Service Planners and Managers," Department of Sociology, University of Wisconsin (1975) (mimeographed).

Hendee, J. "Public Involvement in the United States Forest Service Roadless-Area Review: Lessons From a Case Study," paper presented to Public Participation Seminar sponsored by the University of Edinburgh, School of the Built Environment and Centre for Human Ecology, Edinburgh, Scotland (July 1–3, 1974).

Hendee, J., R. N. Clark, and G. H. Stankey. "A Framework for Agency Use of Public Input in Resource Decision-Making," *J. Soil Water Conserv.* 29 (2), 60 (1974).

Hendee, J. C., R. C. Lucas, R. H. Tracy, Jr., T. Staed, R. N. Clark, G. H. Stankey, and R. A. Yarnell. "Public Involvement and the Forest Service: Experience, Effectiveness, and Suggested Direction," a report from the U.S. Forest Service Administration Study of Public Involvement, NTIS Accession No. PB 234 244/AS (Washington, D.C.: U.S. Government Printing Office, 1973).

Potter, D. R., K. M. Sharpe, J. C. Hendee, and R. N. Clark. "Questionnaires for Research: An Annotated Bibliography of Design, Construction and Use," USDA Forest Service Research Paper PNW–140 (1972).

Stankey, G. H., J. C. Hendee, and R. Clark. "Applied Social Research Can Improve Participation in Resource Decisionmaking," *Rural Sociol.* 40 (1), 67 (1975).

U. S. Forest Service. "Guide to Public Involvement in Decisionmaking," USDA Forest Service GPO 732–283/404 (1974).

8. Codinvolve: A Tool for Analyzing Public Input to Resource Decisions

Roger N. Clark, John C. Hendee and George H. Stankey

INTRODUCTION

In response to laws, agency directives, citizen pressure, and resource administrators' desire to do a better job, the United States Forest Service was among resource-management agencies that developed a variety of programs to promote effective public involvement. The agency has broad resource-management responsibilities, and citizens have expressed increasing concern, often in court, about the allocation of national forest resources and management priorities.

In 1972, the Forest Service initiated an administrative study to review the agency's public-involvement efforts (Hendee et al., 1973). The objectives of this study were: (1) to review public involvement procedures to determine which work best under what conditions, and (2) to develop new techniques for analyzing public input. This chapter describes some results of this major study including: a conceptual framework of public involvement, principles and criteria for analyzing public input and the development and application of the Codinvolve System for analyzing public input.

An early result of this Forest Service study was the development of a conceptual framework identifying processes basic to any public involvement effort. Five main processes comprise the framework: issue definition, public input collection, analysis, evaluation and decision implementation.[1]

Issue Definition

This is the process or stage in resource planning during which managers, working within legal, fiscal, political, resource capability, and environmental constraints, identify the range of alternatives that might require additional public input. The resource base is studied, environmental and resource-capability data are integrated within broad legal and fiscal constraints, and viable management alternatives are identified.

Advice from key members of the public at this stage can assure that no interests or reasonable alternatives are overlooked. But major public input is yet to be collected, and managers must not become locked into any one alternative.

Public Input Collection

The collection process includes all the varied techniques that yield citizen input.[2] The objective of the process is to secure the full range of views from all who are interested or affected. It usually begins with efforts to inform the public about issues, alternatives, and consequences. For their input to be useful, the public must be well informed. Collection also includes efforts to solicit and record citizens' views about the courses of action they prefer.

A wide range of activities is involved. Advisory boards, ad hoc committees, public meetings, opinion leaders, professional contacts, workshops, letters, editorials, opinion polls, petitions, and surveys are possible sources of public views.

There is no single, best way to obtain public input. All collection methods have advantages and weaknesses, and too much reliance on one can distort the range of input. A range of collection techniques is needed.

---

[1] This framework is also described in Hendee *et al.* (1973) and Hendee, Clark and Stankey (1974).

[2] Chapter 7 describes the strengths and weaknesses of a variety of techniques employed for collecting public input.

Analysis

The input must be collected in a form that can be analyzed and evaluated. Collection methods should involve some record of the input to facilitate its use.

Analysis describes (summarizes and displays) the nature, content, and extent of public input so it reflects the ideas, opinions and values it expresses. Wherever possible, analysis should be systematic, objective, and quantitative. It should use processes that can be replicated by independent analysis.

Analysis should focus on questions about the content of input: What was said? By whom? Where did the input originate? How did it vary? How many people provided input? What views did they express? What interests were represented and what ones were not? What were the prevailing opinions and views about management alternatives, general issues, and specific areas? What reasons were given to support the views expressed? What additional issues were raised?

With this information, responsible managers can subjectively evaluate its meaning and implications. But it must be stressed that analysis merely describes public input. It makes no attempt to evaluate the importance of that input. Serious biases result when judgments of importance or "quality" are made in the process of analysis, thereby prematurely screening out certain kinds of input.

Evaluation

Evaluation is the interpretation and weighing of all data collected and analyzed relative to a decision or recommendation. The process is necessarily subjective; no set formula exists to guide it. But when the resource manager presents his decision, he should clearly state the relative importance he placed on the kinds of public input received and why.

For example, where local, regional, and national inputs differ, he should specify the importance attached to each in arriving at the decision and his criteria for such judgments. Likewise, he should clarify the importance he attached to factors other than public opinion (such as resource capability and legal and budgetary constraints).

With a more accurate understanding of public opinion and values, coupled with the other decision factors, decision-makers can better justify decisions and recommendations both to the public and to the agency hierarchy. If each decision-maker clearly states how he weighed the various public input and the relationship of this input to other factors, his judgment can be reviewed more easily by those who question his decision. In time, guidelines for evaluation will evolve from decisions that are accepted and those that are not.

Decision Implementation

When implementing a decision, decision-makers must consider such processes as providing feedback to the public, providing review when necessary, and taking whatever steps are required to translate a decision into an action program. Successfully implementing a public resource decision is not a spontaneous event, particularly when there has been controversy.

It is important to give the public time to react. Reaction to a decision depends on what the public thought the agency would do. When that decision runs counter to public sentiment, untapped opinions can surface again. The "silent majority" suddenly can make itself heard.

Decision implementation should facilitate rather than stymie review when the decision of factors leading to it are seriously questioned. For example, subjective matters such as the importance placed on various factors and input in reaching a decision are legitimate matters for public review and debate. Patience, tolerance, and a good job on the previous processes are the manager's best assets at this stage.

Although these five processes are distinct components, they also are highly interdependent. The way in which any one is conducted can dramatically affect the others (Figure 1). For example, the ability of decision-makers to evaluate data obtained will be greatly affected by the way issues were defined, the collection techniques utilized to tap public sentiment, and the analysis system used to describe and array public input. Likewise the ability to implement decisions into programs that win public understanding and support will largely depend on the decision-maker's ability to explain how all factors affected his decision. Like the proverbial chain and its weakest link, the interdependence of the processes requires comprehensive planning for public involvment to achieve its potential value.

ISSUE DEFINITION

COLLECTION PROCESS
   Public input:
      Public-involvement activities--
      public meetings, advisory
      groups, informal contracts, etc.
   Other input:
      Resource data, legal and budg-
      etary considerations, economic
      data, environmental impact.

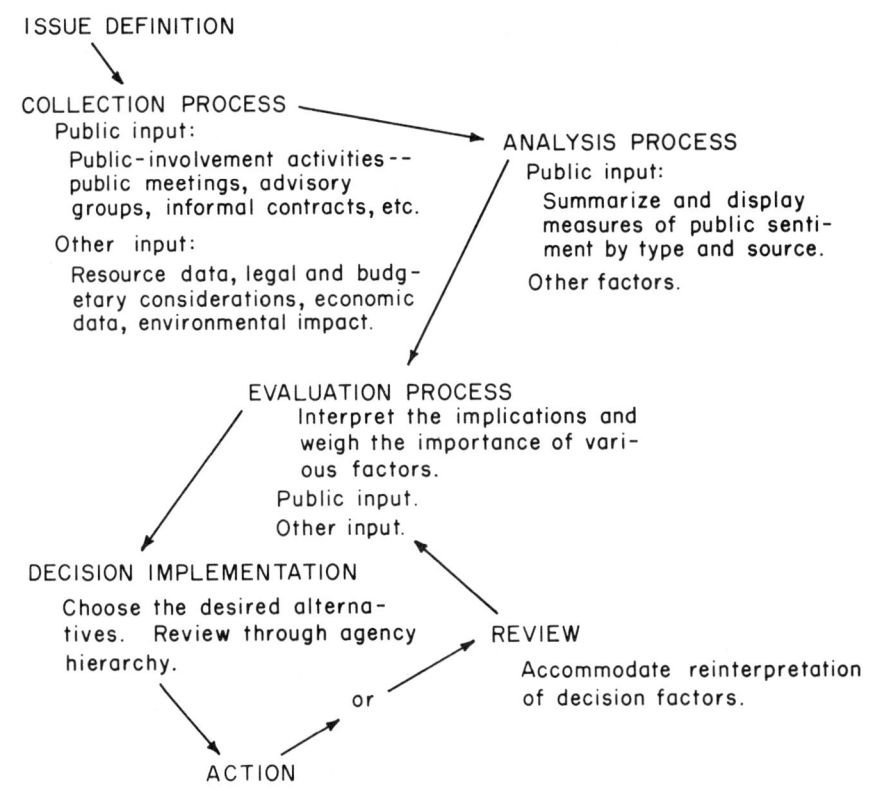

ANALYSIS PROCESS
   Public input:
      Summarize and display
      measures of public senti-
      ment by type and source.
   Other factors.

EVALUATION PROCESS
   Interpret the implications and
   weigh the importance of vari-
   ous factors.
   Public input.
   Other input.

DECISION IMPLEMENTATION
   Choose the desired alternatives. Review through agency
   hierarchy.

REVIEW
   Accommodate reinterpretation
   of decision factors.

or

ACTION

Figure 1. Basic processes of public involvement and their sequential relationship to one another.

DEVELOPMENT OF THE CODINVOLVE SYSTEM

In reviewing Forest Service public-involvement efforts, it became evident that analysis presented a major barrier to effectively utilizing public input. This conclusion was reinforced by the number of requests we received from land managers seeking social scientists' assistance in handling the flood of input from citizens. In many cases, literally thousands of public inputs had been received. The volume of input, coupled with the complexity of the land use issues, made it virtually impossible to make effective use of the information it contained. A systematic, objective, reliable and uniform system for analyzing public input was a high priority. In response to this need, from the broad,.generic methodology of content analysis, we developed an applied content-analysis system called Codinvolve (Clark, Stankey and Hendee, 1974). The system is founded upon a set of principles and criteria geared to yield an accurate, replicable summary of public input. Codinvolve is designed to use edge-punch, card-sorting techniques that are workable at field levels where computer assistance usually is not available. But it is readily adaptable to computer use as well.

The basic concept underlying systematic content analysis of public input is as follows: the common denominators of virtually all public input are the *opinions* offered *for, against,* or *about* the issues in question, along with any *reasons* given to support the views. The number and kind of reasons can vary considerably, even among those given to support the same opinion. This combination of opinions and supporting reasons defines the values the public holds with regard to the issue in question.

Knowing the balance of opinion (numbers for and against an issue) and the supporting rationale (why they are for or against) are both important. The analysis must, therefore, provide an accurate description of all opinions and their supporting reasons in a form for easy review and consideration.

As the case study described later will demonstrate, decision-makers do not always follow the majority rule in land management. But, the analysis of the public input received must clearly identify the alternative values held by the public, and the evaluation must document how those values were balanced against other factors in reaching the decision.

The development of Codinvolve rests on six broad principles as criteria that any analysis system should meet. A discussion of these follows.

Analysis is Separate From Evaluation

Analysis is an objective, replicable process; evaluation is subjective. Issues such as the quality of the input, the relative weights to be assigned to various forms of input, representativeness, and vote counting are matters of evaluation, *not* analysis. Analysis simply provides a descriptive record of the input, a record as accurate and undiluted as possible. The only objective of analysis is to accurately summarize the entire content of the input received. Whether or not the input is representative of potentially affected interests, or whether petitions should be weighted as much as or more than letters must be considered only after the analysis is completed. To confuse these two processes threatens the credibility of the analysis.

Decision-Making Questions Guide Analysis

To make analysis most effective, it is necessary to specify in advance those questions about public input that decision-makers want answered. For example: What is the balance of input—pro, con—for various management alternatives? What reasons support these opinions? How does the input vary according to the residence of respondents?

Often, public involvement programs are initiated with little forethought about specific questions administrators want answered. This severely limits the analyst's ability to provide data describing public input in a form the decision-maker will find useful.

All Input is Relevant and Must be Processed

Because all input expresses human values pertinent to the resources, all of it has implications for decision-makers. Emotional statements as well as detailed site or issue-specific remarks hold potential meaning for decision-makers, and the analyst must make sure his summaries incorporate all inputs.

Analysis Must be Systematic, Objective, Visible, and Traceable

Analysis should follow a structured procedure to check and balance the way input is handled. It must be objective so that independent review would generate the same information. It should be visible so the public can see that citizen opinion plays a significant role as resource decisions are made. Finally, traceability assures that an independent reviewer can "follow" how input was handled.

Identity of the Input Must be Maintained

During analysis, there should be no combining or altering of input. Decision-makers later may wish to review how opinion varied according to the forms in which it was expressed, the locations where it originated, and so forth. Input from personal letters, for instance, should not be combined with input from form letters or petitions. The content of each type of input must be summarized separately so each can be reviewed for its unique implications. To mix different kinds of input in the analysis is to imply they should be weighted equally in their evaluation, something managers may or may not wish to do. The analysis must not prejudice evaluation of the input.

Analysis Must be a Continuing Process

Because many resource-management decisions evolve over extended periods of time, the analysis system must be capable of storing, retrieving, and summarizing information as it is needed. This capability makes the system particularly useful in land use planning underway in several U.S. resource-management agencies. As allocation issues are resolved, management alternatives must be considered. Much public input previously submitted with regard to how much land to allocate to various uses also contains valuable information on how that land should be managed. With this information entered on the edge-punch cards, it is within easy reach of managers and planners at all planning levels. This feature has been pointed out by several managers as a major benefit of analysis. Also, when a series of similar land-allocation issues follow one another, information gained from one can be of considerable value as planners begin to formulate plans for the next.

From these broad principles, we have formulated ten specific criteria for analyzing public input:

1. The method should summarize the extent, content, and nature of public input in relation to the decision-makers' questions.
2. It must be objective.
3. It must be visible and traceable.
4. It must be reliable, in that the opinions expressed are recorded the same way by different analysts.
5. It should provide for uniform application among different administrative units.
6. It should be flexible, to accommodate different conditions.
7. It should have the capacity of handling large quantities of input, have storage-and-retrieval capabilities, and the capacity to assimilate continuing input.
8. It should summarize the balance of opinions expressed and describe variations in each opinion.

9. It should provide other descriptive and qualitative information about the content and nature of input.
10. It should facilitate environmental analysis leading to the preparation of final environmental-impact statements by identifying all significant information and arguments for and against the proposed actions.

Although there is no single ideal method for analyzing public input, the system chosen should satisfy the above criteria. These criteria have guided development and application of the Codinvolve System.[3]

BASIC STEPS IN USING CODINVOLVE

Codinvolve provides for the orderly and systematic transfer of information from any type of written input to a form that is easy to summarize for review. With input in hand, the analyst must provide a summary that answers the decision-maker's questions and objectively describes the full content of that input. The steps in doing this job are described briefly below and are summarized in Figure 2.[4]

Identify Questions for Which Decision-Makers Need Answers

It is essential that the analyst know in advance what information the decision-maker wants from the public input. (Usually this information should be determined early in the public-involvement process.) This is the key to useful analysis. The analyst must consult decision-makers to insure that nothing important is overlooked and that summaries are provided in a useful fashion. Basic questions often asked by decision-makers include: Who said what? What was the distribution of sentiment on the issue? How did it vary by residence of the respondents? What reasons underlie the opinions?

---

[3] Four methods for analyzing public input in addition to Codinvolve were found in use throughout the Forest Service. They were intuitive, simple tabulation, content summary, and content analysis (Hendee et al. 1973, p. 89-92).

[4] For a complete description of the steps readers are referred to "The Codinvolve Users' Manual" by Roger N. Clark, George H. Stankey, Randel F. Washburne, Mary Alice Taylor and John C. Hendee. Available on request from Recreation Research, 4507 University Way N.E., Seattle, Washington 98105.

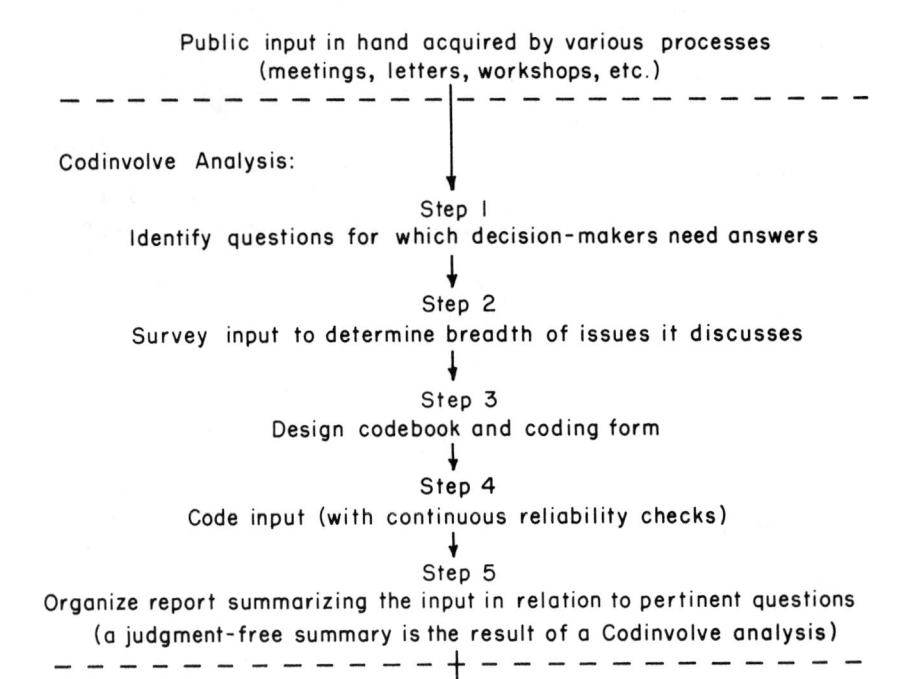

Public input in hand acquired by various processes
(meetings, letters, workshops, etc.)

- - - - - - - - - - - - - - - | - - - - - - - - - - - -

Codinvolve Analysis:

Step 1
Identify questions for which decision-makers need answers

Step 2
Survey input to determine breadth of issues it discusses

Step 3
Design codebook and coding form

Step 4
Code input (with continuous reliability checks)

Step 5
Organize report summarizing the input in relation to pertinent questions
(a judgment-free summary is the result of a Codinvolve analysis)

- - - - - - - - - - - - - | - - - - - - - - - - - -

Evaluation Process: Make judgments about the relative importance of the various kinds of public input in relation to other decisionmaking factors.

Figure 2. Flow diagram focusing on a Codinvolve analysis.

Survey the Input to Determine the Breadth of Issues it Discusses

This step calls for an overview of the input—the issues it discusses and the opinions and information it provides. Although it is important to specify decision-making questions, it is critical that the analytic structure not filter out any new or unanticipated information. In order to respond to the varying nature of input and maintain its integrity, analysis must capture the full breadth of public input so as to summarize it for review.

In order to determine the breadth of issues the input contains, a sample is taken and its content summarized. This content summary is used to define the range and diversity of opinions, supporting reasons, and factual material contained in the input.

Design Summary Form and Codebook

The two basic documents for a Codinvolve analysis, the summary form and codebook, are built around results of the previous step, *i.e.*, the system is designed to incorporate the full range of opinions and ideas expressed in the input.

It is on the *summary form* that information from the input is recorded. Edge-punch cards have been the basic tool utilized for this purpose in most Codinvolve applications. Information from the input should either be coded in punches along the edge of the card or written out in detail directly on the card.

The *codebook* tells the coder how to use the summary form. It contains detailed procedural instructions, definitions, and examples that show where and how information should be coded. It is a basic reference document, and any changes in coding procedures must be noted in it. Reliability or the assurance that each coder's work will replicate that of other coders is crucial to the system's success. In order to insure accuracy, the set of instructions from which all coders work must be clearly understandable and uniform.

Code Input

Coding is the process of transferring the content of public input to a form that facilitates summary. The major objective in coding is to capture, accurately and objectively, the complete scope of information. The principal obligation of the coder is to record only what the citizen said, not what the coder thinks he means.

Perhaps the most difficult part in learning to use the Codinvolve is in maintaining objectivity and not interpreting what the writer means. This often is a problem because many citizens appear confused by the issues under consideration, or base their arguments on faulty logic, or in some cases misinformation. Nonetheless, the analyst must deal *only* with what is said. He must accurately summarize all comments, whether emotional, uninformed, or confusing. Once this job is done, then the evaluation process can begin and responsible personnel can judge the input as a whole rather than sentence by sentence. The analyst may, in fact, ultimately be responsible for evaluating the input, but the key is not to do it during the analysis. Coding is a process that must be entirely objective and replicable. This is possible with careful attention to coding procedures, training of coders, and regular checks for accuracy.

Coding is a demanding job; not everyone can do it. Persons who do not rapidly acquire the necessary skill should not continue coding. Ideal coders, from the standpoints of both accuracy and cost, usually are technical or clerical personnel. Personal or professional knowledge about the issue at hand is not necessary and, in some cases, can actually interfere with accurate coding. Experience indicates that it takes at least three or four days to train a group of coders. During this period, accuracy usually starts at 50 or 65 percent and rises to 90 percent or higher.

The amount of input that a coder can handle without a significant decline in accuracy varies with individuals and with differing types of input. For fairly complex letters, average output per coder usually falls between 30 and 50 inputs a day. Beyond that number, accuracy begins a sharp decline. Structured types of input are easier to code, so form letters and coupons can be handled more quickly, sometimes as many as 150 or 200 a day.

Organize a Report Summarizing the Input in Relation to Pertinent Questions

Upon completion of coding, the analyst summarizes the information into a format easy for decision-makers to use. The process of constructing tables displaying information is done by computer, by hand using edge-punch cards, or both. (For a discussion concerning the relative advantages and disadvantages of these approaches see Clark and Stankey, 1975.)

The end product of Codinvolve is a set of tables summarizing public input. It is particularly important that the analyst provide information about all issues citizens have discussed in their input, and not just that related to the specific questions on which information is sought. This will insure that new or unanticipated information is not overlooked.

The product of a Codinvolve analysis is not a written report. It is the objectively interpreted display of public input.[5] How-

---

[5] Readers interested in examining actual reports based on a Codinvolve analysis are referred to: (1) "Summary of National Public Response to the Roadless Area Review Draft Environmental Impact Statement," a report by John C. Hendee and Roger N. Clark, June 1973, 53 p., mimeo. Available on request from the Director of the Office of Information, U.S.

ever, most decision-makers will request that analysts provide more than a collection of tables. For example, they will be interested in what interpretations the analysts make of these tables, what limitations the decision-maker should consider, and so forth. Writing such reports requires that an analyst interpret the tables with caution to assure that his narrative accurately describes the data.

Quite often, the summary of public input indentifies areas where people might have been confused or misled. Knowing what the confusion is and how it came about can help decision-makers respond constructively. However, if these comments are interpreted or filtered out during analysis, then decision-makers would not have an accurate picture of what their various clients really were thinking. An accurate analysis thus serves as a feedback mechanism to administrators, providing important clues on how well information is diffusing to the public.

To guard against subjective or erroneous interpretations, we have recommended that drafts of the reports be circulated to others for technical review. This review process is invaluable in keeping interpretation accurate and in incorporating points the author might have missed.

A CASE STUDY OF A CODINVOLVE ANALYSIS

Since Codinvolve was developed in early 1972, it has been used in over 75 studies to analyze more than 100,000 public inputs. We have been involved directly in many of these studies working with administrators to apply and adapt the system as necessary to meet their needs. The flexibility built into Codinvolve is a result of this close collaboration between research and manage-

---

Forest Service, USDA South Building, Washington, D.C. 20250. (2) "A Summary of Public Response on the Final Environmental Statement Concerning the Proposed Pelican Butte Winter Sports Development," a report by Lyle E. Jack, 24 p., mimeo. Available on request from the Forest Supervisor, Winema National Forest, U.S. Forest Service, Post Office Building, Klamath Falls, Oregon 97601. (3) "Public Response to the Olympic National Park Draft Wilderness Proposal and Master Plan—Summary and Analysis," a report by the Recreation Research Project, U.S. Forest Service, Pacific Northwest Forest and Range Experiment Station, Seattle, Washington, 94 p., mimeo. Available on request from the Regional Director of the Pacific Northwest Region, National Park Service, 4th and Pike Building, Seattle, Washington.

ment in the application of social science skills to solve a real resource-management problem.

Every application has had unique problems, and has required a slightly different approach (depending on a combination of factors including number and kind of inputs and complexity of the issues discussed). The issues of concern have been varied, ranging from a single, well-defined topic to a broad array of complex issues. In every case, the basic criteria on which the system is based and the five steps, as outlined, have guided analysis.

The Salmon River Wild and Scenic River Proposal, and Idaho Primitive Area and Salmon River Breaks Primitive Area Wilderness Study

The Codinvolve analysis of public input to the Salmon River issue illustrates how flexibility built into the analysis system compensated for the diverse problems encountered.

The Issue

Two interrelated allocation issues were of concern in this example. Approximately 60 miles of the Salmon River in Idaho were under study for possible classification under the Wild and Scenic Rivers Act of 1968. The Forest Service proposed four alternative classification schemes for the river, ranging from classification overlapping the river and adjoining land areas, to no classification for the river whatsoever. Six different alternatives were outlined for the two areas, ranging from a strictly managed wilderness proposal encompassing both areas and the Salmon River on the one hand, to no wilderness classification for any of the area.

This was a complex set of issues, with a large number of possible combinations of river and primitive areas proposals. The objective of the land use study was to develop a proposal for the future management direction of the entire area for submission to the President and to Congress, as required under the terms of the Wilderness Act and the Wild and Scenic River Act. Public comment was requested on both phases of the study.

The complexity of the issues, coupled with the large amount of input received (see Table I), necessitated the use of a computer for completing the tabulations. A special computer pro-

Table I
Type of Input and Number Received

Input		Signatures
Personal letters	544	625
Response forms	2,135	2,229
Workshop input	4,079	5,642
Petitions	1	229
Reports	2	2
Form letters	37	40
Other	7	8
TOTAL	6,805 Inputs	8,775 Signatures

gram has been developed to provide both summaries of input and cross-tabulations of opinions against important variables, such as form of input and residence of respondents.

Strategy of Analysis

As in most other Codinvolve analyses, all opinions and supporting reasons contained in the input were initially entered on edge-punch cards. Opinions on major issues were then transferred to ADP cards for computer analysis.

A special transferring process is necessary to move information punched on edge-punch cards to ADP work sheets for card punching. Although this is a quick procedure, the number of times information has to be handled increases the possibility of error, thus increasing the need for additional time spent on accuracy checks. Supporting reasons that were written on the cards were then summarized by hand from the edge-punch cards.

This combined use of edge-punch cards and the computer allowed several objectives to be achieved. The massive sorting and tabulating process was facilitated by the computer while storage and retrieval of a wealth of public input about many issues and areas was possible using the edge-punch cards. In this particular study hundreds of tables could have been produced arraying the many opinions by important variables such as form of input, who responded, and residence of respondent. While hand sorting of edge-punch cards is possible and has been accomplished in studies of similar size, use of a computer provides economy and additional analytical capability when it is available.

Time Required for the Analysis

Six weeks were required to complete this analysis. Eight coders were employed. The coding rate varied from 30 to 50 inputs per day for letters and about 150 per day for the structured response forms (tear sheet questionnaires from the back of a brochure explaining the issue).

Problems Encountered

In an effort to facilitate broad public participation in the study, the Forest Service team developed several different structured-response forms for the public. Some of the forms asked for a ranking of preference for the various alternatives. Measures of public sentiment obtained from these forms were nonadditive and difficult to compare. This well-intentioned effort to make public input easy to provide through fixed response items was offset by the problems created in analyzing, interpreting and evaluating the meaning of the input.

The Salmon River issue provides an excellent example of the interdependence of all the public-involvement processes. For instance, the overall pattern of sentiment on a land-management issue normally can be shown with only a few summary tables. In the analysis of input, more than a dozen tables needed to be reviewed to obtain this overview because of the way in which the input was obtained.

Many attempts have been made in a variety of studies to structure the form in which the public provides comments. These include response forms, check lists, and questionnaires. In most cases, the motivation for structuring the input seems to have been to make the analysis process easier, *i.e.*, it's easier to count boxes than to decipher comments in an unstructured personal letter.

Unfortunately, as the Salmon River example illustrates, such structuring does not ensure useful input. Our experience and that of many land-manager colleagues indicates that the nature and quality of information obtained is severely restricted when obtained by structured input. With the availability of a system like Codinvolve, much of this structuring would appear unnecessary. Efficient and accurate analysis is possible even with diverse forms of unstructured input.

Thus, we feel that structuring how the public provides comment is inappropriate and unnecessary in most cases because personally written letters generally provide a more detailed picture of the writer's views. It is better to provide sufficient information about the issues for which comments are being solicited and urge citizens to respond in their own language. It also should be made clear that other comments also are welcome.

Response forms are best used to focus public comment on the important issues rather than structuring how the input is to be provided. Response forms or questionnaires should always be combined with well-publicized opportunities for unstructured public comment. With Codinvolve, accurate analysis is still possible regardless of the form in which public input is received.

Balance of Opinion

A complex picture of public sentiment on the two issues emerged from the analysis.[6] With regard to the Salmon River, most persons who utilized structured-response forms favored no classification at all. Protection of local land-owner rights and the local economy were common reasons for this position. Most support for a "wild" classification came from nonlocal residents and generally was in personal letters.

A similar pattern emerged in response to the six Primitive Area proposals. Again, there were significant differences in opinion obtained from different types of input. For instance, input obtained from public meetings reflected greater support for restrictive classification than did written input.

The analysis also revealed a significant minority position that advanced its own proposal for the areas under study. A coalition of conservation groups proposed a substantially larger wilderness proposal than the Forest Service proposed.

Outcome

After the public input was analyzed, the Forest Service prepared a proposal regarding the area's future management for submission to the President and Congress. The proposal calls

---

[6] For a detailed discussion of the input, see "Analysis of Public Inputs to the Salmon River Study and the Idaho and Salmon River Breaks Primitive Areas Study," a report by Joel Dahlin, Ray Hunter, Karl Haaser, and Harold Bolt. Available on request from Forest Supervisor, Bitteroot National Forest, 316 N. 3rd, Hamilton, Montana 59840.

for classification of a 1.5 million-acre Wilderness with the Salmon River managed under the Wild and Scenic Rivers Act. The proposal was presented to the public in early 1974 and nearly 10,000 additional inputs were received which were analyzed using Codinvolve. The final outcome is pending action by Congress.

The outcome of this case to date demonstrates two important aspects of public involvement. First, the use of public involvement in decision-making is more than a matter of vote-counting. The tentative decision made by the Forest Service was contrary to the aggregate measure of public opinion, which called for no classification of the area. The extent to which the agency has made defensible "evaluation" of the input awaits legislative and possible judicial review. In any case, the visibility and traceability of the Codinvolve analysis process will allow proponents as well as opponents of the Forest Service to draw their own conclusions about what the content of the public input received means for the decision.

Second, the different opinions surfacing from different types of input, as well as the variations in sentiment according to residence, are examples of the need to maintain the identity of the input throughout the analysis. There were distinct patterns of support for and opposition to the Forest Service proposal, which correlated directly to such things as form of input. In the evaluation process, Forest Service officials were able to review this differential pattern of opposition and support and make judgments accordingly about the relative significance of the various perspectives.

This case example represents one of a range of issues for which a Codinvolve analysis has been conducted. The procedures used and problems encountered are typical of other applications. The number and kind of inputs, number and complexity of issues discussed, and level of analysis required for other applications are variables analysts must consider in determining the specific approach best suited for the job at hand. In all cases, however, the criteria and basic steps outlined earlier in this paper should guide the conduct of the analysis.

ACCEPTANCE OF CODINVOLVE BY MANAGERS AND THE PUBLIC

Response by decision-makers who have used the Codinvolve system has been enthusiastic. The system has provided a way to contend with large quantities of diverse input. Their response, however, has been tempered by the extent to which they understand the principles and criteria upon which the system is built, and on how the output of the system is to be utilized.

Early in the development and use of the system, we frequently encountered instances in which managers assumed the Codinvolve System would perform evaluation functions. For example, during the design stage, several managers asked that the system be designed to categorize the "quality" of information, or that only "substantive" information be coded. As we have already discussed, this would require judgments about the importance of inputs, and that is not a function of the analysis process. The analysis phase delivers information to the decision-maker in an undiluted, nonjudgmental state; it is the responsibility of the decision-maker to gauge the importance to place on different input.

However, once decision-makers have understood the analytic role of Codinvolve their support of the system has been high. They have stressed the value of being able to review the diversity of public input. Where decisions are in line with public wishes, it is possible to clearly document this. When decisions run counter to expressed public will, managers can more accurately outline the rationale for their decision because they can identify specifically the character and extent of public opposition as well as support.

Citizens likewise have generally endorsed the Codinvolve system. Presentations on the system, the principles and criteria upon which it is based or how it can be used, have been made to a variety of citizens groups. Public support of the system has, as in the case of managers, been contingent upon understanding what it does. A particularly important feature of Codinvolve that citizens have favorably responded to is its treatment of all input as important, its recognition and recording of general expressions of values, as well as site- or issue-specific information. Also important is the ability for the citizen to see how his input has been handled and the fact that the emotional content of input has been retained. On numerous occasions citizens have been invited to see how Codinvolve treats their inputs. Most seemed impressed with how their views were protected so they surfaced in summaries, and that their comments were not simply reduced to numbers. The visibility of the system's operation, and seeing that it doesn't make decisions, seems to have been a major reason for public acceptance of it.

CONCLUSIONS

Citizen participation in decision-making has become a fact of life for resource-management agencies in the United States. The Codinvolve System for analyzing public input is a tool to facilitate public participation that evolved from the adoption and application of social science methodology. Practitioners in one field—resource management—received increased capability from applied social research as a result of our involvement in their problem. We think this involvement of researchers in a management problem was the key to developing a workable system and urge our manager and social scientist colleagues to join in similar ventures for the most mutually gratifying results (Stankey, Hendee and Clark, 1975).

Analyzing the content of public input might appear deceptively easy. Often we've been asked to "drop by this afternoon to show me how Codinvolve works.... I want to analyze 5,000 letters tomorrow." However, as with most analysis systems, learning and using Codinvolve requires an investment of time and money on the part of managers, technicians, and coders. As the Salmon River study demonstrates, the analysis of public input cannot be a last-minute, add-on item. Sufficient time and budget must be allowed early in the land-use planning process to insure an adequate job.

A decision to use Codinvolve, or any other system capable of providing similar information, is a decision to commit funds and people. However, in most cases, using the system involves a rather minor expenditure (as little as 5 percent in one instance) in relation to the total investment in any land-use planning study. The potential benefits in quality land management seem well worth the cost.

REFERENCES

Clark, R. N., G. H. Stankey, and J. C. Hendee. "An Introduction to Codinvolve: A System for Analyzing, Storing, and Retrieving Public Input to Resource Decision," *USDA Forest Service Research Note*, PNW-223, (Portland, Oregon: Pacific Northwest Forest & Range Experimental Station, 1974), 16 pp.

Clark, R. N., and G. H. Stankey. "Analyzing Public Input to Resource Decisions: Criteria Principles, and Case Examples of the Codinvolve System," *Natural Resources J.* (forthcoming, 1975).

Hendee, J. "Public Involvement in the United States Forest Service Roadless-Area Review: Lessons From a Case Study," paper presented to Public Participation Seminar sponsored by the University of Edinburgh, School of the Built Environment and Centre for Human Ecology, Edinburgh, Scotland (July 1–3, 1974).

Hendee, J., Roger N. Clark, and George H. Stankey. "A Framework for Agency Use of Public Input in Resource Decisionmaking," *J. Soil Water Conserv.* 29 (2), 60 (1974).

Hendee, J. C., R. C. Lucas, R. H. Tracy, Jr., T. Staed, R. N. Clark, G. H. Stankey, and R. A. Yarnell. "Public Involvement and the Forest Service: Experience, Effectiveness, and Suggested Direction," a report from the United States Forest Service Administration Study of Public Involvement, NTIS Accession No. PB 234 244/AS (Washington, D.C.: U.S. Government Printing Office, 1973).

Stankey, G. H., J. C. Hendee and R. Clark. "Applied Social Research Can Improve Participation in Resource Decisionmaking," *Rural Sociol.* 40, 67 (1975).

9. Rational Participation and Public Involvement in Water Resource Politics

John C. Pierce, Kathleen M. Beatty, and Harvey R. Doerksen

INTRODUCTION

What moves people to participate in water resource politics? The answer is important, for the motivation to water politics participation affects the nature of the demands on policy-makers and the success of public involvement programs. To a large extent, the causes of individual participation will govern the amount of conflict in water policy processes. If participants are motivated solely by dissatisfaction with policy, for example, there will be greater conflict with policy-makers. If both satisfaction and dissatisfaction with policy are motivators, there will be conflict among participants, and policy-makers will have potential allies in the public. In short, the characteristics that distinguish participants and nonparticipants have critical implications for programs designed to increase public involvement.

This study examines the ability of one model of political behavior to explain levels of water policy participation. The model employed here is that of rationality. A preliminary answer is proffered to the question of whether water policy participants are distinguished by their greater self-interest in water policy outcomes and their apparent ability to perceive the connection between those outcomes and their self-interest. Assumptions of rationality are made, and predictions on the basis of those assumptions are tested. If the predictions hold, the presumption is in favor of the assumption of rationality with which the analysis began.

WATER POLITICS AND RATIONALITY

Water resource political participation is not an easy task. Water resource issues usually are rather complex, with technical questions at the heart of evaluations of policy alternatives. Opportunities for public participation are irregularly available, often depending on the initiative of those who make the policy. Public hearings, for example, are established by legislators or agency personnel, and special effort is required by members of the public to attend them. Moreover, water resource questions do not regularly dominate the mass news media. There is no routinized, inexpensive source of water resource information available to the general public. Unlike voting, participation in water resource politics is generally not taught as one's civic duty (Campbell, et al., 1960). Because participation in water resource politics requires rather special effort and motivation on the part of the individual, people who do participate should be distinct from those who do not.

What can explain the behavior of people who do make the choice to participate? Social scientists employ a variety of frameworks to explain political participation. In various studies, participation is related to social and economic characteristics (Verba and Nie, 1972), psychological and attitudinal variables (Lane, 1959), socialization processes (Beck, 1974), and formal rules and procedures (Matthews and Prothro, 1966).

One framework enjoying increasing use as an explanation of political behavior is the rational choice approach. The concept of rationality is used, for example, to gain insight into voter behavior (Downs, 1957), legislative coalition formation (Riker, 1962), and organizational participation (Olson, 1965).

A common thread among definitions of rationality is that individual behavior is motivated by self-interest. There are several alternatives affecting that interest, and the individual possesses sufficient information or ability to calculate the consequences of the alternatives. In the voting context, Straatman (1974) says that

> Rational behavior ... is implied by the voter's ability to calculate logically the benefits that the various alternatives might be expected to yield, and rational choice is effected when the voter opts for the alternative that he thinks will provide him with the greatest benefit.

Goldberg (1969) defines rationality more generally:

> Put most simply, being rational in a decision situation consists of examining the alternatives with which one is confronted, estimating and evaluating the likely consequences of each, and selecting the most attractive set of expectations.

In this study, the alternatives available to the individual are the levels of participation in water resource politics, ranging from abstention to intense and multidirectional participation. Self-interest, in terms of potential costs and benefits from participation, is present when the individual has an identifiable stake in water resource policy outcomes. Since political processes influence water resource policy, the general hypothesis is that *the rational behavior of the individual with a personal stake in water resource policy is participation in attempts to influence the direction of policy.*

The water resource policy process is amenable to the rational model of participation for several reasons. First, as noted above, participation is not easy in water resource politics. More than convention, habit, or social norms is necessary to stimulate activity. Moreover, water resource policy allocates a number of readily identifiable costs and benefits to the public. These costs and benefits are the incentives to participation. Generally, incentives are either collective or selective (Olson, 1965). Collective benefits (costs) generally apply to everyone, such as the production of hydroelectric energy. Selective benefits (costs) apply only to individuals who meet certain conditions, such as the setting aside of certain waters only for canoeing. Selective benefits are greater stimuli or incentives to participation because the individual receives direct gains or losses from the policy, gains or losses that are not shared with others not in the same condition. Thus, the rational framework would suggest that participation would be greater among individuals with selective benefits or costs to be derived from water resource policy.

The skeletal model of rational participation presented here possesses three basic variables, in addition to participation itself. First, there is some assessment of the degree to which the individual has a selective stake in water policy outcomes which would move that person to participate. That is, there must be an identifiable incentive to which it would be rational for the individual to respond. Second, there is some indication of the extent to which the individual currently perceives benefits or costs to that individual's interest emanating from water policy. Third, there is some measure of the ability of the individual to calculate costs and benefits from policy. The variables chosen to represent those elements of the model are waterfront property ownership, water resource policy satisfaction, and level of education.

Waterfront Property Ownership

The variable most directly relevant to the question of selective costs and benefits from water resource policy that is available in this study is whether the individual owns waterfront property. Waterfront property can be employed by the individual for a wide variety of uses—agricultural, recreational, aesthetic, or business. The extent to which those intended uses are met and, hence, the extent to which the individual can derive benefits or suffer costs is structured by present or proposed policies. Thus, the rationality framework would hypothesize that people owning waterfront property would be more likely to participate in attempts to influence water resource policy.

Water Policy Satisfaction

The level of policy satisfaction appears in rational choice literature as a motivator to participation. V. O. Key argues that in voting, individuals primarily "... reject what they have known, or they may approve of what they have known" (1966). Hence, political participation is at least partially an expression of support for or opposition to existing policy. Brody and Page (1973) suggest that a useful distinction can be made between indifference toward policy and either positive or negative orientations to the policy. They argue that individuals with *indifferent* attitudes about policy are less likely to express support for the system or opposition to the system than either those who are satisfied or those who are dissatisfied with policy. And, participation in political processes is one mechanism by which those system orientations can be expressed.

Anthony Downs (1957) presents an argument that would refine that of Key and Brody and Page. Again, the neutral public would be less likely to participate. However, given support for the present policy and perceiving no threats to the status quo, Downs would predict also that there would be less participation among the satisfied public. Thus, one would predict that political participation in the rational framework would be highest among the dissatisfied public. It would be low among the satisfied and indifferent public. Yet, the assumption of no threat to the status quo on the part of the satisfied public's perceptions is unlikely. Water resource policy is in a state of continual flux. The changing nature of that policy emphasizes that there are indeed many threats to the status quo. Thus, those satisfied with policy would experience some motivation to participate, although less so than the dissatisfied public.

Education

Goldberg argues that a person's rationality depends on the ability to calculate costs and benefits (1969). Thus, rationality should increase as the level of education increases, for "education increases rationality in the special senses of lowering information costs and developing innate intelligence toward its fullest potential" (Goldberg, 1969). Thus, given the appropriate conditions for rational participation—selective costs and benefits and perceptions of policy satisfaction or dissatisfaction—that participation should be higher among individuals with higher levels of education.

In summary, then, the basic rational participation model presented here is hypothesized to discriminate among individual participation levels according to the person's education, policy satisfaction, and ownership of waterfront property. Accumulating across variables, the greatest participation should occur among the highly educated, dissatisfied, waterfront property owners.

THE DATA

The data for this analysis were obtained from a mail questionnaire survey of residents in Washington State from October 1974 through January 1975. Four separate mailings were employed. The original sample contained 1,300 potential respondents; 173 questionnaires were undeliverable, or returned uncompleted because the respondent was deceased, aged, or infirmed. Of the remaining 1,127 in the sample, 687 returned questionnaires at least partially completed and 48 returned the questionnaire but refused to complete it. The return rate of 61 percent is comparable to other studies using similar methods (Dillman, 1972).

The dependent variable in this analysis is an additive index of water resource political participation. Each respondent indicated whether he/she had participated in one of the following activities in an attempt to influence water resource policy: attending a public hearing, contacting a legislator, contacting a government agency, joining a group, or joining a citizen advisory committee. Table I shows the percentage participating in each of those activities. No more than 18 percent participated in any of the activities, and 10 percent or less participated in the other four. This evidence supports the earlier position that water resource political participation is a relatively infrequent occurrence, and by implication, something that requires special motivation.

Table I
Public Participation in Five Activities for the Influence of Water Resource Policy

	Attending Public Hearing	Contacting Government Agency	Contacting Legislator	Joining Group	Citizen Advisory Committee
Percentage Participating	18%	9%	10%	7%	3%

The index of political participation ranges from 0 to 5. The mean position on the index for the total sample is 0.462. Two education categories were created: high education includes individuals with more than 12 years of education, and low education includes individuals with 12 years or less. The ownership of waterfront property is a dichotomy, those who own and those who do not. Policy satisfaction is divided into three categories: satisfied, not sure, and dissatisfied.

RESULTS

Within each of the independent variables—education, policy satisfaction, and waterfront property ownership—the difference between categories in the average level of participation is statistically significant (p <0.001). The results are shown in Table II. Thus, each element of the rationality framework exhibits a separate effect on participation. But, what happens when the independent variables are combined with each other?

The average participation score within each of the combined categories of education, property ownership, and policy satisfaction is shown in Figure 1. In general, the hypothesis suggesting that the level of water policy participation can be explained through the use of rational choice variables is supported. Tracing the breakdown of the level of participation in the combinations of the independent variables is illustrative. People in the high-education group participate more than people in the low-education group (0.581 versus 0.325).[1] Within the low-education group, waterfront property owners participate slightly more than nonproperty owners (0.351 versus 0.321). Within the high-education group, however, the property owners participate substantially more than the nonproperty owners (0.970 versus 0.478). Even so, the high-education nonowners participate more than either of the low-education groups. Clearly, then, the educated property owners, as predicted, exhibit the greatest participation. In terms of this study's framework, the explanation is that property owners have a greater interest (greater potential for selective costs and benefits) in water policy outcomes, and education allows them to perceive the relationship between that interest, water policy, and the potential impact of participation.

Introduction of the policy satisfaction variable generates even greater range in the average level of participation. As predicted, the dissatisfied high-education property owners participate at the highest average level (1.688). Of the categories with more than ten cases, the two next most participating groups are (1) the high-education satisfied property owners (0.933), and (2) the high-education dissatisfied nonowners (0.789). The lowest

---

[1] The averages are slightly altered from those shown in Table II because the Table II figures are based on all individuals for whom education level is available. In Figure 1, however, the data are based on individuals for whom data on all three independent variables is present. People with missing data on any of the variables were omitted from the latter analysis.

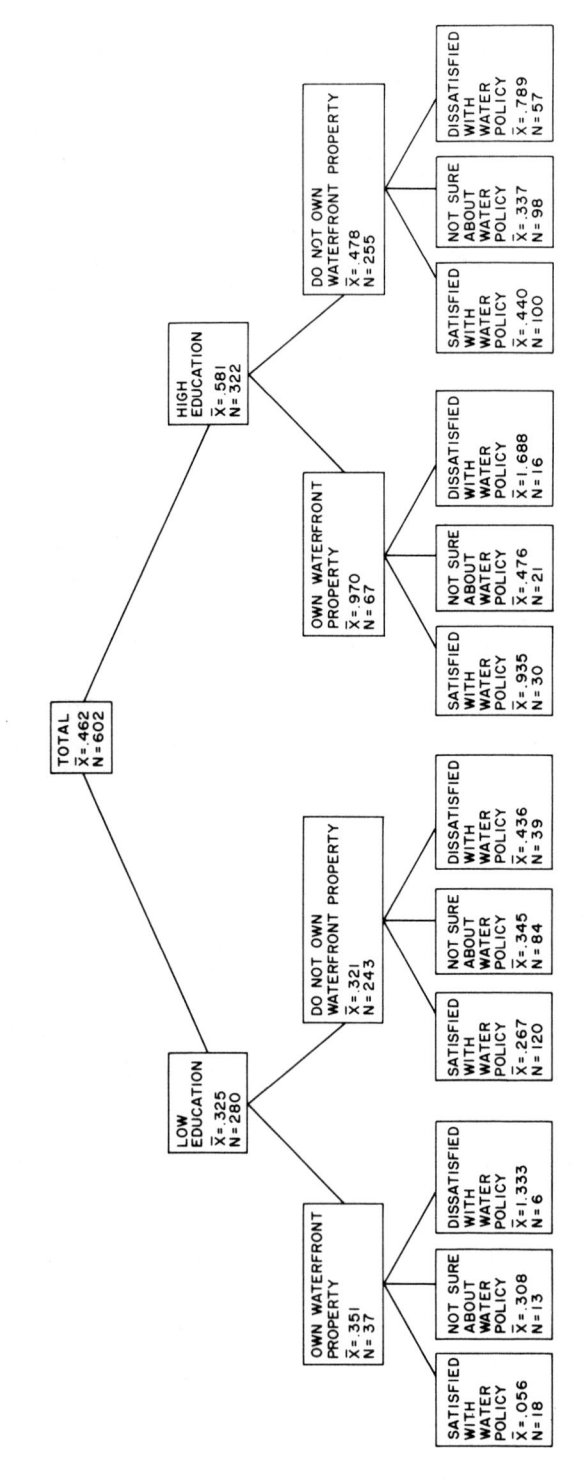

Figure 1. Average level of water politics participation among high- and low-education respondents, controlling for level of water policy satisfaction and water front property ownership.

Table II
Average Levels of Water Politics Participation in Categories of Education, Property Ownership, and Policy Satisfaction

Categories	Participation Number	Participation Mean Level	Statistical Probability
Education			
High	344	0.587	$p < 0.001$
Low	294	0.340	
Waterfront property ownership			
Yes	108	0.796	$p < 0.001$
No	520	0.400	
Water policy satisfaction			
Satisfied	281	0.391	
Not sure	229	0.354	$p < 0.001$
Dissatisfied	129	0.845	

levels of participation are found among the low-education satisfied property owners (0.056) and the low-education satisfied nonowners (0.267).

The rational framework for participation used here discriminates quite well among individuals according to their level of participation in water resource politics. With only three variables entered into the analysis, rather wide differences in participation are found. The three variables were chosen because they are suggested in the nonwater politics literature, and the results support the hypotheses generated there. The results are the strongest when the independent variables are taken together. Thus, even though when taken separately each independent variable affects participation, obvious interaction takes place so that the addition of each variable results in even greater levels of participation.

CONCLUSION

Patterns of public participation in water resource politics fit into a rational decision framework. Participation is highest among the highly educated dissatisfied waterfront property owners. That is, participants are more likely to be able to perceive the impact of policy on their selective water resource interests, are dissatisfied with current policy and hence motivated to change it, and have an identifiable interest in water resource policy. These findings have implications for the nature of water resource politics and for public involvement programs.

The correlates of water resource policy participation reflect on the nature of future water politics. Present water politics is widely seen as full of conflict. If the water resource policy process continues to be open to public involvement, and the correlates of public participation hold, the present pattern of conflict will continue unabated. For example, that the participants are more likely to be dissatisfied with present policy means that policy-makers will be subject to continued challenge and controversy. While many policy-makers may view public involvement programs as an opportunity to build agency support, it is unlikely that public involvement programs will have any significant impact in that direction. Persuasive communications are most effective on people who are uncertain, and least effective on people who are strongly negative toward the content. Thus, agency arguments would be most convincing with people who are neutral about present water resource policy. Yet, as this study has shown, "neutrals" are the very people who are least likely to participate in water resource politics. Moreover, those who are most likely to participate—the dissatisfied—are the least likely to be effectively swayed by the agency personnel.

In the long run, it appears important that public involvement programs provide participants with feelings of efficacy with regard to selective benefits. That is, participants should feel as though their involvement has some impact or potential impact on policies that affect their interests. Symbolic rewards of participation will not be sufficient. If water policy participants are rational, they will be sensitive to the costs and benefits of a public involvement program. As noted earlier, the costs of water policy involvement appear to be substantial. Participants also will be looking for selective benefits. If the benefits are not forthcoming, rational participants will withdraw and devote their energies to more fruitful political avenues. Thus, if the purpose of a public involvement program is only to increase support for an agency and not to actually involve the public in decisions, the public involvement program itself will suffer.

The success of public involvement programs is a function of the interaction between the participant public and the agency. In the first place, it depends on the degree to which the concerned public avails itself of the opportunities for involvement. In the latter case, it depends on the degree to which the policy process is flexible enough to accommodate demands and information from a rationally involved public.

ACKNOWLEDGMENTS

The research on which this chapter is based was supported jointly by Washington State University and the U.S. Department of the Interior, Office of Water Resources Research as authorized under the Water Resources Act of 1964 (P.L. 88-379).

REFERENCES

Beck, P. A. "A Socialization Theory of Partisan Alignment," *The Politics of Future Citizens*, Richard G. Niemi, Ed. (San Francisco: Jossey-Bass, 1974).

Brody, R. A., and B. I. Page. "Indifference, Alienation, and Rational Decisions: The Effects of Candidate Evaluations on Turnout and the Vote," *Public Choice*, 15, (1973).

Campbell, A., P. E. Converse, W. E. Miller, and D. E. Stokes. *The American Voter* (New York: John Wiley and Sons, Inc., 1960).

Dillman, D. A. "Increasing Mail Questionnaire Response in Large Samples of the General Public," *Public Opinion Quart.* 36 (2), 254 (1972).

Downs, A. *An Economic Theory of Democracy* (New York: Harper and Row, 1957).

Goldberg, A. S. "Social Determinism and Rationality as Bases of Party Identification," *Amer. Pol. Sci. Rev.* 63 (1), 5 (1969).

Key, V. O., Jr. *The Responsible Electorate* (Cambridge, England: Belknap Press, 1966).

Lane, R. E. *Political Life: Why and How People Get Involved in Politics* (New York: The Free Press, 1959).

Matthews, D. R., and J. W. Prothro. *Negroes and the New Southern Politics* (New York: Harcourt, Brace and World, 1966).

Olson, M., Jr. *The Logic of Collective Action* (Cambridge: Harvard University Press, 1965).

Riker, W. *The Theory of Political Coalitions* (New Haven, Connecticut: Yale University Press, 1962).

Straatman, W. C. "The Calculus of Rational Choice," *Public Choice*, 18, 93 (1973).

Verba, S., and N. H. Nie. *Participation in America* (New York: Harper and Row, 1972).

10. Public Opinion and Water Policy

Douglas D. Rose

PUBLIC PREFERENCES FOR WATER USE

Considerable progress has been made in the past few years in understanding the structure of opinions, of which the three main ingredients are: (1) *attitudes* toward some object, consisting of pro-con evaluations, (2) *beliefs* about the connections between objects, consisting of information perceived to be true, and (3) *values*, consisting of pro-con evaluations of goals. The simplest and most basic opinion unit is the combination presented in Figure 1.

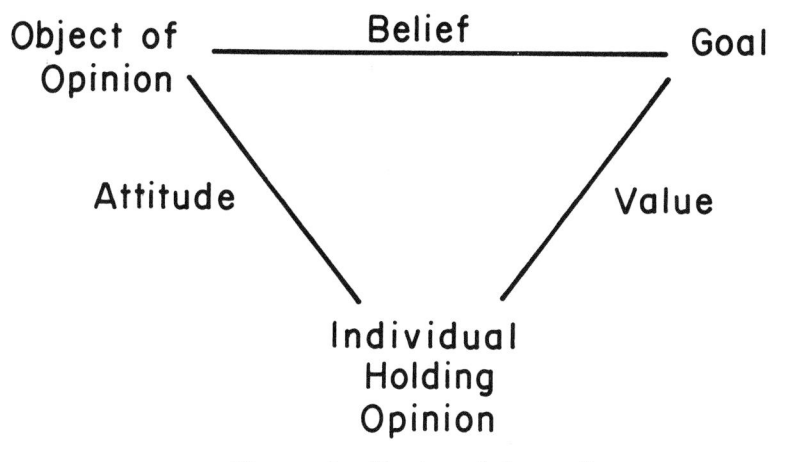

Figure 1. Basic opinion unit.

180 WATER POLITICS AND PUBLIC INVOLVEMENT

Attitudes, beliefs and values are the three relationships between the three elements of an individual holding an opinion, a goal, and an object of an opinion. A value is how the individual evaluates the goal, a belief is what the individual perceives to be the relationship between the goal and some object, and an attitude is the evaluation of the object. The three relationships are causally connected in the ways presented in Table I: attitudes are the results of values and beliefs. For instance, if an individual desires security for his family and believes that social security will produce the security, he will be in favor of social security. The simplest unit is expanded in practice to include more individuals (the public), more goals, more objects, individuals (including the individual holding the opinion) as objects, beliefs linking goals, beliefs linking objects, missing beliefs, and other complications.

Table I
Possible Opinion Structures

Value ×	*Belief* =	*Attitude*
Positive	Positive	Positive
Positive	Negative	Negative
Negative	Positive	Negative
Negative	Negative	Positive

We will examine opinions where uses of water are objects. The uses themselves are not the final objects, however; policies which consist of promoting some uses and restricting other uses, are the final object of opinion. In the simple case, the opinion units for water policy are, as shown in Figure 2, comprised of attitudes toward policy based on beliefs about what uses are promoted by the policies, beliefs about what goals are served by the uses, and values.

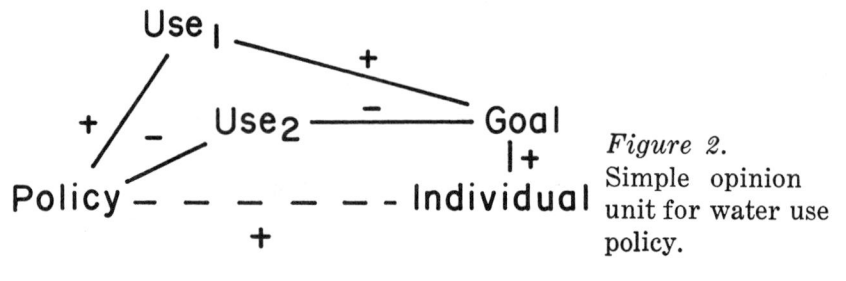

Figure 2. Simple opinion unit for water use policy.

The policy does not only promote some use, it promotes some use for some people. The policy itself is relational. When the individual holding the opinion is the user, Figure 2 remains adequate to describe the opinion unit. When the individual is not the user, however, we must consider the relationship between the individual holding the opinion and the user. The goals being served by use are no longer those of the individual with the opinion; hence, we must inject the user as an object, as in Figure 3, and consider the attitudes toward the user (identification).

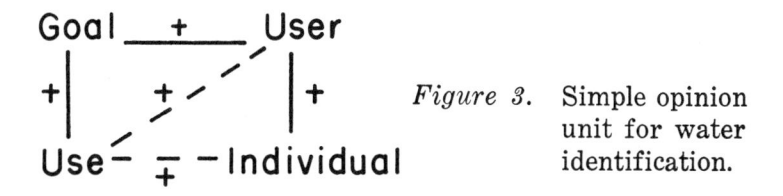

Figure 3. Simple opinion unit for water identification.

Finally, as in Figure 4, the uses described by the policy may serve the goals of a nonuser individual (or those with whom he identifies). If the uses and users are derivative, we shall call them "indirect" and secondary benefits of the policy; if the uses and users are prerequisite, we shall call them "administrative"; in both cases, we use the models in Figures 2 and 3, replacing the direct uses with indirect or administrative uses.

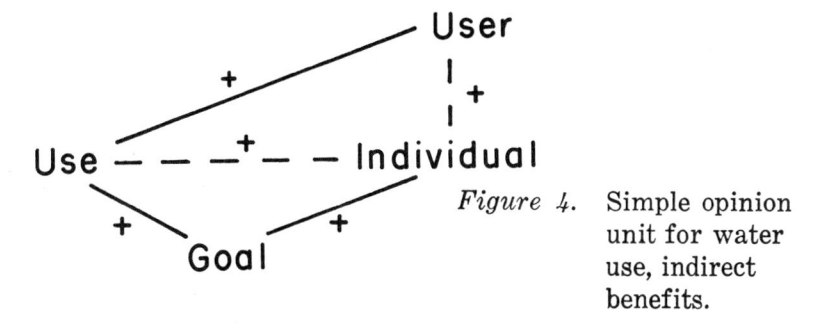

Figure 4. Simple opinion unit for water use, indirect benefits.

Method

The main dimensions of public water policy preferences are expected to be a function of (1) values, (2) water uses, and (3) identifications. To investigate the structure of public opinion on water policy, results were used from a mail questionnaire given to a random sample of the public in the State of Washington in late 1974.[1] Two-thirds of a thousand questionnaires were returned (a response rate of 61 percent), coded and made available to the author. While the survey probed many aspects of water policy opinion, we are mainly concerned here with four types of items. The respondents ranked seven uses of water in order of priority (agricultural, domestic, energy, industrial, preservation, recreation, and transportation); this is the measure of policy preference. As with the other variables, the ranks have been converted to scores on a zero-to-one continuum, with one as the highest or best score, by treating the ranks as intervals. The respondents also indicated whether they used water for four purposes (irrigation, recreation, business, and transportation); it is assumed that they all used water domestically and that they all used water-derived energy.

A third set of questions concerned whether groups (big business, consumers, farmers, environmentalists) had too much, too little, or about the right amount of power; we will treat this as a measure of attitudes toward (identification with) the groups, controlling for actual differences in power by considering only relatively high or low identification; five identification variables are measured: pro-business ("about right"), pro-consumer ("too little"), pro-farmer ("too little"), pro-environmentalist ("about right") and strongly pro-environmentalist ("too little").

Finally, respondents ranked 18 terminal values or goals of which we will use 5: family security, a comfortable life, an exciting life, pleasure, and a world of beauty (Rokeach, 1973). A further instrumental goal, personal survival, is assumed to have a very high ranking, as it is a necessary condition for the enjoyment of most of the other high-ranking goals. The value ranks were converted to a zero-to-one interval by treating ranks as intervals.[2] The measurement conversions are for convenience, as we will only be looking for general notions of direction and strength of relationships, rather than absolute impact, and because we use physical controls for complex relationships, the

---

[1] The data were collected by John Pierce and Harvey Doerksen of Washington State University.

[2] The value ranks certainly do not represent interval differences (see Rokeach, 1973), but the use of intervals for ranks does not impede correct conclusions because (1) the errors in scoring are symmetrical, hence impacts are not created by the scoring, and (2) the errors are greatest for middling ranks, hence impact is systematically being underestimated. The basis for these statements is an unpublished analysis by Douglas Rose of Rokeach's results.

measurements themselves should have little impact on our conclusions.

Policy Preferences

The outstanding characteristic of the public's policy preferences is the general agreement among the public. Table II presents the mean preference scores for each use. Agriculture and domestic uses average 80 percent, while the maximum for the top two uses would be an average of slightly over 90 percent; similarly, transportation and recreation uses average between 20 and 25 percent, while the maximum for the lowest two scores would be slightly under 10 percent. Altogether, the consensus on uses (the mean ranks) accounts for 45 percent of all ranks (variance).

Table II
Mean Preference Scores for Seven Water Uses

Agriculture	0.783
Domestic	0.778
Energy	0.668
Industrial	0.402
Preservation	0.400
Transportation	0.242
Recreation	0.227

As indicated in Table III, what disagreement exists occurs almost entirely on values of approximately the same overall rank, while values of quite distinct overall ranks are ordered with a unanimity (*e.g.*, 96 percent) belying the measurement error usually involved in complex rankings. In fact, the reliability of pair rankings follows directly from differences in their overall mean scores. A single overall dimension corresponding to the mean scores accounts for 96.3 percent of the variance in the pair rankings (thus, 43 percent of the variance of all rankings). The overall dimension reverses the mean rankings of recreation and transportation (not much of a change), but otherwise reflects the mean rankings almost exactly.

This domination of use preferences by a single ordering suggests that the public largely agrees in preferring a public policy corresponding to the mean scores. In terms of opinion structure, this suggests a consensual belief system about what goals are

Table III
Respondents Whose Ranking Agrees with Overall Ranking, by Pairs of Values, in Percentages

	Domestic	*Energy*	*Industrial*	*Preservation*	*Transportation*	*Recreation*
Agriculture	44%	64%	89%	84%	96%	92%
Domestic		67%	84%	81%	90%	89%
Energy			86%	72%	88%	86%
Industrial				55%	73%	72%
Preservation					61%	70%
Transportation						46%

served by what uses for what users and a consensual value system about those goals. While this is a boon to politicians, it is difficult to analyze empirically. The lack of variation makes proof highly difficult, as proof usually consists of showing that something is present when it is expected and absent when it is unexpected; when something is always present (consensus) or always absent, empirical evidence is incomplete.

Water Users, Identifications, and Values

The distribution of water use is indicated in Table IV; recreation use is very widespread, while agricultural, transportation and business uses all involve sizable minorities of the public. Uses tend to overlap, however, because transportation users are often disproportionately also business or recreation users, and some uses get counted twice as agricultural and business. Almost all the population uses water in a number of major ways, domestic, energy, and recreation being the primary ways. Further, the indirect uses deriving from agricultural, energy, and industrial uses are nearly universal. As a result, use patterns and identifications should not be a consideration for most uses. For two of the uses, agriculture and domestic, the most basic instrumental goal of survival is involved in indirect and direct use because safe drinking water and food result; because survival is assumed to be a highly valued instrumental goal, the population should be, as it is, fairly unanimous in desiring a policy giving priority to these uses. While water uses for energy and business do not serve quite so essential values, their direct and indirect benefits are highly diffuse and ubiquitous; in Washington, those benefits are more directly linked to water use for energy than for business.[3] Differences in users and values are thus reduced to a subsidiary role.

Table IV
Mean Usage Scores for Four Water Uses

Recreation	0.69
Transportation	0.25
Agricultural irrigation	0.24
Business	0.15

Identifications vary considerably, as indicated in Table V. The public strongly identifies with consumers (largely a matter of self-identification). Both farmers and environmentalists benefit from identification and, as these groups are actually distinct minorities, the identifications are presumably based on the indirect benefits these groups produce for the public. Few in the public strongly identify with environmentalists or identify with big business. Identification with big business is negatively related to the other identifications, suggesting a group of identifiers quite distinct from the rest of the population in their perceptions of direct and indirect benefits. Identification with farmers is unrelated to the remaining identifications, which are positively related to each other. The bases for these patterns lie outside the bounds of this inquiry; we take them as given and expect that the differences in identification will have policy consequences.

The five personal values selected for analysis have quite characteristic differences, seen in Table VI. Excitement, pleasure and beauty are largely of tertiary importance as goals, while comfort is a major incentive and family security a highly valued

---

[3] This can be compared with Louisiana, for example, where gas and oil are dominant in energy, and water is a major source of food and business. While we would expect energy uses of water to be important in Washington, we would expect other uses to be more preferred in Louisiana.

Table V
Mean Identification Scores for Five Groups

Consumers	0.80
Agricultural (farmers)	0.57
Environmentalist	0.44
Strongly environmentalist	0.17
Business	0.12

goal. By and large, the values are not strongly related to each other. Comfort and pleasure are related to excitement and thus to each other, and beauty and excitement are mildly related, with mild negative relations to family security. For the most part, however, differences among the mean scores dominate the variance: values as consensual goals are more important than different patterns of value preference.

Table VI
Mean Value Scores for Five Values

Family security	0.75
Comfort	0.50
Beauty	0.35
Excitement	0.31
Pleasure	0.29

Because identification with users is self-identification for the users themselves, we expect that use will promote identification. Table VII gives the results for five use-identification patterns. The reader can see that while the impacts are small, they are consistently in the right direction, suggesting that our measures are valid but not error-free.[4] The small impact reflects both

---

[4] As all variables have been measured from zero to one, the units are the same for all variables. The impact (regression coefficient) is the share of the maximum difference on the dependent variable that would be produced by a maximum difference on the independent variable. For a universal scientific law, the impact as measured here would always be one. In the special case of use, which is a dummy variable, the impact is the difference between users' and nonusers' scores on the dependent variable. All other impacts have been arranged in similar format, so that (except for rounding error) the impact is the difference between the expected dependent variable scores for the highest (one) and lowest (zero) independent variable scores. The measure of impact is similar in both intent (standardized regression coefficient) and results to beta weights.

the complexity of the actual processes and the presence of measurement error in measures with little true variance (consensus). As we wish to avoid the sophisticated operations required to handle such complexity and error, we will accept moderate-sized impacts as evidence confirming the simple models tested. For use and identification, the impacts support the notion of self-identification as a somewhat more powerful version of identification with other people.

Table VII
Use by Identification in Percentages

Use	Identification	User's Identification	Nonidentification	Regression Coefficient (Impact)
Business	Big business	16%	11%	0.06
Recreation	Strongly environmentalist	21%	10%	0.11
	Environmentalist	46%	41%	0.05
	Consumer	82%	74%	0.07
Irrigation	Farmers	62%	47%	0.15

If the benefits from an activity are a reason for users to support the activity politically, they ought also to be a reason for the use itself. For several goals, Table VIII indicates that values have an apparent impact on who uses an activity (though the reciprocal influence cannot be ruled out). Recreation users tend to be drawn from the part of the public most oriented to beauty, pleasure, and excitement. Business users of water are risk-takers, while farmers irrigating their crops tend to be strongly oriented to family security. The use of water transportation, on the other hand, does not indicate a different pattern of personal goals. These patterns are unsuspicious.

If use serves a goal for the user or indirectly serves someone else's goal, then identification with users should increase as the value attached to the goal increases. Table IX presents some of the results. Most obviously, a concern with beauty leads to identification with environmentalists, presumably because preservation serves beauty. Less obviously, a concern with comfort leads to an identification with economic producers. While this pattern

Table VIII
Use by Value, in Percentages

Goal	Use	High Value Use	Low Value Use	Impact of Value
Comfort	Transportation	27%	23%	0.03
Family security	Business	13%	5%	0.08
	Agriculture	27%	16%	0.10
Pleasure	Recreation	76%	16%	0.19
Beauty	Recreation	77%	66%	0.10
Excitement	Recreation	76%	67%	0.09

Table IX
Identification by Value, in Percentages

Goal	Identification	High Value Identification	Low Value Identification	Impact of Value
Comfort	Business	12%	10%	0.01
	Consumer	77%	84%	−0.08
	Farmer	48%	41%	0.07
Beauty	Strongly environmentalist	42%	5%	0.37
	Environmentalist	61%	37%	0.24

is real enough and has been commented on as an ideology, we include it here only to indicate the empirical problems posed by complexity: the connection is highly contingent on sex and economic role, with accompanying beliefs and identifications well beyond anything having to do with water policy. We shall try to avoid and control for such complexities by restricting ourselves to combinations whose relevance to water policy is obvious.

Policy and Use Preferences, Identification, and Values

Whatever goals are served, the use of water should lead to the user's supporting a policy of that use. As Table X indicates, the expectation is confirmed. Every user group prefers its use more than nonusers do. Note, however, that the overall ranking of use

Table X
Policy Preference by Use

Policy	Use	User's Preference	Nonuser's Preference	Impact of Use
Agriculture	Irrigation	0.83	0.77	0.06
Business	Business	0.43	.039	0.04
Preservation	Recreation	0.45	0.30	0.15
Recreation	Recreation	0.27	0.14	0.13
Transportation	Transportation	0.27	0.23	0.04

preferences remains largely the same; only uses virtually tied on the overall scale (recreation and transportation, business and preservation, and agriculture and domestic) have their relative rankings reversed. Though use has the expected impact, that impact dwarfs before the commonality of preference across the public.

Table XI
Policy Preference by Identification

Policy	Identification	Identifier's Preference	Non-identifier's Preference	Impact of Identification
Agriculture	Farm	0.82	0.76	0.06
Energy	Business	0.72	0.66	0.06
	Consumer	0.63	0.67	−0.04
Business	Business	0.48	0.39	0.09
Preservation	Strongly environmentalist	0.63	0.35	0.28
	Environmentalist	0.41	0.31	0.10
Transportation	Business	0.27	0.24	0.03
	Consumer	0.23	0.34	−0.11

Identification also has the expected impacts on policy preferences. Identification with the groups directly using the water yields support for those uses. The only unexpected note (in Table XI) is that both energy and transportation are seen as producer rather than consumer uses. Policy preferences also follow values, as shown in Table XII.

Table XII
Policy Preferences by Value

Policy	Goal	High Value Preference	Low Value Preference	Impact of Value
Domestic	Comfort	0.82	0.74	0.07
Energy	Family security	0.66	0.68	−0.02
Preservation	Beauty	0.69	0.26	0.43
Business	Comfort	0.44	0.36	0.08
Recreation	Pleasure	0.34	0.18	0.16
	Beauty	0.32	0.19	0.13
	Excitement	0.31	0.20	0.12

Recreation Preferences

The model presented earlier for a simple opinion structure indicates that users' preferences for water use will depend on the use serving some goal and upon the value the user puts upon the goal. Table XIII presents simple opinion structures for three goals for recreation users' recreation preferences. The values increase the preference for recreation substantially among users. Beauty, in particular, is a strong incentive among users to support a policy promoting recreation use. For nonusers who iden-

Table XIII
Recreation Preference by Recreation Use, Environmental Identification and Values

Value	High Value Preference	Low Value Preference	Impact of Value
Recreation Users			
Beauty	0.39	0.20	0.19
Pleasure	0.37	0.25	0.12
Excitement	0.34	0.24	0.10
Nonusers, Environmental Identifiers			
Beauty	0.19	0.12	0.07
Pleasure	0.30	0.10	0.20
Excitement	0.34	0.09	0.25
Nonusers, Nonidentifiers			
Beauty	0.04	0.18	−0.14
Pleasure	0.24	0.09	0.15
Excitement	0.20	0.13	0.07

tify with environmentalists (there are too few nonusers who *strongly* identify with environmentalists for analysis), beauty is not a strong incentive for supporting recreation use but pleasure and excitement are effectual values. Though support among nonusers does not reach the levels for users, suggesting that self-identification is stronger than identifications with other people, most of the support that does occur depends on the two values of pleasure and excitement. Among nonusers who do not identify with environmentalists, the value assigned to pleasure considerably increases the support for recreation indicating some identification with recreation users. Excitement, however, is not a major factor. Beauty is a negative factor; nonusers who are nonidentifiers and who value beauty do not prefer recreation as a policy. For all three groups, values play the expected role.

The three goals are strong incentives to use recreation and to identify with environmentalists. Their impact is thus twofold: they promote and maintain use and identification, which by themselves have some diffuse impacts on policy preference, and they have impact among users and identifiers to support recreation use policy. While we are, in this analysis, missing evidence on the belief linkages between recreation use and the goals, for pleasure and excitement they appear consensual and have a face validity. Thus the opinion model even in a simple form appears to illuminate recreation use preferences.

Preservation and Domestic Water Uses

Easily the most striking success of the simple opinion structure model occurs for preservation preferences. As specified in Table XIV, recreation users split sharply in their preferences for preservation policy depending on their attitude toward beauty. Users who strongly value beauty strongly support preservation; users who do not strongly value beauty give preservation the lukewarm support of nonusers and nonidentifiers. Environmentalist identifiers also divide their preferences according to beauty, but the impact is diluted through identification. Nonusers who are nonidentifiers do not divide on beauty. Aside from the value assigned to beauty, the groups do not divide on preservation, giving it uniformly low ratings when beauty is not valued. Again, beauty also operates as an incentive for use and identification, but its impact is one-dimensional, as there are few diffuse benefits from preservation to users and identifiers.

While there are diffuse benefits to preservation (future users advantaged over present users), they are neither major nor divisive.

Table XIV
Preservation Preference by Recreation Use, Environmental Identification, and Beauty

Value	Recreation Use	Environmental Identification	High Value Preference	Low Value Preference	Value Impact
Beauty	Yes	—	0.76	0.28	0.48
	No	Yes	0.57	0.25	0.32
	No	No	0.27	0.23	0.04

Easily the most striking nonsuccess of the simple opinion structure model occurs for domestic use. There are three reasons for the lack of demonstration. First, the public overwhelmingly prefers domestic use because they are almost all users and the use involves the fundamental instrumental value of survival. There is simply little variance on these matters, so proof is not available: we don't have people who like themselves or others to die from lack of drinking water. Second, for the secondary uses of domestic water that serve secondary goals, we do not have information on either the use or the goals. We don't know, for instance, which Eastern city residents would be grumpy about requests not to water their lawns or not to take showers on hot summer days or why they would be reluctant to comply.

For comfort and the instrumental value of cleanliness, the impact on domestic use preference is shown in Table XV. Even without these lesser values, support for domestic use is high. Third, the variance in domestic use preferences appears to involve differences in beliefs about the relationship of the policy to use. The relationship of the amount of domestic use to the goals served is not linear: the provision of small amounts of water serves the essential needs for safe drinking water, additional amounts are used for less essential purposes (cooking, bathing, sanitation) and yet additional amounts are used for even less important purposes (washing cars, watering lawns, cleaning dishes, washing clothes).

Table XV
Domestic Preference by Comfort and Cleanliness

Value	High Value Preference	Low Value Preference	Value Impact
Comfort	0.82	0.74	0.07
Cleanliness	0.81	0.75	0.06

Thus, the evaluation of use differs for two different types of priorities: (1) cutting back present use—domestic use is easily cut back with little harm, and (2) providing any use—domestic use is perhaps top priority for the first water. Respondents appeared to differ in how they viewed the ranking system: some viewed it as changes from present policy, some viewed it as policy from scratch. Because no opportunity was given to discriminate priorities for different amounts of uses, beliefs about the policy appear to be affecting the domestic rankings. As the domestic uses are most multipurpose and have the greatest differences in benefits depending on specific levels and uses (by comparison, agricultural irrigation is fairly linear: more water, more and juicier food), beliefs about the policy have the greatest impact on the domestic use.

Transportation, Energy, and Business Use Preferences

For both transportation and business uses of water, we have user groups, have seen that the uses tend to be identified with economic producers, and have indicated that the public's identifications do not lie with producers, except for a small segment seeing production as the key to highly valued comfort. While users and identifiers might be expected to support producer uses from economic motives, the public at large should be relatively detached from these considerations.

The results for transportation, shown in Table XVI, indicate that transportation is not very important for anyone, users included. While comfort is at least a minor motive for users, the rest of the public (including all types of producer and consumer identifiers) sees water transportation as at most a minor discomfort. In many ways transportation is the converse of domestic use: it is never perceived as very important, its ranking varies least among the seven uses, and it confers at best marginal benefits that can usually also be obtained from alternative sources. Fresh water transportation is perceived as a minor matter in Washington; historically, water transportation has often played a more crucial role and perhaps public views in the past were different. At present, the variance that does occur in the ranking of transportation is largely the by-product of other concerns: it is last or next to last except when the more volatile recreation and preservation uses are low-ranked, or when the other producer uses (especially energy and business) are high-ranked.

Table XVI
Transportation Preferences by Comfort and Use

Value	Use	High Value Preference	Low Value Preference	Value Impact
Comfort	Yes	0.29	0.25	0.04
	No	0.23	0.24	−0.01

The business use equations indicated in Table XVII show the more direct impact of economic considerations. For users, continued use means family security and comfort, and the support for use follows the concern with these goals. To some degree, everyone has a perceived security and comfort stake in business use, but this is more minor for nonusers than for users. Finally, business identifiers clearly have values other than comfort in mind when they support business use, though the analysis has

Table XVII
Business Preference by Comfort, Family Security, Use, and Business Identification

Value	Use	Business Identification	High Value Preference	Low Value Preference	Value Impact
Family security	Yes	—	0.51	0.28	0.23
	No	—	0.42	0.32	0.10
Comfort	Yes	—	0.53	0.36	0.17
	No	Yes	0.50	0.47	0.03
	No	No	0.42	0.34	0.07

not presented evidence on what these values are. They appear clearly to be indirect benefits, rather than the benefits gained by users. Such an ideology of indirect business benefits has long been associated with conservatives and the Republican party.

While the entire population can be considered energy users, the public identifies energy use most often with economic producers. Not surprisingly, the public's economic identifications have some impact on the manner in which they evaluate energy use. Identifiers with consumers see no net comfort benefits to themselves from preference for energy uses (Table XVIII), while those who do not identify with consumers do see benefits and evaluate energy use partly on the basis of their concern for comfort. Business identifiers show a slight inclination toward energy uses on the basis of comfort benefits, while nonidentifiers show no such inclination. Such marginal concerns do not, however, explain the high ranking of energy; energy has diverse specific uses serving diverse goals in the specific instances, so that bases for supporting energy use are probably too diffuse to be caught by our simple model.

Table XVIII
Energy Preferences by Comfort and Consumer and Business Identification

Identification	High Value Preference	Low Value Preference	Value Impact
Consumer	0.65	0.68	−0.04
Nonconsumer	0.72	0.63	0.09
Business	0.73	0.70	0.03
Nonbusiness	0.66	0.66	0.00

Agricultural Preferences

For agriculture, users have a direct economic stake in the use, and the value of comfort has some impact, as shown in Table XIX. The rest of the population has no economic stake, indeed, personal economic considerations argue for preference for other uses. Nonusers' prime motives concern indirect benefits of agricultural use, most notably food. As with business identifiers, identifiers with farmers support agricultural use because of the indirect benefits. Though the motives vary somewhat from group to group, everyone gives high preferences to agriculture, almost without exception.

Table XIX
Agricultural Preferences by Irrigation Use, Farmer Identification, and Comfort

Value	Use	Farmer Identification	High Value Preference	Low Value Preference	Value Impact
Comfort	Yes	—	0.86	0.82	0.05
	No	Yes	0.75	0.87	−0.12
	No	No	0.72	0.78	−0.06

Competition Among Uses and Policy Preferences

Each use has been treated separately because the basic evaluation in some absolute terms depends on the separate evaluations. For policy purposes, though, the uses must be related; in any scarcity situation, some uses must be preferred to others for there is a fixed sum of resources to be allocated. In the model here, the separate evaluations of the uses should be combined via the links between uses and policy in evaluating policy. The most preferred policy would favor the most preferred uses (which in turn serve the most preferred goals). The need to compare uses in effect leads to a rescoring of the benefits from any use toward a fixed-or-zero-sum. Thus, the "score" given a use in preference rankings is as likely to be high because some other score is low as it is to be high because of its associated high benefits. Though the measure of preference used so far has included this zero-sum aspect, we have ignored it so far.

From a preference point of view, half of the variance in rankings must be spurious. That is, because every time the rank of some use goes up, the rank of some other use(s) must go down, any variance or change is counted twice. We should be able to explain at best half the variance by considering each use separately, for the other half is due to the ranking procedure. These ranking effects are expected to produce a negative correlation and impact of −0.17 between any two uses. These ranking effects have obscured some of the impacts of goals, identifications and uses in the previous analysis. They also obscure the relationship among uses.

To examine the relationships among use preference, we first correct for the ranking effect by removing the estimated impact of a use on a change in rank of another use. After correction, the major relationships are as in Figure 5. The two major negatively related clusters are preservation and recreation, on the one hand, and business and energy use on the other. Recreation and preservation are preferred, as we have seen, by users and identifiers oriented to beauty, pleasure and excitement. Business and energy uses are preferred by a different group of users and identifiers oriented to comfort and family security. Two additional "producer" uses, agriculture and transportation, are mildly related to business and energy use, though they have minor user clienteles oriented, again, to comfort and family security. These relationships among uses are about what we would have expected from the simple opinion structures we have described for each use separately. The policy adds nothing new, except for the forced ranking procedure.

Public Preferences Overall

The overall patterns of public preferences are reviewed in Figure 6. Most of the variance in evaluation traces to the direct and indirect benefits produced for the entire population. Agriculture and domestic uses are ranked high because they serve essential goals for everyone. Energy and business uses directly and indirectly serve less important goals, hence are lower ranked. The other three uses do not, in themselves, serve any goals of the entire public.

The next largest determinants of preferences follow identification patterns and depend on the size of the identifying group, the extent of identification, and the goals served. These identifications largely set the ordering of the middle-ranked uses, and the rankings tend to follow the evaluation of the goals served.

Finally, the benefits residually depend on special users and their values. Only preservation and recreation, the large user groups, are much affected by user considerations. The actual rankings, by forcing comparison of benefits, double the amount of variation and produce negative relationships between the evaluation of one use and the evaluation of another.

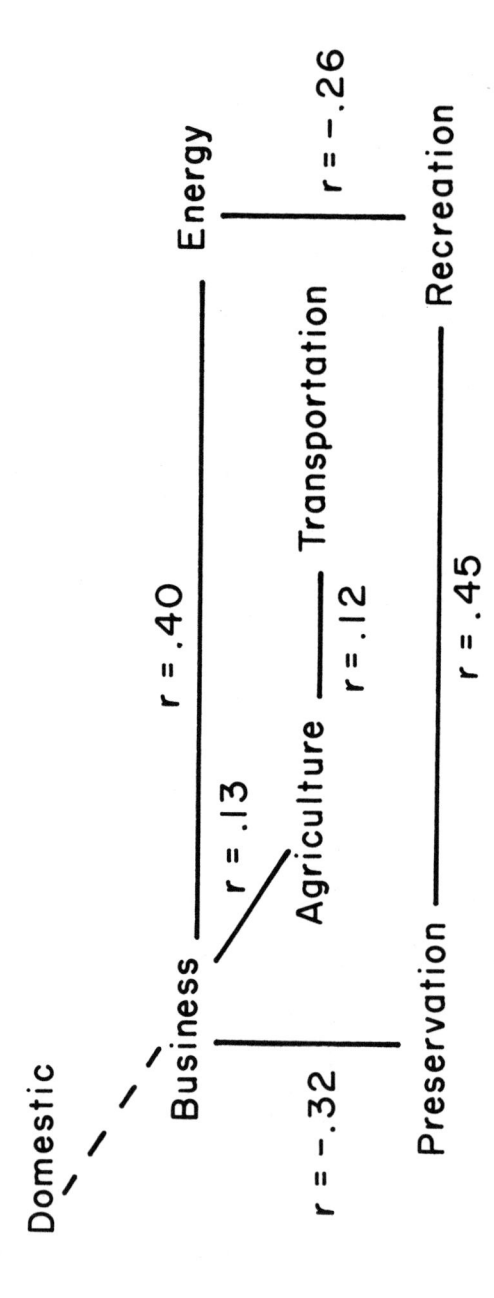

Figure 5. Major relationships (corrected for forced ranking) between use preferences.

a) Whole Public

	Agriculture	Domestic	Energy	Industrial	Preservation	Recreation	Transportation
Preference	↑	↑ ↑	↑	↑			
		Direct	Direct				
Identification	Farm			[Producer]			
		/ \					
Value	[Survival]	Comfort	Family	Security			

b) Identifiers

	Agriculture	Domestic	Energy	Industrial	Preservation	Recreation	Transportation
Preference							
		↑ ↘			↑	↑	
Identification		Consumer	Business		Environmentalist		
Value		Comfort			Beauty	Pleasure Excitement	

c) Users

	Agriculture	Domestic	Energy	Industrial	Preservation	Recreation	Transportation
Preference	↑			↑↑	↑	↑ ↑	↑
Use	Agricultural			Business		Recreational	Transportation
			Family				
Value			Security	Comfort	Beauty	Pleasure Excitement	

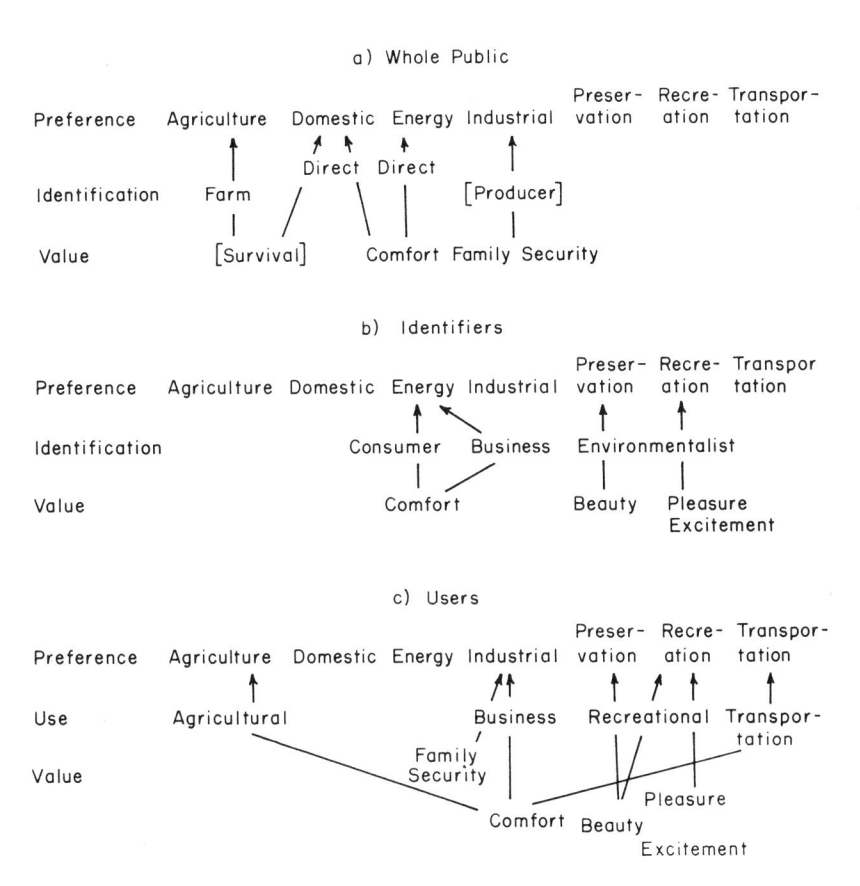

Figure 6. Summary of public opinion sources.

CONCLUSION

In sorting out public opinion, the most important difference is between the uses serving essential goals for the entire public and everything else. Second, the difference between uses serving generally high-valued goals for the public and the remaining uses provides the next largest clue to public opinion. Next are the differences between uses with sizable direct beneficiaries and those uses whose clientele is largely indirect and through identification; direct benefits are evaluated more highly. The remaining calculations depend on the size of user and identification groups and the relative ranking of goals served. Beliefs about the relationships between policy and uses, as well as uses and goals, can usually be expected to be consensual, and hence not a major source of differences. What public opinion in large represents are the *stakes* in the policy held by the public.

REFERENCES

Rokeach, M. *The Nature of Human Values* (New York: The Free Press, 1973).

11. Participatory Democracy in a Federal Agency[1]

Daniel A. Mazmanian

INTRODUCTION

For virtually every federal agency, direct public involvement is an inconsequential part of their operations. When important policies or programs are being assessed, the general public is typically kept in the dark and only informed well after the commitments are made. Typical is the conclusion of a recent study of the Atomic Energy Commission that "the decision to build [nuclear reactors] remains one that has already been made by the time citizens are afforded an opportunity to express their views on the matter." Only after "considerable capital expenditures have already been made and others arranged for, a site has been acquired, the staff of the AEC, the applicant and the vendor have worked out the details of construction, and the Preliminary Safety Analysis Report has been submitted... do citizens become privy to the plans" (Ebbin and Kasper, 1974).

These criticisms repeatedly have been made of the Army Corps of Engineers. With the emergence of the environmental movement on a national scale in the 1960s, the Corps came under

---

[1] An earlier version of this paper titled "Citizens and the Assessment of Technology: An Examination of the Participation Thesis" was presented at the 1974 Annual Meeting of the American Political Science Association, Palmer House, Chicago, Illinois, August 29 - September 2, 1974.

the most virulent attacks for both the substance of its decisions, and the secretiveness with which they were made. By the end of the decade even some within the agency began to concede that the general public was effectively excluded from the agency's decision-making process. As one of the Corps' own District Engineers stated:

> The traditional way engineers go about planning a public works project leaves little room for the citizen to be heard. Engineers would first define the "problems" then "objectives" or "goals." Finally, they would develop "The Plan" to attain these goals.
> Of course eventually, the public gets a look at "The Plan" in public meetings or hearings: Presentation is oral. And a thick study document is available for inspection, should some persistent citizen have the energy to labor through it. Oftentimes, engineers do not show the public alternative plans; and if they do, written copies are not available for public scrutiny. Questioned about alternatives the planner is likely to answer: "We looked at other ways to solve the problem, but there was little support for any of them" (Sargent, 1972).

Therefore, it came as a surprise to many when in 1970 the Chief of Engineers announced a turnabout in the Corps' policy toward the role of the public in the planning of its projects. Speaking in early 1971 he declared: "I consider public participation of critical importance in the Corps' effectiveness as a public servant. It is ... an area I won't be satisfied with until we can truly say that the Corps is doing a superb job" (Dodge, 1973).

The Chief's pronouncement marked a signal break with the past. Between 1970 and 1973 a number of comprehensive public participation programs were initiated on a variety of Corps project studies. The public was informed at the outset that the studies were underway; informal meetings, workshops with small groups, and large public meetings were all used to discuss and debate alternatives. Throughout the process, newsletters and brochures were mailed to interested citizens so that they could keep abreast of developments, and summaries were provided of the lengthy and technical study documents. In most cases, the Corps' planners withdrew, at least publicly, from being proponents of a specific plan, adopting the posture of arbiters between competing local, state, and national interests. When compared to the dearth of such efforts by other agencies, the Corps' new public participation efforts have been extraordinary.

Now, after three years of experimentation, the agency appears to be losing interest, or at least it is no longer aggressively pursuing the program. All too frequently one hears said of one or another of the new public participation efforts that "the planning effort was a great program, but we won't be trying it again." It is said that they are too costly and require too many man hours for too little output. There are exceptions of course, such as in the San Francisco and Seattle Districts, where the creed of public involvement is more ingrained. But these are unrepresentative of the response in other districts and in Washington, D.C. The Corps' coolness to public participation appears in deed more than in word. It has not changed its regulations nor has it publicly altered its views. Yet, neither is it pushing for greater experimentation with different forms and methods of public participation or attempting to institutionalize fishbowl or other open planning techniques agencywide. The downgrading is reflected not only in the programs but in the curtailment of the Corps' Institute of Water Resources Technical Assistance Program and staff support for project level open planning. However, broad public participation remains a part of "urban studies" general investigations.

There are many conceivable reasons for the dwindling support. Bureaucratic backlash against new programs may be a factor. Recent tightening of the budgets throughout the federal government may be another. The dampening of public outcry with the Corps' performance, in part attributable to the agency's public participation program, has reduced the pressure to continue and expand the program. The shifting political focus within the United States away from concern with conservation and environmental issues to "solving the energy crisis" that surfaced abruptly in the winter of 1973 may have also played a part.

There is an even more fundamental explanation. For reasons that the Corps seemingly cannot fathom, while the most extensive public participation efforts have won public acclaim and credibility for the agency, they have more often than not failed to build a consensus on the plans that emerge out of the planning process. And, of course, without a local consensus the best agency image may be of little avail in winning congressional approval of projects, the lifeblood of a public works agency. Moreover, the failure to win a consensus contradicts all the agency has been led to expect of the public participation program from the professionals who designed it, the social psychologists and human relations experts, and from its own in-house advocates.

What follows is a brief review of the "participation thesis" as it has evolved out of social psychology and organizational theory. The Corps' uncritical adoption of the thesis to its planning process in the early 1970s will be examined next, and its expectations of how public participation would build a consensus around its project proposals, hereafter referred to as the Corps Model of Public Participation. The validity of the participation thesis is not universally accepted and, therefore, a plausible alternative to the Corps Model, the Expanded Model of Public Participation, is also presented. To judge which of the two models best depicts the actual workings of public participation in an agency's decision-making process, a survey has been conducted of citizens who participated in five Corps planning studies. The results are used to evaluate the applicability of the two models.

THE PARTICIPATORY DEMOCRACY THESIS

A central tenet of social psychology and human relations theory is the salutary effect of involving, in the decision-making process, all those affected by an organization's decision. In the words of Herbert Simon (1955): "We now have a considerable body of evidence to support the participation hypothesis that significant changes in human behavior can be brought about rapidly only if the persons who are expected to change participate in deciding what the change shall be and how it shall be made."

The accepted basis for this belief reaches back to the pioneering experimental work of Mayo, Lewin, Lippit, and White in the 1920s and 1930s. Stated briefly, these studies found that members of participative (democratic) groups were much more satisfied with the experience in group decision-making than those in nonparticipative (authoritarian and laissez-faire) settings. They showed a greater interest in their work and were far less aggressive. They were more committed to the task and, interestingly, showed a higher level of originality and creative thinking in working out the group goals. Finally, members showed greater respect, and a marked preference for the leaders of democratic groups (White and Lippitt, 1953 and 1960; and Verba, 1961).

These results are explained by five psychological reactions of the individuals to the decision-making setting. First, participation in decision-making within a group encourages "identification" with (a) the group and (b) the group task. Second, identification takes the form of goal congruence between the individual and the group's goals. Third, goal congruence leads to activity or behavior consistent with this congruence. The individual, in effect, willingly works for the group goal. Fourth, overall organizational climate, improved by widespread goal congruence and reinforced by congruent behavior, contributes to persistance of behavior and increases productivity. And fifth, goal congruence and joint activity have integrative functions, reducing distinctions in such areas as power and status (Mosher, 1967; and Lewin, 1951).

These conclusions were not the inductions of democratic philosophers, but the findings of empirical researchers, and this was to make a profound difference both in their credibility and their acceptability among the burgeoning experimentally oriented and scientifically bent social scientists emerging in the United States in the 1930s and 1940s. The importance of the distinction was not lost upon the professional community:

> ... the empirical demonstration of the functional superiority of a democratic form of organization ... suggests that democracy can find rational grounds for asserting its worth. Even to a limited extent, it can be seen that science can bolster the claims of a democratic form of authority, and it would therefore seem that on scientific grounds it is the duty of scientists to take the side of fostering democracy ... (Wolpert, 1959).

Lewin and others were not espousing participation as ideology or public morality, but as a rational scheme of organizational management.

Following World War II social psychologists continued the work begun by Mayo, Lewin, and others and the participative thesis withstood further scrutiny. One of its noted contemporary advocates is Rensis Likert, until recently director of the University of Michigan's Institute of Social Research. Likert (1967) expands Lewin's original authoritarian-democratic dichotomy of organizational climates to four major systems of organization: "exploitive authoritarian," "benevolent authoritarian," "conservative," and "participative." Based on a series of performance characteristics, Likert concludes that the participative system exceeds all others: the most productive management system is the one that most meaningfully includes the participants, those who must live with and implement decisions, in the planning and execution of the organization's task. "These organizations mobilize both the noneconomic motives and economic needs so that all available motivational forces create cooperative behavior focused on achieving the organization's objectives. The enterprise is a tightly knit, well-coordinated organization of highly motivated persons" (Likert, 1967).

Two basic criticisms of the participation thesis have been raised, significantly, by those outside the mainstream of social psychology and organizational management. Normative democratic theorists have attacked the kind of leader-dictated group atmosphere central to Lewin's participative process as not truly democratic. The process does not allow for the free and creative expression of the individual, but creates an atmosphere where peer pressures and the appearance of leader objectivity are subtly used to bring about submission of the individual to the will of the group. Such participative decision-making orchestrated from above may only be an instrument of persuasion in the hands of leaders, or pseudo-democracy (Kariel, 1956). At best this is procedural, not genuine democracy, and at worst it can be the conscious manipulation of the citizenry by those in positions of authority.

The second criticism is directed at the applicability of the thesis to complex real life situations. Based on a series of case studies of the decision-making process leading to reorganizations of a number of public agencies, Mosher (1967) concludes that Lewin's participation thesis is of limited applicability: the degree of participation had no discernible effect on goal attainment or group performance in reorganizations within public agencies. The instances of high participation did reveal greater employee support for the agency reorganization programs, with the greatest resistance experienced where there was no employee participation at all. Also, while not conclusive, the evidence seems to indicate that participation is more effective the earlier it begins.

Of greatest interest is Mosher's explanation of why the participative mode apparently failed to produce better performance and implementation. It had little to do with the decision-making climate but with the degree of divisiveness over substantive concerns among the participants, a conclusion contrary to the wealth of prior studies in experimental settings and industry. Effective implementation depends on the extent of mutual benefit that will flow from successful completion of the group task as perceived by the participants:

> That participation is more effective toward reorganization when the anticipated effects appear to increase the complementariness of individual goals with reorganizational goals among participants. Participative processes were most likely to be pursued where such complementariness could be anticipated. And where individuals were likely to be hurt by reorganization, participation was generally avoided (Mosher, 1967).

This affirmed Verba's earlier insight that there may be severe contextual limitations to the applicability of the participation thesis. According to Verba (1961), the thesis holds to the extent that the "no-conflict" assumption is true: "there is a single group goal or single method of attaining a group goal that is in the best interests of all concerned—both leaders and followers." The assumption may have been valid for most experimental studies, and even in industrial work group situations. But as demonstrated in the cases of reorganization in public agencies, consensus on goals and perceived mutual benefits are not always present. When conflict over goals does emerge, the most participative process cannot insure agreement, cooperation, and effective implementation of the group task.

THE CORPS' ADOPTION OF PUBLIC PARTICIPATION

The Corps' embrace of public participation in the 1970s followed from a realization that concern with environmental degradation was mushrooming into a national cause. This resulted in a fairly intense and active segment of the public opposing the Corps' massive channelization, dam building, and other water-related public works projects. Indeed, during the period of the late 1960s and early 1970s the Corps was a central target of the environmentalists. And, antipathy toward the agency resulted in an increasing number of rejections of Corps proposed projects by the states and local communities around the nation.

The Corps was not the first agency to turn to participative decision-making as a solution to this kind of situation. The concept was basic, for example, to the "war on poverty" of the 1960s.

However, for a group of professional engineers, adoption of the ideal of interactive consultation with diverse segments of the community, especially those hostile to them, was unusual. Yet, this was the path chosen by the Chief of Engineers. The agency was encouraged in this direction from within and by outside professionals, who apparently did not fully appreciate the warnings of Verba and Mosher. Rather, in the tradition of Lewin, Likert and others the agency was persuaded that a positive participative setting would generate favorable attitudes toward the agency on the part of the public and overcome resistance to its goals by bringing all those affected into the decision process. This was the message spread through the writing and recommendations of the Corps' Institute of Water Resources (IWR), its in-house "think tank," and by consultants from major universities in the area of water resource planning and public relations, from whom IWR personnel took their cues. A case in point are the studies often cited by Corps planners, prepared for IWR in 1970 (Borton, Warner and Wenrich) and the National Water Commission in 1971 (Warner), in which planners and social psychologists from the School of Natural Resources and from Likert's Institute of Social Research at the University of Michigan assured the Corps that the participation thesis could readily be applied to the agency's water resources planning. They argued:

> One major reason that government planning agencies have undertaken more extensive involvement activities has been *to generate greater public understanding and support for eventually recommended plans. Public participation in the actual formation of such plans is also a primary means by which these plans can be made more publicly acceptable*—that is, they can thereby more adequately reflect the needs and preferences of those being planned for. Also through a public involvement process, potential opponents of the eventual plan are provided with means through which they may exert influence to have their concerns addressed and dealt with more acceptably in the plan formulation process (Warner, 1971).

Meanwhile, the theme was being reiterated by leaders in the field of public administration. One finds as prominent a figure as Roger C. Crampton, Chairman of the Administrative Conference of the United States, arguing that broadened public participation in agencies will improve administrative decisions and give them greater legitimacy and acceptance (1972).

THE CORPS' MODEL OF PUBLIC PARTICIPATION

This concept of participatory decision-making as a mediating factor in the planning process, provides a basis for a causal formulation of the process of policy formation in a public works agency.

Figure 1(a) represents an initial causal model based on the Corps' view of the state of affairs as of the late 1960s.[2] The three components, of course, represent a simplification. But they depict the factors pertinent to introduction of participatory decision-making: A vocal group of citizens with environmental concerns were distressed with the prevailing lack of ecological sensitivity and the growth mentality among their fellow citizens and government agencies. This placed them in conflict with the traditional mode of thinking and activities of the Corps, which in turn led to negative evaluations of Corps projects.

$$a. \overset{(-)}{X_5} \longrightarrow \overset{(-)}{X_3} \longrightarrow \overset{(-)}{X_1}$$

$$b. \overset{(-)}{X_5} \longrightarrow \overset{(-)}{X_3} \longrightarrow \overset{(+)}{X_2} \longrightarrow \overset{(+)}{X_1}$$

Figure 1. The Corps' conception of participatory decision-making in the planning process. X_1 = evaluation of proposed project, X_2 = evaluation of experience in public participation program, X_3 = orientation towards Corps, and X_5 = extent of environmental concern. The sign above each factor indicates Corps' view of how it was or would be affected by each.

---

[2] Although environmentalism is used as the measure of concern in the model, environmentalists naturally are not the only segment of the community interested in Corps projects. If those with commercial or flood protection or other concerns were inserted in the model, their orientations toward the Corps and their evaluation of planning and of projects could be expected to differ from those with environmental concerns. A number of interests in a community can usually be counted upon to support Corps activities. Their inclusion in participative planning, it could reasonably be assumed in light of the participation thesis, would enhance their positive image of the Corps and enthusiasm for its projects.

The model depicted in Figure 1(b) shows the anticipated effect of adding participative decision-making to the planning process. It would not necessarily change concerns or orientations toward the Corps, at least not in the short run. However, it would change evaluations of specific Corps projects, and over time, should bring about greater satisfaction with the agency *per se* and public cooperation in the accomplishment of the goals agreed upon in the participative arena.

AN EXPANDED MODEL OF PUBLIC PARTICIPATION

In a number of ways the context within which the Corps was attempting to implement the participation thesis is different than those described by Lewin and others. It was not an experimental setting where the substantive outcomes would be of little or no consequence to participants. To the contrary, the participants who made the effort to attend the Corps' planning sessions could be expected to come with very definite objectives. Nor could it be assumed that the participants concurred on who should be the ultimate judge. They were not members of the organization and did not feel bound by its assumed authority in rendering ultimate decisions on water resources projects or in determining general agency policy. This can be contrasted to the earlier settings experienced by Lewin and others where the participants were presumably indifferent to the usurpation of authority by the experimenter, or the industrial setting where workers, although given a voice, seldom challenge the inherent right of management to make final decisions.

Viewed in the light of the cautions of Verba and Mosher on just such contextual limitations, most likely these differences mean that the linkage between the participative experience (X_2) and project evaluation (X_1) is not as direct as the Corps might wish. Involvement in the planning of a project may increase credibility and trust in the agency. Participants may develop an effective rapport with the engineers and respect their earnest effort to arrive at a consensus decision. However, the greater the extent to which participants enter the planning process with fundamental disagreement over goals and objectives, the less likely there will ever be a consensus on the proposed project. When views are polarized from the outset, the best efforts at compromise and consensus building can fail. Indeed, in extremely divisive situations, if the Corps fails to side with one of the contending groups and attempts to split the difference between factions, its plan may be acceptable to none.

Figure 2 depicts an Expanded Model of Public Participation, with a multiplicity of direct and indirect linkages leading to X_1. In essence, it is the Corps model with two important modifications. First, "Citizen Power"—the propensity of participants to want more decision-making powers delegated to citizens and away from public agencies—has been included as an independent causal factor affecting the succeeding factors in the planning process. In an era of "power to the people" this factor could be expected to stand out as an independent influence, particularly affecting evaluation of the Corps' public participation program and the underlying predispositions toward the agency.

Second, as indicated by the Mosher study, when interests or concerns of the participants are likely to generate incompatible objectives, participation *per se* will not bring about generalized support for a plan. Thus, the linkage to X_1 is assumed to run along both X_2X_1 and X_3X_1. Consequently, one cannot assume, as did the Corps, that a positive experience in planning will in and of itself result in a positive evaluation of a proposed project.

Absent from both the Corps Model and the Expanded Model are feedback loops that, if included, would add a dynamic component. They might indicate, for example, that changes in the kinds of projects the Corps undertakes should eventually bring about

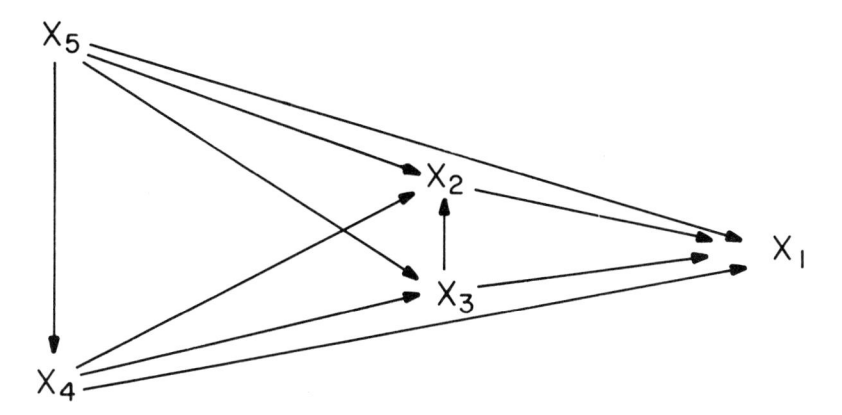

Figure 2. An expanded model of participatory decision-making. X_4 = citizen power.

changes in the public's attitude toward the Corps, or that changes in Corps planning should eventually dampen demands for citizen power, and so on. They are not included because for a given episode of project planning the process is presumably static, with orientations and evaluations remaining fairly constant. Since the Corps' studies examined herein are single episodes, possible feedback loops are not considered.

A COMPARISON OF MODELS

The Data Base

A comparision of the two models is made on the basis of data collected through a survey of the participants of five Corps of Engineers project studies,[3] a majority of which were selected largely because they had attempted to implement various methods of participative decision-making. From among the approximately 3,000 persons who participated in public meetings, seminars, workshops, discussions, and planning in the five studies, over 900 were randomly selected and sent questionnaires about their experience in December 1973 and January 1974. The questionnaire required about 50 minutes to complete. The overall response rate was 53 percent.[4]

---

[3] Two hundred questionnaires were mailed to participants of the Wastewater Management Study for Cleveland-Akron and Three Rivers Watershed Area in Northern Ohio; 200 to the Unit L-15 of the Missouri River Levee System Study, just north of St. Louis; 195 to the Mississippi River-Gulf Outlet New Lock and Connecting Channel Study, just south of New Orleans; 138 to the study of flood control and related water resources problems on the Wildcat and San Pablo Creeks, Contra Costa County, California; and 184 to the study of flood control problems along the Middle Fork of the Snoqualmie River, located approximately 20 miles east of Seattle.

[4] An examination of the returned but unscored questionnaires indicates that some of the older and less well educated—those with less than a high school education—had difficulty in completing the questionnaire. It must be assumed therefore that this segment of the participant population in Corps planning is underrepresented in our response set. The education factor may also account for the unusually low response rate from the San Pablo Creek Study, a case where many participants come from the model cities area of San Pablo and Northern Richmond. This would also explain why 14 of the 35 unscoreable questionnaires were from participants in that study.

Whether the respondents are representative of all those who participated in Corps planning or of the broader public attentive to water resources issues is not known. Every effort is made to bear this in mind when reporting the findings of the survey. Nevertheless, inference will be drawn on the general nature of the decision-making process in attempting to highlight some of the most probable implications of the available data. Given the paucity of systematically gathered information about the Corps' public participation program, or of any other agency for that matter, at a minimum the conclusions should prove provocative and a starting point for further inquiry.

Items included on the questionnaire were mainly of the closed-ended format, with respondents asked to rate each on a four-step ladder. Information was elicited about general orientations toward the Corps, the proper role of citizens in water resources planning, the level of direct participation desired, the extent of participation actually achieved, and motives for participation.

Measures of Model Components

From the battery of questionnaire items that focused on reasons individuals participated in the planning process, three types can be identified: those who were primarily concerned with the environmental impacts of proposed projects, those with personal property or commercial and economic interests, and those who appear to have been motivated out of curiosity with the new forms of public decision-making being introduced by the Corps, that is, the public minded.[5]

Taking the mean of a respondent's ratings across all the items that distinguish a given type provides one good measure of his or her level of concern. These means, hereafter referred to as scale scores, provide a measure for comparing respondents, for example, on the extent to which their involvement is based on concern with environmental issues or on their own economic well-being. The three measures tap quite distinct interests. The Pearson product moment correlation between the environmental and the economic benefit measures a negligible 0.05, that between the enviromental and civic-minded is a somewhat higher yet still minimal 0.12, and that between economic interest and civic-

---

[5] A complete list of items comprising each scale used in this analysis is given in the APSA version of the paper.

minded is 0.07. The level of significance of the three correlations is 0.09, 0.01, and 0.17, respectively.

In examining models of the planning process, environmentalism (X_5) will be used as the measure of concern. This is done because of the centrality of environmentalists to the Corps' efforts. Using other concerns has virtually no effect on the structure of the models.

The component of the Expanded Model not considered in the Corps Model nor in prior applications of the participation thesis is the propensity of citizens to want to share authority in public policy decisions. As will become evident, the greater this propensity, the less likely the public will be satisfied with any decision-making process that leaves the major decisions in the hands of a governmental agency. This component is measured by items that statistically cluster together into a "Citizen Power" scale (X_4), such as, "Citizens should have a greater voice in the planning of water resource projects," and the inverse of, "The decisions over which water resource projects are to be built should be left in the hands of the experts." Clusters (scales) were determined by grouping items according to their highest pair-wise correlation coefficient (for details on the method, see Leavitt, 1971).

An individual's general orientation toward the Corps (X_3) is measured by a series of questionnaire items that cluster in an "Orientation Toward Corps" scale.[6] The items ask about the Corps' openness and tone and its receptivity to citizens. For example, if one believes that "The Corps is making an honest effort to reconcile the many community interests," he is also likely to believe that "The opinions of citizens greatly influence the actions taken by the Corps," while disagreeing with the statement that "The Corps goes through the motions of consulting citizens but is not sincerely interested in obtaining their views."

Throughout the planning process participants naturally formed opinions about many aspects of the process: which modes of participation are to be preferred, the seriousness of the Corps in consulting with the public, and how effectively information and ideas are communicated by the Corps to the public. This is reflected in part in the preferences for some modes of participa-

---

[6] The term "orientation," as used herein is synonomous with "attitude," as used in psychology, which is defined as "learned predispositions to respond to an object or class of objects in a favorable or unfavorable way" (Fishbein, 1967).

tion over others. In order to test the models of participative decision-making, an operational indicator of the participants' overall evaluation of the planning experience is needed. For this, a group of items inquiring into the substance of the Corps' participative planning program as actually experienced by the respondents cluster together as an "Evaluation of Planning" scale (X_2). The items attempt to gauge what actually transpired at the planning sessions and to what extent the respondents felt that the agency had included them in a meaningful planning effort. The measure includes items such as "The information provided by the Corps can easily be understood by the layman," and the inverse of that, "Corps personnel usually tried to avoid any open discussion at public meetings of the most controversial issues surrounding the proposed project."

The most difficult component to measure is the evaluation of the Corps' recommended project because some districts had not announced their recommendation by the time the questionnaire was administered. Or, as in the Cleveland-Akron Study, the district formally presented a series of options among which political leaders could choose. Though it is evident that the experience in the planning process left impressions on virtually all of the participants about which was the Corps' preferred plan, nevertheless, when asked to react to the Corps recommended project proposal many of the respondents were forced to rely on an educated guess of what the proposal was going to be. Approximately 5 percent of the respondents failed to express an opinion as to their like or dislike of the proposed project, a figure equivalent to the "no answer given" proportion for most other items on the questionnaire.

Asking respondents to judge a proposed project before it is formally announced obviously presents some problems in interpreting the results, especially since the official recommendation may differ from what is anticipated, and this could alter a respondent's project evaluation. For the test of the two models, however, the issue is immaterial. If the planning effort was perceived to be a positive one, then under the assumption of the participation thesis the respondent would approve of and be committed to what he believed to be the project proposal, whether or not the recommended project had been announced.

Two items cluster together to form the "Evaluation of Project" scale (X_1). Since all respondents were asked to answer both items, and since they ask diametrically opposing questions, it is conceivable that one could respond very favorably to the first item—"I am in favor of the project the Corps proposed"—and similarly high on the second—"I oppose the proposed plan." In the 11 cases where respondents did so, the observation was deleted from the analysis under the assumption that the items either were misread or answered mistakenly. The reverse does not logically follow. That is, a low rating on both items could simply be an indication of indifference to the project, not confusion, and these cases were therefore retained.

Test of the Models

With operational measures of X_1 through X_5, it is now possible to return to the discussion of the adequacy of the Corps' model of the planning process. Once again, the Corps felt that it could involve the public in a successful participatory planning program. This proved to be the case. The scale score mean of X_2 is equal to that of concern with environmental issues and higher than all other scales: on the four-point ladder the mean for $X_2 = 2.93$ whereas $X_1 = 2.20$, $X_3 = 2.74$, $X_4 = 2.78$, and $X_5 = 2.94$. Evidently the public regarded the public meetings, workshops and other activities undertaken to be a fairly comprehensive and sincere effort at including citizens in the planning process.

Yet this is only part of what the Corps expected. They also assumed that the greater one's environmental concern the more antipathy toward the agency, that this antipathy was directly related to project evaluation, and the interjecting participatory decision-making would produce a positive evaluation of agency projects. These assumptions will be tested first through use of simple correlation coefficients between the model components, followed by a path analysis of the model's major causal linkages.

The correlation coefficients of adjacent components of the Corps Model, shown in Figure 3, reveal some anticipated and one rather surprising finding.[7] As expected, Figure 3(a) shows that the $X_3 X_1$ relationship is strong. If citizens hold the corps in low regard, this will be reflected in project evaluation. Also, Figure

---

[7] Arrows have been deleted from Figures 3 and 4, which show only measures of association, to avoid confusion with the earlier discussions of the models, where the most probable causal paths were being described, and the path analysis to follow, where arrows are used to explicitly identify an inferred causal path.

a. $X_5 \xrightarrow{(-.09)} X_3 \xrightarrow{.50} X_1$ ($R=.523$, $R^2=.278$)

b. $X_5 \xrightarrow{(-.09)} X_3 \xrightarrow{.77} X_2 \xrightarrow{.42} X_1$ ($R=.531$, $R^2=.282$)

Figure 3. Correlation coefficients of the Corps model of participatory decision-making. Coefficients significant at the 0.01 level except those in parentheses.

3(b) shows that the X_2X_1 relationship is strong, as expected, though the X_3X_2 relationship is even stronger.

If it is true as the Corps assumed that those with environmental concerns hold the Corps in low regard, then there should be a high negative correlation between the measures of environmental concern and of orientation toward the agency. Contrary to this expectation, the X_5X_3 relationship is a negligible -0.09. Although the sign is negative and thus in the direction expected, the relationship is so low as to be meaningless. There seems to be no *direct* link between concern with environmental issues and attitudes toward the Corps.[8]

Simple correlations provide a good overview of relationships between model components, but do not indicate to what extent participatory decision-making has a *direct* impact on project evaluation. The statistic useful here is R^2, the multiple correlation coefficient squared, which gives the proportion of the variation in a dependent variable, in this case X_1, accounted for by one or more independent variables. The R^2 for the initial Corps Model in Figure 3(a) is 0.278; that is, X_5 and X_3 account for approximately 28 percent of the variation in X_1. What does X_2 add to this? With X_2 included the R^2 rises to 0.282, a minuscule increase of 0.004. In other words, X_2 adds virtually nothing to the explained variance.

An examination of the Expanded Model provides equally interesting results. As with the Corps Model, a direct X_5X_3 link is

---

[8] A similar result followed when the same analysis was run on a subset of 78 self-identified environmental group representatives (in contrast to those with environmental concerns). The zero order correlation between the "Environmental Concern" measure of the environmental representatives and "Orientation Toward Corps" was a mere -0.14, with a significance level of 0.11.

assumed, but also, that the relationship is mediated in part by X_4. And as with the Corps Model, it assumes that the all-important X_2X_1 link exists, but in addition that there are direct links between X_5, X_4, and X_1. The complex nature of the relationships is borne out in the correlation coefficients in Figure 4.

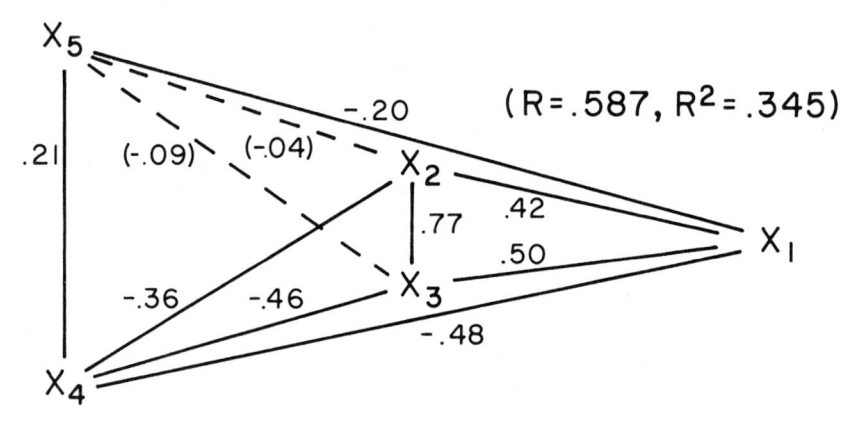

Figure 4. Correlation coefficients of the expanded model. Coefficients significant at the 0.01 level except those in parentheses.

It appears that the Corps is correct, after all, in expecting the antipathy of those with environmental concerns. It is just that their negative feelings about the agency are filtered through, and exacerbated by, belief in citizen power. This is indicated by the positive X_5X_4 relationship, followed by the negative X_4X_3 one.

The inability of the very effective public participation efforts to carry over into project evaluation is explained to some extent by the Expanded Model. Yes, there is an X_2X_1 relationship. Yet X_3X_1 is even stronger. Quite independent of one's experience in the participatory programs, then, one's initial attitude toward the agency appears to dictate to some degree one's project evaluation.

Figure 4 also helps to clear up the maze of probable linkages hypothesized by the model. The nil X_5X_2 and X_5X_3 relationships eliminate them as meaningful links, and will no longer be depicted as part of the model.

With the weakest links eliminated from the model it is appropriate to ask which of the remaining relationships are nonspurious. Path analysis provides the answer. The technique determines the unique effect of each independent causal factor on the specified dependent variable. In essence, the relationship between the two is calculated while "holding constant" all others. Each arrow in Figure 5 represents the presumed causal linkage or paths of causal influence remaining in the Expanded Model. Through the use of standardized regression coefficients, the strength of each path is estimated.

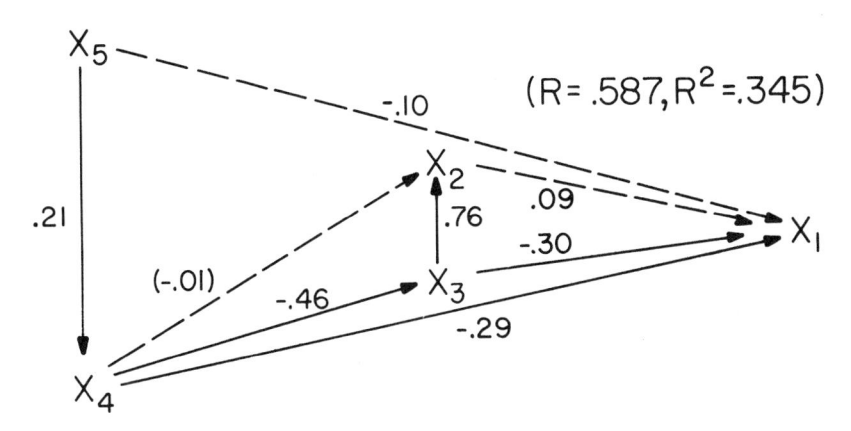

Figure 5. Path coefficients of the expanded model. Coefficients significant at the 0.01 level except those in parentheses.

The picture that emerges is somewhat surprising in light of the correlations in Figure 4. $X_4 X_2$ reduces almost to zero, leaving X_3 as the only direct factor influencing X_2. More importantly, X_4 and X_3 clearly emerge as the two equally dominant determinants of X_1, while the relationships of X_2 and X_5 to X_1 shown in the correlation analysis (0.42 and -0.20) have no appreciable impact.

One final question remains: Does the addition of X_4 in the Expanded Model add to the variance in X_1 accounted for by the components of the Corps Model? With only X_5, X_3, and X_2 as the independent variables, $R^2 = 0.282$. Inclusion of X_4 increases the R^2 to 0.345. While there is no hard and fast rule to judge by, this seems to be a significant increase.

SUMMARY AND CONCLUSION

It should now be clear why the Corps of Engineers has become disillusioned with its new public participation program. In the tradition of Lewin, Likert and other social psychologists and organizational theorists, the Corps assumed that a well-intentioned positive open planning process would result directly in greater satisfaction with the organization among the participants, which would in turn foster greater congruence on goals between the individual participants and the organization, and finally, facilitate more effective implementation of the organization's (the group) goals. Instead, for the five studies examined, the participants clearly distinguished between the open planning activities of the Corps, with which they appeared satisfied, and the Corps' project proposals, which they rated relatively low. This lack of carry-over from satisfaction with the decision-making process to the evaluation of project proposals appears to have baffled and disappointed the Corps.

The failure of the program to produce the anticipated carry-over can be explained by two factors. First is the uncritical acceptance by the Corps of the participation thesis. The Corps assumed, at least implicitly, that its environment was analogous to that of the experimental and industrial settings where the efficacy of the participation thesis had been demonstrated. It assumed that if all members of the group, defined by the Corps as all people interested in a particular water resource project, were brought together in the decision-making process that an identification with the group and the group goals (which the Corps believed would be congruent with its goals) would result. It assumed that the participants in the decision-making process of a public agency would be as accepting of the authority of the Corps as were Lewin's experimentees of the authority of group leaders assigned to them, and as are workers in industry of the authority of management. Also, the Corps assumed that the kind of *esprit de corps* generated among the members of the small groups where the participation thesis had been demonstrated could be replicated in its planning program. However, there were numerous participants in the planning program, most of whom were from outside the agency, and they were therefore far less susceptible to pressures to conform to the "group goal" and adopt a team spirit.

The differences between the Corps' environment and those where the participation thesis had been successful are crucial. Most participants came to the Corps' planning program with strong views about the substantive issues under consideration. And many felt the need for a greater sharing of responsibilities between the citizen and the Corps engineers in the decisions being made. Their substantive concerns, belief in sharing responsibilities, and general predisposition toward the Corps all affected their evaluation of the Corps' proposed projects. These factors were operative despite their rapport with the engineers and appreciation of its efforts to open its decision-making process that emerged through open planning. In short, the participants in the five studies judged the project proposals far more by what they thought of the Corps and what they wanted the agency to do or not do than according to reactions to the planning process through which the proposals were developed.

Second, and related to the first, many of the participants in the five studies, particularly the environmentalists, began with negative attitudes toward the Corps. They believed that the Corps was not especially sympathetic to their concerns, and that there was little chance that they could influence the agency's behavior. Therefore, despite the open nature of the planning program, their initial low evaluation of the Corps made their low evaluation of the Corps' proposed projects almost a foregone conclusion.

Still, it is not unreasonable to assume that "Evaluation of Planning" and "Orientation Toward Corps" are interactive. Thus the positive evaluation of planning that has been expressed by the participants in the present generation of studies will feed back and affect positively their attitudes toward the Corps. The more numerous the open planning programs experienced, the higher their eventual regard for the agency might be.

"Evaluation of Project" and "Orientation Toward Corps" are most likely also interactive. Thus, to the extent that the Corps modifies the nature of its project proposals to accommodate the demands of environmentalists and its other critics, this too will feed back and positively affect attitudes toward the agency, quite likely, even more so than will a continuation of open planning. The more accommodating the projects, the more positive will be the public's orientation toward the Corps.

If there is one lesson learned from the studies examined, it is that favor cannot be won for old project ideas or even some innovative ones, such as massive land treatment for sewage sludge disposal, simply by undertaking elaborate public participation programs. However, if the Corps views open planning as a long-term educational process for both itself and the public, it may strengthen support for the agency and its proposals. But, if it continues to view the program as a short-term strategy for coalescing divergent factions around existing missions and projects, it will continue to prove a disappointment.

ACKNOWLEDGMENTS

The author wishes to express appreciation to Paul Iannacone, Herbert Kaufman, Judith V. May, Allen Mazur, Barry M. Mitnick, and John D. Sullivan for their helpful suggestions during the drafting of the paper. The material presented is part of a Brookings Institute study, "Citizen Participation: The Case of Environmental Policy," being conducted by the author.

REFERENCES

Borton, T. E., K. P. Warner, and J. W. Wenrich. *The Susquehanna Communication-Participation Study: Selected Approaches to Public Involvement in Water Resource Planning*, a report, submitted to the U. S. Army Corps of Engineers Institute for Water Resources (December 1970).

Crampton, R. C. "The Why, Where, and How of Broadened Public Participation in the Administrative Process," *Georgetown Law J.* 60 (3), 525 (1972).

Dodge, B. H. "Achieving Public Involvement in the Corps of Engineers' Water Resources Planning," *Water Resources Bull.* 9 (3), 448 (1973).

Ebbin, S., and R. Kasper. *Citizen Groups and the Nuclear Power Controversy: Uses of Scientific and Technological Information* (Cambridge, Massachusetts: The Massachusetts Institute of Technology Press, 1974).

Fishbein, M. "A Consideration of Beliefs, and Their Role in Attitude Measurement," in *Readings in Attitude Theory and Measurement*, Martin Fishbein, Ed. (New York: John Wiley and Sons, Inc., 1967).

Kariel, H. S. "Democracy Unlimited: Kurt Lewin's Field Theory," *Amer. J. Sociol.* 62 (3), 280 (1956).

Leavitt, M. "MULTYP/Multiple Typal Analysis: A Clustering Program," *Behavioral Sci.* 16 (4), 417 (1971).

Lewin, K. *Field Theory in Social Science* (New York: Harper and Row, 1951).

Likert, R. *The Human Organization: Its Management and Values* (New York: McGraw-Hill, 1967).

Mosher, F. C. "Participation and Reorganization," in *Governmental Reorganization: Cases and Commentary*, Frederick C. Mosher, Ed. (Indianapolis, Indiana: Bobbs Merrill Co., Inc., 1967).

Sargent, H. L., Jr. "Fishbowl Planning Immerses Pacific Northwest Citizens in Corps Projects," *Civil Eng.* 42 (9), 54 (1972).

Simon, H. A. "Recent Advances in Organizational Theory," in *Research Frontiers in Politics and Government*, Stephen K. Bailey et al., Eds. (Washington, D. C.: The Brookings Institution, 1955).

Verba, S. *Small Groups and Political Behavior: A Study of Leadership* (Princeton, New Jersey: Princeton University Press, 1961).

Warner, K. P. *A State of the Art Study of Public Participation in Water Resources Planning*, Final Report, prepared for the National Water Commission (June 1971).

White, R. K., and R. Lippitt. "Leader Behavior and Member Reaction in 'Three Social Climates,' " in *Group Dynamics: Research and Theory*, Dorwin Cartwright and Alvin Zander, Eds. (Evanston, Illinois: Row, Peterson and Co., 1953).

White, R. K., and R. Lippitt. *Autocracy and Democracy: An Experimental Inquiry* (New York: Harper and Row, 1960).

Wolpert, J. F. "Toward a Sociology of Authority," in *Studies in Leadership: Leadership and Democratic Action*, Alvin W. Gouldner, Ed. (New York: Harper and Row, 1959).

12. Prospects for Public Participation in Federal Agencies: The Case of the Army Corps of Engineers[1]

Daniel A. Mazmanian and Jeanne Nienaber

INTRODUCTION

Environmentalists today are among the strongest advocates of direct involvement of citizens in the life of the polity. Dissatisfaction with the performance of public agencies charged with overseeing the nation's natural resources has led to a fairly broad-based movement for direct participation. The assumption is that the public, as opposed to private and special interests, is seriously underrepresented and that only through a sustained effort by concerned citizens can the political system be made to work for the common good. The history of American politics is replete with such well-intentioned efforts. But few have survived the initial flurry of activity, and seldom have they left a lasting imprint on the decision-making processes of the institutions they rose to challenge (McConnell, 1966).

There are at least two persuasive theories that explain the short-lived nature of such efforts. Economists and rational choice theorists see the dearth of citizen participation as a logical consequence of individual benefit-cost calculations. Organization theorists have an equally plausible explanation, based not so

---

[1] An earlier version of this paper titled "Bureaucracy and the Public" was presented at the Midwest Political Science Association Annual Meeting, Chicago, Illinois, April 25-27, 1974.

much on the calculus of individual actors but on the immutable laws of organizational behavior. In the following chapter our intention is to analyze the Army Corps of Engineers' citizen participation program from both perspectives, with a view towards bridging the gap between research on social choice and organization theory. As we will try to demonstrate, the two complement each other quite well; deficiencies on one side are compensated for or explained by the other.

The Free Rider Problem

A common view of the citizen-as-participant, which is inferred from the short-lived nature of movements for greater citizen participation, is that he is apathetic. The sporadic outpouring of people concerned with public issues is thus attributed to the nature of the conflict: the political stakes are high, the issue is highly visible, and a significant segment of the population feels itself genuinely excluded, disaffected, and disadvantaged. But once the sense of outrage or of injustice at being excluded is alleviated, citizens will return to preoccupation with their daily lives, thereby leaving the more mundane and time-consuming resolution of public problems to the ever-enduring special interest groups and to public officials.

Economists provide a somewhat different explanation. The condition prevails because issues of general welfare, those that are known as public goods, give rise to the well-known problem of freeriding,

> a situation wherein people have little incentive to expend substantial resources to avoid what appears to be insignificant individual costs, even though they could benefit from collective action and could not be prevented from enjoying the benefits. The inclination here is to take a free ride by "letting George do it" (Wandesforde-Smith, 1972).

Thus, individuals do not participate in the public decision-making process because the cost of participation outweighs an individual's share of the public good to be gained. This is a problem accentuated as the size of the population with an interest in common increases. The political consequence of this latter fact, as Olson indicates, is that the very persons who have some of the most pressing common interests, the so-called "forgotten group" of society, go unrepresented in the policy process (Olson, 1965).

Finally, it is noted by Riker and Ordeshook (1972) that due to a diminishing feeling of personal efficacy the tendency to participate is universally reduced with the increasing size and complexity of society.

The logic of the individual rationality theory is straightforward, and its insights are of profound consequence for a democratic society, particularly if Riker and Ordeshook are correct in identifying the long-term direction in participation. But the increasing size and complexity of modern society has not led to an eclipse of a wide range of participatory activities; not everyone is freeriding. For example, over the past half century the absolute turnout of eligible voters in presidential elections has increased to the point where nearly 75 million persons voted in 1972. On the local level there is evidence that an appreciable proportion of the population takes an active hand well beyond voting. In their nationwide examination of participation Verba and Nie (1972) show that at least three out of every ten Americans participate in community affairs.

Gauging the potential for citizen involvement in the decision-making of an agency of fairly limited activity, such as the Army Corps of Engineers, exclusively on the basis of the above figures would be unwarranted. A more appropriate guide is available: a recent survey covering the metropolitan St. Louis area showed that with specific reference to the kind of water resource issues pertinent to the Corps, 18 percent of the population said it was "very interested" in participating in water resource management planning for that area (Fleishman-Hillard Opinion Research, 1973). Even discounting this figure for the probable drop-off between expressed interest and actual participation, and for the possibility that this may not be a representative sample of nationwide attitudes, the finding seems impressive and indicative of a fairly large pool of untapped participation-minded citizens.

Bureaucratic Resistance

It seems appropriate, then, to look beyond the freerider problem when asking why citizen involvement in agencies is negligible, and, when it does come about, why it is typically short-lived. Another perspective on this issue is presented by bureaucratic and organization theory. It is asserted that bureaucracy is resistant to change; agencies pursue the wrong policies; they are responsive to only an elite and not to the general public; they make their decisions behind closed doors; and only the threat of litigation will force bureaucrats grudgingly to allow ordinary mortals to participate in the decision-making process. The notion of encouraging outsiders to participate actively in agency policy-making or to pass judgment on their programs and policies runs counter to the bureaucratic laws of conservatism, hierarchy, expanding control, imperialism, and self-serving loyalty (Laws identified by Downs, 1967).

While this view may be shared by many people challenging traditional decision-making prerogatives, those within the agency have their complaints and grievances as well. In other words, the view from within may not correspond to the view from without, for very good reasons. Or, bureaucrats and the public may share similar attitudes but give different reasons for holding those opinions. It may not be a Jekyll and Hyde situation at all; rather, it may be a case of two Hydes (or two Jekylls), one sitting within the agency and one standing without, each eyeing the other with suspicion.

While from their divergent perspectives social choice theory and organization theory both seem to explain the general paucity of citizen participation, they have also overlooked many interesting exceptions. One such exception may turn out to be the recent surge of participation by citizens and environmentalists in the planning operations of the Corps of Engineers. Not that citizens have come to share with or have authority over Corps activities, but in the space of a few years the Corps claims that citizens have assumed an important and permanent role in policy formulation and project planning. They have assumed this role through their participation in public meetings, seminars and workshops, citizen advisory boards, and a growing informal network of communication channels at the district, division, and national level. A measure of its effort to encourage this involvement is the extent to which the Corps is reformulating its traditional citizen participation procedures to facilitate representation by *all* interested publics.

CITIZEN PARTICIPATION AS A COMPONENT OF THE CORPS OF ENGINEERS' PLANNING PROCESS

The Army Corps of Engineers is a public works agency, and until recently, uniformly dedicated to the planning and construction of water-related projects. It builds dams, channelizes rivers, nourishes beaches suffering from erosion, dredges harbors, and so forth. It has done this by congressional statute for the furtherance of "national economic efficiency." Corps personnel and supporters of the agency, for example, claim to have helped create a system of waterborne transportation and thus to have contributed to the economic productivity of the country. The agency's other activities, such as flood control, are also justified primarily by the economic criterion.

The Corps gained notoriety among social scientists when Arthur Maass published his book, *Muddy Waters*, in 1951. In this classic, Maass analyzed the role of the Corps and uncovered an anomaly among federal agencies: the Corps is an organization that is theoretically a part of the Executive Branch but is in practice an extension of the Legislative Branch. No other federal agency appeared to be so independent of the Executive and so closely allied with Congress. Numerous administrations have attempted to sever this close connection between the Corps and Congress, but so far without success. Thus the Corps' program became the classic example of "the pork barrel." It operated with impunity within administrations dedicated to a manner of decision-making more rational than that of selecting projects that would aid Congressmen in getting reelected.

Challenges to the Status Quo

The environmental movement of the late 1960s and early 1970s presented a significant challenge to the Corps. The demand that federal agencies take into account the "environmental effects" of their actions followed closely on an earlier demand voiced by various groups in the mid- to late 1960s: that the government in general and the bureaucracy in particular should make more "public" the decision-making process so that decisions would no longer be lost within the corridors and confines of those gigantic structures housing the federal agencies. Instead, decisions and policy would be made out in the open, in public view, and with increased participation by those anxious to participate. It was to be a new game: the players were to be changed (involve the public, not just the traditional interest groups) and then the rules (consider the environment, or, in the language of the economists, the "externalities" of one's activities).

Citizen participation and environmentalism were thus a two-pronged attack on the old way of doing things. How did the Corps respond?

"The Corps Cares": A New Motto

Public participation in governmental decision-making can take many forms. Voting in elections, letter-writing, attending city council meetings, lobbying, and so on are all recognized forms of participation in the political process. The branches of government, as well as the various levels of government, have evolved certain forms of participation more or less appropriate to their functions and their relative position in the political structure. For the Corps, as with virtually every other federal agency, direct public investment had been an inconsequential part of its operations. The public was typically told about the Corps' intentions at a not-too-well publicized or sparsely attended public hearing. Few attempts were made to include citizens directly in the planning process. Few citizens cared to be involved.

It came as a surprise to many, therefore, that in recent years the Corps of Engineers responded to demands for a more open planning process in a forceful and energetic manner. In 1970, the Chief of Engineers announced his policy with respect to this aspect of the Corps mission:

> We will encourage as broad public and private participation as practical in defining environmental objectives and in eliciting viewpoints of what the public wants and expects as well as what it is projected to need (U.S. Army Corps of Engineers, 1973).

Thus the mandate from the Chief's office was clear: to consider environmental effects fully and to broaden the agency's public involvement program. The mandate, however was easier said than done. As anyone familiar with the bureaucracy knows, enunciating policy is one thing; translating it into action or implementing it is quite another. The years intervening between the Chief's initial statement and the present have been referred to frequently within the agency as a "period of transition."

The task of implementing this new policy fell to the 38 districts (including two operating Divisions: New England and Pacific Ocean) that together comprise the local level of organization in the Corps. In the Corps' decentralized organization, district offices have considerable autonomy, and decisions on water resource projects have almost always been made in light of local needs and conditions. Undoubtedly the most crucial variable in determining whether a Corps project will or will not be built, or whether an agency-wide policy will or will not be successful, is the immediate environment—physical, social, political—within which the district operates. Thus one would expect to find some significant differences in the way in which these policy guidelines have been implemented Corps-wide.

And one does. For example, with the public participation program, certain districts began reformulating their procedures prior to the time that the word came down from Washington. The Baltimore District, in working on its comprehensive plan for the Susquehanna River Basin, attempted innovative participation techniques by holding workshops and seminars throughout the planning process. This was in 1969, and it may have provided a model for other districts. Overall, however, most changes in this program occurred subsequent to 1970.

PUBLIC INVOLVEMENT: REDEFINING ROLES AND REORGANIZING

Seen from within, the Corps' new thrust into public participation and environmental planning has had a number of interesting consequences. Based on in-depth interviews and data collection at eight district and three division offices, a picture emerges of an agency trying to orient itself to new objectives as well as to a new way of doing things. Though there appear to be interesting comparisons to be made among district offices (which we will explore in a following section), some overall observations are in order.

New programs mean reorganization. Since the mandate to involve the public was interpreted as a new "program" within the Corps, this meant that someone, some groups or some division within the office, must have primary responsibility. In a number of districts, this function devolved upon a newly formed environmental resources unit (called a branch or section). In most district offices, these environmental resource branches were instituted between 1970 and 1972, in order to handle the requirement of the National Environmental Policy Act (NEPA) and, frequently, the public participation program. Usually, they evolved from the agency's old recreation units. Personnel were added to the few landscape architects or recreation planners in the district office, the name was changed and, to some extent, the functions performed by the unit changed as well. Also, in many districts, the so-called planning unit shared or had primary responsibility for the public participation program.

The planning units were involved in the new program because the planning branch is responsible for initial project formulation, and since the common grievance was that the public was generally confronted with an "after-the-fact" plan, early involvement was deemed essential. Iron out the problems at the start, it was felt, and then let the engineering and design people take care of the rest. Planning has become, to borrow from Aaron Wildavsky, the battleground for unresolved conflicts.

The environmental people are frequently involved in the participation program because much of the demand for citizen involvement has come from the environmental community; it is the environmental branch's document (the Environmental Impact Statement) that is most accessible to the public and thus the document over which many recent conflicts have revolved.

Whether the commanding officer of the district (the District Engineer) will spend much of his time on this activity is highly variable. Prior to the expansion of the citizen involvement program, the job of the District Engineer was largely defined in terms of "meeting the public," and probably still is. However, many District Engineers (as well as other Corps employees) make an implicit distinction between this program and their "normal" public duties, such as attending luncheons given by local business or professional groups, meeting with local economic interests, coordinating with other governmental bodies, and the like. In other words, this program is perceived as just one channel of communication to the public, and generally to a specialized public at that: the environmental interests. Therefore, most District Engineers replied in the negative when asked whether they spend much of their time at public hearings, workshops, and seminars. Obviously they spend a great deal of their time in meeting with interest groups, and in other public relations-related activities, but the norm appears to be to view the new program as serving a particular clientele, and not as the single or best way of reaching The Public, except, again, in those areas where environmental issues are of overriding importance.

Also highly variable is whether the chief of the engineering division involves himself in the expanded citizen involvement effort. This person is regarded as the highest-ranking civilian

PARTICIPATION PATTERNS AND EVALUATION 233

employee in the office, and so his support, or lack of it, could be viewed as one indicator of the importance attached to the program. From a sample of nine district offices, only one or two chiefs interviewed personally handled this program and made attendance a normal part of his job.

In most cases, responsibility for the program has devolved upon the planning and environmental staffs. The reasons are numerous, but the conclusion seems to be that the agency perceives this effort as one of tapping not *the* public interest but a specialized part of it. We will elaborate on this point later.

District mailing lists for the participation program may run to 5,000; they are coded as to geographic area, area of interest(s), and so on. New groups and individuals, those "suspected" of having an interest in the project, have been added to the lists. Unlike the procedure during less controversial times in which the announcement of a public meeting may have been tacked up on the bulletin boards of the post office and city hall, the Corps now mails out hundreds and sometimes thousands of these announcements. The format of the document has similarly changed; it used to be a one-page sheet, composed largely of a citation from the Congressional study authorization. Now it is a three-to-four page document with a much fuller, and more glamorous, summary of the proposed project.

Obviously the public participation program, together with the preparation and writing of Environmental Impact Statements (as required by NEPA), has meant that agency resources such as personnel, money, and time must be allocated to these activities. New personnel have been brought into the agency, and people with nonengineering backgrounds have been recruited to perform these functions.

To most people interviewed in the district offices, the establishment of an environmental resources unit, staffed with biological- and social science-oriented personnel, illustrated the changing orientation of the Corps with respect to its basic mission.

In the planning and environmental units of the field offices one finds a preponderance of nonengineering disciplines, or at least a sufficient number of them so that they can "compete" with the engineers in those units and also not feel like the token social or biological scientist on the staff. A fairly typical environmental branch will include such disciplines as economics, fisheries biology, wildlife biology, and geology. The planning unit will be staffed with people from such disciplines as sociology, urban planning, landscape architecture, and forestry, as well as with civil and sanitary engineers.

Thus we find new people in the agency, new functional units, and the formal enunciation of new objectives. The next question is, obviously, how these three factors relate to one another in reality and not just on the organization charts. For, as Victor Thompson has noted:

> If new activities cannot be blocked entirely they can at least be segregated and eventually blocked from the communications system if necessary. Typically, the introduction of technical innovative activities into modern organizations is by means of segregated units, often called research and development units. Segregating such activities prevents them from affecting the *status quo* to any great extent. The organization does not have to change (Thompson, 1969).

The cynic or skeptic could thus argue: All right, you have brought new people, with diverse backgrounds, into the agency; new units are created to handle the Corps' new objectives of expanded public participation and environmental awareness; a great deal of time, money, and effort is being expended on these activities and programs. Nevertheless, as Thompson suggests, you still have not proven that this great flurry of activity has changed anything to any appreciable extent. What, the critic may ask, do you say to that?

Our answer is that we cannot yet tell with any great certainty whether these internal agency changes have produced changes in the agency's "output." One cannot tell primarily because of the ongoing nature of the civil works program: most of the agency's workload at any given time is composed of projects already underway and in various stages of completion. On the average, it takes six years to complete just the *planning* of a project (Wolff, 1971). Construction may then take another ten years. The impact, therefore, of new programs and methods on this ongoing work is almost of necessity minimal, and any changes that do take place as a result of internal pressures for change will invariably be "at the margin." We are not dodging the issue of change, but simply pointing out the difficulty of evaluating the extent of change when one is studying an ongoing, "live" program.

The available data are the essentially subjective, personal

opinions of those affected by these new programs, both within the agency and without. For the purpose of this research, we are measuring change primarily by what the participants say (or don't say) about the Corps' changing missions.

How do those within the agency, the field and division people, feel about these new programs? Have they been a success? Are they valuable or a waste of time? Do those with nonengineering backgrounds feel useful, or isolated and segregated, from the real decision-making process? The following is a brief summary of responses to these questions, as perceived by agency people.

A mixed picture emerges. In short, there is a rather thoroughgoing ambivalence as to the efficacy, or utility, of the Corps' expanded public participation program and of its new environmental procedures. Most people felt that the agency was still in a "period of transition" and that the optimal solution to these new concerns, or demands, had yet to be discovered. On the one hand, they felt that the Corps had responded admirably to these external pressures for change; they were, on the whole, satisfied with the agency's response record. On the other hand, there was not much feeling that these were vital or important functions of the agency. With one or two exceptions, most agency people were less than satisfied with the new programs.

On the question of involving the public in the planning process, very few agency people were wholeheartedly enthusiastic about it. Those that were often included the District Engineers themselves; they seemed to be highly sensitive to the public nature of the Corps' programs and frequently expressed concern that there be "widespread public acceptance" of the agency's projects. Not that others didn't express similar sentiments, but it was the District Engineer who very often had the most positive statements to make on these new programs of the Corps.

"Public involvement is a difficult concept for an agency to handle," one person lamented. And this rather accurately reflects the feelings of those directly dealing with the program. They felt that it was on the whole necessary but that not a great deal of useful information was obtained by these meetings; that "the public" who turned out for public meetings did not represent the entire public; that generally opponents of Corps' projects showed up, not the proponents; that environmental groups were using the environmental issue to mask their real interests; and that frequently projects turned out to be worse, not better, after endless rounds of meetings with "the public." From the perspective of the bureaucracy, then, the greatest utility of the citizen involvement program is probably that it has alerted and sensitized the agency to its potential opposition. It has derailed possible lawsuits, and, to some extent, satisfied the opposition.

This is not to say that the program is merely symbolic; there have been substantive changes made in projects as a result of the public input. Each district visited invariably cited one or two cases of changes in Corps' projects resulting from the combination of public input and environmental awareness. Some felt that projects were better as a result, while others felt the changes were either negligible or for the worse. We thus did not find unanimity of opinion, within the agency, as to whether the new planning process resulted in better projects. Personnel did feel, however, that it tended to result in "greater public acceptability" of projects, and that is not an unimportant criterion.

CITIZEN PARTICIPATION IN FIVE COMMUNITIES

Whether the Corps' recent efforts have broadened participation in the public policy process is an open question. A partial answer may be found in an examination of citizen participation in the planning of five of the Corps' project studies. The criteria for selection of this example were: (a) the major portion of the public participation activities must have occurred since passage of the National Environmental Policy Act of 1969; (b) the studies be located in different geographical regions of the United States; (c) at least one be of a dam study, one a levee study, one a channelization study, and one a pilot wastewater management study; and (d) cooperation for the study by the district office must be assured. Those chosen were the Wastewater Management Study for Cleveland-Akron Metropolitan and Three Rivers Watershed Areas in Northern Ohio (Cleveland-Akron study); the Unit L-15 of the Missouri River Levee System Study, just north of St. Louis, Missouri (L-15 Levee Study); the Mississippi River-Gulf Outlet New Lock and Connecting Channel Study, just south of New Orleans (MR-GO Study); the flood control and related water resource problems study on the Wildcat and San Pablo Creeks, Contra Costa County, California (San Pablo Creek Study); and the Middle Fork of the Snoqualmie River Study, located approximately 20 miles east of Seattle (Snoqualmie River Study).

Although these studies exemplify major types of Corps projects, they are not a representative sample of dam building or channelization or flood control activities in any strict sense, nor are they representative of a total range of citizen participation programs. Most of the studies were chosen because they demonstrated the far-reaching efforts that an agency can undertake. once motivated. This should be taken into consideration when interpreting our findings.

From among the approximately 3,000 persons who participated in the public meetings, seminars, workshops, discussions, and overall planning in the five studies, up to 200 names for each study were drawn at random from the meeting attendance list kept by the Corps; questionnaires about their experience in December of 1973 and January of 1974 were mailed to these names.[2] The present analysis is based on the scoreable responses returned as of February 15, 1974.[3]

Who Participates?

Taken in aggregate the respondents are not "average" Americans. They are older (with a mean age of 49.9 years), wealthier (with a mean family income of about $15,000), more educated (with a mean of 14.6 years of education), male (77.9 percent), and established residents of the community (the mean years at their present address is 14.5 years, and their mean years in the state or region 34.1 years). But these characteristics are typical of the general activist-oriented segment of the population (Verba and Nie, 1972).

Environmental and business interests were well represented in all the studies. On the whole environmentalists comprised one-fifth of the sample, reaching as much as 30 percent in the L-15 Levee Study. Businessmen comprised one-seventh of those participating, reaching 28 percent in the San Pablo Creek Study. Moreover, those who are usually underrepresented were well accounted for: environmentalists and concerned citizens repre-

---

[2] Two hundred questionnaires were mailed to participants of the Cleveland-Akron Study; and 184 to the Snoqualmie River Study.

[3] The overall response rate for the questionnaire as of February 15 was 53 percent, varying by study from 35 percent to 59 percent: 35 percent for the San Pablo Creek Study, 47 percent for the MR-GO Study, 58 percent for the L-15 Levee and the Cleveland-Akron Studies, and 59 percent for the Snoqualmie River Study.

sent almost four-fifths of the total sample. This alone indicates that the freeriding problem can be overcome at least to some extent if an agency is willing to reach out to all segments of the community by actively soliciting their views: by maintaining contact with community, citizen, and environmental groups; by publicizing its planning program through the mass media; by making even preliminary plans available for review; and finally, by providing a public forum for discussion and the exchange of views.

Why Participate?

Participation in Corps planning was not the result of habit. Those surveyed indicated that they had had little previous experience or opportunity in the planning process of water resource agencies. They were not coerced, although many were prompted by friends and associates. And they were not paid by the Corps for their time and efforts. Why did they bother? When asked, the reason given most frequently (by 71.3 percent) was their "concern over the environmental effects of the proposed plan." This was followed in degree of concern by the possible effects to one's home or other properties that the proposed project might have; this reason was identified by 55.4 percent. The third-ranked item was concern with wastewater management.

Two additional features of the response to this question are noteworthy. First, a number of the most salient issues for the public were those affecting the general welfare of the community —the environment, wastewater management, and preservation of wilderness areas—precisely the kinds of issues that are not supposed to, or have not previously, generated extensive public participation. Second, a familiar criticism of citizen participation programs by agency personnel is that they tend to draw only project opponents, while proponents stay at home.[4] The evidence bears this out, although the point seems to have been exaggerated. In our sample, opponents of the Corps' plan outnumbered proponents by only a four-to-three margin, with the

---

[4] Rarely considered by these critics is that the preponderance of negative sentiments expressed at public meetings may be a function of opportunities; the public meetings provide one of the few forums open to opponents of a plan, whereas proponents have numerous "informal" channels of access.

pro-Corps item ranking sixth and the con-Corps item ranking fourth among the ten concerns selected by respondents.

Evaluating the Participatory Experience

It is exceedingly difficult for the public to gauge its impact on the Corps: How receptive is the Corps to the ideas of citizens? To what extent has the Corps changed its way of approaching problems as a result of the public's participation? And, to what extent are the views of the heretofore underrepresented segments of the community becoming a part of Corps' decision-making? When asked, "Do you know if the Corps has modified or changed its plans for the project you participated in as a result of suggestions made by citizens?" an exceptionally large 47.1 percent of the respondents answered "Don't know." Nevertheless, the public does have opinions about the Corps and the Corps' predisposition to favor one set of interests over others. These opinions, in turn, are associated with the public's opinion about the proposed project, their evaluation of the quality of information about the project provided by the Corps, and their view of the proper role of citizens in water resource planning.

An individual's general predisposition toward the Corps is tapped by a number of our questionnaire items. These items have been identified and statistically grouped together through use of a pair-wise clustering technique (technique reported by Leavitt, 1971). The technique shows that if one believes that "The Corps is making an honest effort to reconcile the many community interests," he will also be likely to believe that "The opinions of citizens greatly influence the actions taken by the Corps," while disagreeing with the statement that "The Corps goes through the motions of consulting citizens but is not sincerely interested in obtaining their views." Taken together, these and like items form a scale that measures the respondent's underlying "Orientation Toward Corps."

Table I, "Four Attitudinal Scales, By Subgroups," shows the differences in the orientation toward the Corps by study, self-identified role type, and substantive interest. The comparison in the last category reveals a distinctively lower evaluation of the Corps by those concerned with the environmental effects of the projects as opposed to those who see the Corps providing flood and other protection for their property. The mean scores of the two groups are 2.66 and 2.96 respectively, statistically sig-

Table I
Four Attitudinal Scales, by Subgroups

Subgroups	Orientation Toward Corps	Evaluation of Project	Citizen Power	Civic Duty	n
1. *Study Location*					
Cleveland-Akron	3.03	1.97	2.88	3.56	(108)
L-15 Levee	2.51	2.33	2.65	3.60	(111)
MR-GO	2.65	2.05	2.92	3.54	(75)
San Pablo Creek	3.20	2.58	2.66	3.70	(30)
Snoqualmie River	2.75	2.01	2.71	3.66	(93)
2. *Self-Identified Role Type*					
Environmental or Conservation	2.47	1.61	3.10	3.75	(76)
Concerned Citizen	2.76	2.27	2.81	3.53	(240)
Business	3.08	2.19	2.37	3.71	(54)
3. *Substantive Interests*					
Environmental Effects[a]	2.66	1.75	2.95	3.68	(244)
Direct Personal Benefit[b]	2.96	3.32	2.40	3.42	(44)

[a]Persons who score 4 (on a 4-step ladder) on the item "I am concerned over the environmental effect of the proposed plan," but less than 4 on the item "My home (or other properties) was recently flooded and I may benefit from the proposed project."

[b]Persons who score 4 on the second item in notation *a* but less than 4 on the first item.

nificant at the 0.01 level. The same kind of difference exists between self-identified role types. The average rating of the Corps by businessmen (3.08) is much higher than that by environmentalists (2.47), and well above that of the concerned citizens (2.76). The difference between the groups is significant at the 0.01 level.

The mean scale scores by study are more difficult to interpret. It is conventional wisdom that businessmen rate the Corps higher than any other group. Also, as a proportion of the respondents, they are most represented in the San Pablo Creek Study. The combination of these factors surely helps explain why the Corps received its highest study-wide rating at San Pablo Creek. Similarly, the low rating in the L-15 Levee Study is explained in part by the preponderance of environmentalists (30.2 percent of the respondents) who participated there.

Above all, the study-wide means on the orientation towards the Corps indicate that the evaluation of the Corps' intentions and performance is not based so much on the extent of its public participation program as on other factors such as the predisposition of the respondents. Environmentalists typically distrust and dislike the Corps while businessmen look favorably upon the agency. Scale scores are undoubtedly also influenced by the respondent's view of the proposed project. Otherwise the extensive efforts at holding workshops and public meetings, and the attempts by the Corps to present a number of viable alternatives in the L-15 and Snoqualmie River studies ought to have resulted in a much higher "Orientation Toward Corps" ratings. Likewise, with its single public meeting, MR-GO would have been rated lowest of all (see Table I).

Although the aggregate data show no clear relationship between the extent of a public participation program and the public's orientation toward the Corps, qualitative analysis does. The view expressed by a number of environmental and civic leaders who have monitored the Corps over a number of years is that in the last two or three years certain Corps districts have become more open in their deliberative process and more receptive to environmental interests. Bringing these findings together, it appears that an open and comprehensive public participation program is not in and of itself sufficient to overcome the deep-rooted distrust of the Corps where it exists or to overcome opposition to a proposed project. But, as reflected in the views of a number of leading environmentalists and civic group leaders, the Corps has gained recognition and respect in those districts where a reasonable effort to include all factions, and to accommodate the conflicting interests in the community, have been seriously undertaken. A key variable thus appears to be a "genuine" effort on the part of the agency.

That a good public participation program does not assure a consensus on a project plan is underscored by responses to the scale measuring "Evaluation of Project." The ratings shown on the table for the Cleveland-Akron and Snoqualmie River studies make this clear: with two of the most extensive public participation programs, they managed to receive the two lowest project ratings among the five studies: mean scores of 1.97 and 2.01 respectively.

Even though the environmentalists are the most vocal critics and the least trustful of the Corps, they are also the most committed to sustained involvement in Corps planning. This is shown by responses to items that cluster together to measure attitudes on the proper role of citizens in the planning of water resource projects, as shown in the "Citizen Power" scale. Environmentalists are far more prone to respond that "Citizens should have a greater voice in the planning of public water resource projects," and disagree with the statement, "The decision over which water resource projects are to be built should be left in the hands of the experts." The highest citizen power score among the five studies is for MR-GO, with a mean score of 2.92. The participants in the MR-GO Study apparently feel the greatest need for more direct citizen control over the Corps and over decisions affecting water resource in their area.

Two items combine to form a "Civic Duty" scale. When asked to rate the item, "I intend to participate in future project planning programs," along a 4-step ladder, 59.2 percent of the respondents marked step four ("agree"), and an additional 18.5 marked step three. The intention to participate was even more pronounced when the same was asked in reverse; that is, when respondents were asked to rate the item, "I see no reason for taking part in any future Corps sponsored citizen involvement programs." In this instance 83.4 percent marked step one ("disagree") and 9.0 percent marked step two. As indicated by the scores on this scale, presented in the table, there is only a slight difference between subgroups: environmentalists and businessmen are more inclined to continue participating than concerned citizens, and those with environmental interests more so than those seeking direct benefit, but the differences are significant at the 0.01 level.

Most striking about the Civic Duty Scale is that it is virtually uncorrelated with the other scales that have emerged in our analysis. (And the variables comprising it are not strongly associated individually with any others in the questionnaire.) The scale is not related to the position of respondents on the proposed plan, or their predisposition toward the Corps, or their feeling about whether citizens should be more active. Nevertheless, the high scale scores clearly indicate that, if given the opportunity, the overwhelming majority will continue to participate in Corps planning.

SUMMARY AND CONCLUSIONS

We have been concerned in this chapter with recent efforts by the Corps of Engineers to include a broad range of interests in the policy-making process, and the success of the efforts. For a number of reasons that have been discussed at great length by political and social scientists, bureaucracies tend, over time, to become closely allied to their "natural" clientele: they overlook, ignore, and/or minimize the significance of other interests that may appear to them to have little to do with their programs. In the case of the Corps, the public interest traditionally has been identified with local waterways interests, and with the Congressional authorization process which, by and large, reflects this local development orientation.

In recent years, however, the Corps has made a serious effort to include a wider spectrum of interests in its planning process. The impetus for this reform came principally from the Office of the Chief of Engineers. However, its implementation naturally depended upon, and is the responsibility of, the local district offices. What follows is a brief summary of: (a) the success of the public participation program in bringing new interests into the Corps; and (b) the likelihood of its survival as a dynamic, rather than a purely formalistic, process.

Environmental awareness and the demand for citizen involvement have brought new interest into the Corps. Within the agency, the planning and environmental units represent interests and values that are new to the traditional, "structural" approaches generally taken by the Corps. Viewed in the aggregate, there is presently a sizable group that is pushing, from the inside, for what are considered innovative solutions to water resource problems. But whether they have had much influence on actual Corps projects appears to vary considerably from district to district. In some offices these units are isolated and the new people spend their time writing Environmental Impact Statements (or running the public involvement program!). In other offices, they appear to have much greater importance. The variation appears to depend on two factors: (1) the support for innovative solutions outside of the agency, and (2) the degree of support given by the top civil and military personnel within the office. Lacking these, there is not a great deal that the planning and environmental units can do to alter decisions and policy effectively.

In terms of tapping previously underrepresented interests in the society, here, too, we feel that the program has been a qualified success. In most Corps districts, thousands of participants have been drawn into the planning process in a way seldom achieved by any federal agency. However, as the data show, the participants are not representative of every segment of society: they are disproportionately middle class, and representative of local concerned citizens (activists), business, and environmental groups. The poor are chronically underrepresented, as are ethnic minorities. Nevertheless, the above-named groups that do participate indicate that the Corps is reaching people and listening to views that it did not consider before. The balance sheet is mixed.

The Corps has put much time and money into both its participation and environmental programs. It provides write-ups of proposed alternative plans, plus technical assistance and information. The district office also provides the forum for the participants, as well as doing the organizing and publicity for the meetings. The resources expended on the preparation of environmental assessments and impact statements have also been considerable. Exact figures on the monetary costs are lacking, but some districts estimate that approximately 10 percent of their planning budget goes into just the citizen involvement program. An impact statement, frequently prepared by consultants, may run into many thousands of dollars. The paper work generated by these programs is frequently overwhelming, and so a number of agency people wonder whether the benefits do in fact outweigh the costs.

There are benefits, of course, but to date they have been

largely symbolic, nonmaterial, and often within the area of "public relations." Few projects have changed as a result of these new policies. However, new programs, if they can be successfully integrated into the agency, mean new constituencies and hence greater public support and acceptance. No one wants to be caught wearing the black hat in an era of "environmental awareness," and the Corps has indeed been sensitive to this charge. Further, by expanding its range of operations, which it is currently doing, it may be assuring its survival in a period of changing national priorities. One has only to compare the Corps' performance (and budget) with other water resource agencies on this score to appreciate the importance of flexibility. Generally speaking, it is far better to be a multipurpose agency than a single-purpose one, and the umbrella of "public works" is sufficiently general to allow for the introduction of new programs and new planning styles.

In short, the Corps' new program is evidence that the problems of freeriding and collective action can be overcome, to some extent, *if* an agency is willing to underwrite information gathering and organizational costs that have usually served to impede participation in the public policy process by all but the well-organized, wealthy, and the development-oriented.

The program also indicates that a large organization can change, but that it takes sustained pressure from both within and without the agency; good ideas, new people, reorganization, and so on are not enough. Political support or pressure from outside of the agency is essential.

Will the new programs continue or perish? Can widespread participation in agency decision-making survive? If history and our analytic theories are guides, probably not. First, we have no evidence that the public will want to participate on a continued and sustained basis; the program is still too new to determine this. Judging from past participation efforts, however, there is every reason to believe that it is of a sporadic or cyclical nature.

But even if the public was willing, the benefits to the agency are still seen as less important than the costs: time and money, the challenge to bureaucratic expertise and professional judgment, the sharing of power. We do not, however, wish to rule out the possibility of a happy union between bureaucracy and widespread citizen involvement. For such a program to survive there must be, first, positive feedback and support for the agency from the interests who gain access through this process. This is important if one expects the Corps, or any other agency, to willingly underwrite information and organization costs. Second, there may need to be a legal mandate, from Congress or the President, requiring that public participation be an integral part of the decision-making process of all agencies, a process that goes beyond the holding of public hearings. Sanctions for noncompliance would need to be a part of the mandate to assure its implementation, although hopefully they would be seldom employed. They would serve only to insure that the spirit as well as the letter of the law be carried out.

Taken together, the positive benefits an agency could receive if it implemented a meaningful program, and the sanctions to be imposed if it did not, provide the necessary incentives to agencies to assure the survival of public participation in agency decision-making. The new balance of interests that this would represent within the policy process would not alleviate the problems of conflicting and competing interests, but it could assure that many interests that are underrepresented today will receive a more equitable hearing.

REFERENCES

Downs, A. *Inside Bureaucracy* (Boston, Massachusetts: Little, Brown and Company, 1967).

Fleishman-Hillard Opinion Research. "Attitudes of Residents and Leaders of the St. Louis Metropolitan Area Toward the Management of Water Resources," a report presented to the Army Corps of Engineers, St. Louis District (October 1973).

Leavitt, M. "MULTYP/Multiple Typal Analysis: A Clustering Program," *Behavioral Sci.* 16 (4), 417 (1971).

McConnell, G. *Private Power and American Democracy* (New York: Alfred A. Knopf, 1966).

Olson, M., Jr. *The Logic of Collective Action: Public Goods and the Theory of Groups* (Cambridge, Massachusetts: Harvard University Press, 1965).

Riker, W. H., and P. C. Ordeshook. *An Introduction to Positive Political Theory* (New York: Prentice-Hall, Inc., 1972).

Thompson, V. "Bureaucracy and Innovation," in *Organization Concepts and Analysis,* William Scott, Ed. (Belmont, Calif.: Dickenson Publishing Co., 1969).

U. S. Army Corps of Engineers, Directorate of Civil Works. *Environmental Program* (EP 1105-2-500, June 1973).

Verba, S., and N. H. Nie. *Participation in America: Political Democracy and Social Equality* (New York: Harper and Row, 1972).

Wandesforde-Smith, G. "Environmental Watchdogs: The Promise of Law and Politics," Environmental Quality Series, No. 8, University of California, Davis, Institute of Governmental Affairs (April, 1972).

Wolff, R. D. "Involving the Public and the Hierarchy in the Corps of Engineers Survey Investigation," Report EEP-45, Stanford University, Program in Engineering-Economic Planning (November 1971).

13. Citizen Advisory Committees: The Impact of Recruitment on Representation and Responsiveness

John C. Pierce and Harvey R. Doerksen

INTRODUCTION

The quest for public involvement in water resource politics leads in many directions. One route increasingly well traveled is the citizen advisory committee (Dodge, 1973; Felton, 1968). In the water resource arena, a citizen advisory committee is a formal mechanism designed to link the general public and those who make water resource decisions. In principle, the citizen advisory committee (CAC) should allow for public involvement, reflect the various water resource interests found in the public, and communicate those interests to public officials. In turn, those who make decisions will be more responsive to the public. They will possess more information about public preferences because those preferences will have been communicated to them directly and the officials can communicate directly to representatives of the public.

The efficacy of the citizen advisory committee model of public involvement is therefore based in two linkages. The first is between the public and the CAC members themselves. Crucial questions are the extent to which the CAC is open to general public involvement and the degree to which those who are involved on the CAC actually mirror the distribution of interests in the general public. If some interests in the public are underrepresented and others are overrepresented, the image of the public received by policy-makers will be distorted and the linkage thereby weakened. Thus, the first linkage is one of *representation*.[1]

The second linkage deals with the relationship between the citizen advisory committee members and the public officials with whom they interact. Many public officials view public involvement programs as an opportunity to proselytize among the public or to provide a cathartic experience for probable opponents (Wilson, 1973). Yet, if public officials are unresponsive to the views of CAC members, CACs perfectly representative of the general public will fail in their purpose. Thus for public involvement to succeed through the citizen advisory committee, there also must be public official *responsiveness*.

The number of influences potentially affecting representation and responsiveness is large (Jewell and Patterson, 1973). The process by which CACs are selected is one variable that may have an impact on both representation and responsiveness. Recruitment, according to Seligman, *et al.*,

> gives expression to various subcultures and interests and translates them into the decision-making process. The politics of recruitment determine the actors in decision-making and shows how they will act in decision-making roles. Whether cleavages will be aggravated or reduced and how policies will be enacted is directly and indirectly determined by the recruitment processes (1974).

Although the above words were written to describe recruitment to a state legislature, they can also be applied to water resource citizen advisory committees. Water resource politics is full of conflict, and public involvement programs are in the midst of that conflict. There are cleavages in the public as articulated by the various water resource interests such as preservationist, industrial, agricultural and energy. Citizen advisory committees are one location where those cleavages and interests are collected and presented to public officials. Recruitment is important be-

---

[1] To be sure, the conception of representation as the degree to which distributions of interests in the public are matched by distributions in a "representative" body is only one of several. The philosophical and political literature is replete with extended discussions of the true or alternative meanings of representation (Pitkin, 1967; Dixon, 1968; Wahlke, *et al.*, 1962).

cause members of a citizen advisory committee can be selected through a variety of mechanisms: selection by public officials, designation by specified organizations or corporations, election at public meetings, or "first come, first served" volunteering.

Almost by definition, those recruitment processes in which CAC members are selected by public officials or by companies and organizations are closed to the general public. Those processes in which there is the opportunity for people to volunteer or to be elected at public meetings are more open. To this point, however, there exists little information as to whether greater openness of the recruitment process makes any difference. This chapter reports one study of the impact of recruitment on CAC representativeness and on members' perceptions of public official responsiveness. Thus, the hypotheses of this study are that *the more open the recruitment process the more representative the citizen advisory committee (in the sense of mirroring the distribution of public preferences) and the less responsive the public officials are perceived by CAC members.*

More open recruitment processes should promote representation of public preferences on citizen advisory committees. Traditional criticisms of the water resource policy process emphasize the extent to which the process is closed to the general public. Some critics claim that decision-makers systematically select for advice and support those individuals and organizations with whom they most often interact and on whom they generally rely for political alliances. Thus, in the selection of CAC members, public officials would focus on visible water resource interests, those presently involved in the policy process. Certain interests in the public would be omitted. More open processes—those taken away from the discretion of the public official—would allow for citizen advisory committees more representative of the general public.

Likewise, in closed recruitment processes, public officials may select individuals and organizations with whom they traditionally interact. They would be more likely to share a common framework, perceptions of the same problems, and the same range of potential solutions. On the other hand, the open processes may recruit individuals new to the process, people without previous interchange with policy-makers. Moreover, they may represent interests more likely to be in opposition to the goals and missions of the public officials. Thus, they should be less likely to perceive public officials as responsive to them.

THE WASHINGTON STATE WATER PROGRAM

The Washington State Water Program is one attempt to provide for public involvement through the citizen advisory committee framework. This chapter examines the relationship of representation and responsiveness to recruitment processes in five river basins involved in that program. The five citizen advisory committees examined in this study were selected from among seven which participated with the State Department of Ecology and the Washington State University Cooperative Extension Service as part of the State Water Program authorized under the Washington State Water Resources Act of 1971.

A project associate was hired for each river basin CAC to coordinate the activities of each committee. The project associates had a number of responsibilities, among which were to organize the citizen committees, to communicate needs for technical and educational assistance to the Department of Ecology and the Extension Service, to provide assistance to the Department of Ecology and the Extension Service, to provide assistance to the CACs in communicating goals to DOE, to keep the public informed of the State Water Program, and to consult with government officials (Pace, 1974).

The intent of the CACs was to develop a process whereby local residents could influence water planning and policy for their own river basin. This purpose was to be accomplished by the organization of citizen groups in designated river basin study areas, leading to broadly based lay-citizen participation in the planning process. The Extension Service and Department of Ecology worked cooperatively with the CACs. The Extension Service would develop an organizational framework within which local people might improve their knowledge, understanding, use and appreciation of the water resources planning process. They also would assist in identifying problems, determining objectives, setting priorities, and choosing among alternatives needed to achieve river basin objectives. The Department of Ecology was to integrate recommendations of the citizen groups into the State Water Program. The Citizen Advisory Committee program was, therefore, intended both to help to educate the public regarding water resources problems and to solicit their input to the planning process (Pace, 1974).

DATA COLLECTION

The data analysis is based on mail questionnaires sent to all members of the five CACs and a sample of the public in the following river basin areas: Walla Walla, Yakima, Big Bend, Spokane, and Southwest. Official lists of all CAC members provided the target groups, the size of which ranged from 18 in Yakima to 98 in Big Bend. The method included an original questionnaire, a one-week postcard reminder, a three-week letter with replacement questionnaire, and, a seven-week letter with replacement questionnaire. Within each river basin a public sample of 120 names also was drawn. The same four-stage process of obtaining responses was employed. Completion rates for the CACs ranged from about 60 percent (Walla Walla and Spokane) to 100 percent (Yakima). For the general public, completion rates ranged from 52 percent in Yakima to 64 percent in the Walla Walla and Southwest river basins.

MEASURING REPRESENTATION

The measure of representation employed here is the degree to which the distribution of water policy preferences in the public is matched by the distribution of those preferences in the respective citizen advisory committee. This section describes the specific measure of representation and presents the results with regard to the degree to which the CACs differ in their level of representation and the degree to which representation varies by the water policy interest being examined.

The CAC members and the river basin public samples were asked to rank seven alternative uses of water resources in the order of their personal preference. The seven alternate uses included: agriculture, preservation, domestic, energy, industry, recreation, and transportation. Operationally, representation is assessed by the degree to which the rankings of each use by the public in a river basin are matched by that basin's CAC members' rankings. The measure chosen to assess the level of representation is the Gini Index of Inequality (Alker, 1965; Schneider 1975). The Gini Index provides a single score that indicates for the total distribution the degree to which CACs differ in their preferences from their publics. The measure ranges from 0.0 to 1.0. As the Gini Index is a measure of inequality, perfect representation occurs when it has a value of zero. Complete lack of representation is indicated by an index of 1.0. Thus, perfect equality (a Gini Index score of Zero) would occur when the citizen advisory committee in a river basin and the public in that basin both have the same distribution of ranks for a policy emphasis, such as preservation.[2]

The Gini Index of Inequality was calculated for each river basin for each of the seven policy preference rankings. Thus, the level of inequality in representation can be compared across substantive policy emphases and across river basins. Table I presents the average level of inequality of representation in each of the five river basins, based on seven Gini Index scores. Differences among the river basins in the level of representation are statistically significant at the 0.001 level, as calculated by one-way analysis of variance. Much of that variation is due to two basins, Big Bend and Spokane, which exhibit CACs the most representative of their publics. On the average, Walla Walla, Yakima, and Southwest river basins are closely grouped in their levels of representation.

Table I
River Basin Gini Index Averages[a]

	Spokane	*Walla Walla*	*Yakima*	*Southwest*	*Big Bend*	
Gini Index Averages	0.317	0.367	0.365	0.379	0.221	$p \leqslant 0.001$

[a]The entry in each cell is the average Gini Index for that river basin, based on seven Gini Index scores, one for each of the policy preference rankings.

Overall, what can be said about the level of public representation on citizen advisory committees? At a minimum, the citizen advisory committees fall short of approaching perfect representation in water policy preferences. Only the Big Bend CAC

---

[2] For a description of the method of calculating the Gini Index of Inequality, the reader is referred to Alker (1965).

exhibits less than 30 percent of the possible inequality in representation. On the other hand, no river basin is more than 38 percent of the way to perfect inequality of representation.

A second question is the degree to which the level of representation varies among the different policy emphases, across all five river basins. The average Gini Indices for the seven different policy emphases are shown in Table II. That table shows a rather wide variation in representation according to the policy emphasis. CACs are most representative on the rankings of transportation and domestic uses of water. They are least representative on the rankings of energy, recreation, and preservation.[3] Again, the differences among the alternative uses are significant at the 0.001 level.

Table II
Policy Emphasis Gini Index Averages[a]

	Agriculture	Preservation	Domestic	Energy	Industry	Recreation	Transportation
Gini Index Average	0.325	0.359	0.259	0.458	0.315	0.383	0.218

Note: $p \leqslant 0.001$

[a] The entry in each cell is the average Gini Index of Inequality for that water resource policy use across the five river basins.

Thus, the level of representation as measured by the Gini Index of Inequality varies among the river basins and among the policy emphases. That some variation exists opens the question of the impact of other river basin characteristics on representation. A subsequent section looks at the relationship of recruitment processes to representation. First, however, attention is turned to the measurement of public official responsiveness.

---

[3] Generally, the citizen advisory committees overrepresent supporters of preservation and recreation as water use priorities and underrepresent the supporters of energy as a water resource use.

PUBLIC OFFICIAL RESPONSIVENESS

Earlier it was noted that a second crucial link in the role of the CAC as a mediator between the public and policy-makers is the responsiveness of the policy-makers to the citizen advisory committee members. Perfectly representative CACs may be ineffectual if policy makers do not respond to them. For several reasons, this analysis examines public official responsiveness as *perceived* by the CAC members. First, the measurement of actual responsiveness is difficult at best. It would demand the acquisition of unavailable data, such as movement in public officials positions on issues, and the quality of the interaction between officials and CAC members. Second, the members' perceptions of public official responsiveness is important in itself. It is important to the officials, for one of the purposes of public involvement programs is to increase public support for those who make policy. Third, important to the operation and success of democratic systems is the feeling among citizens of political efficacy, that government responds to their participation (Campbell, et al., 1960). Thus, perceptions of official responsiveness are central to the full pattern of linkage.

Perceived responsiveness is measured by responses to the following questions: "How often do you think public officials have been influenced by the views of the members of the Citizen Advisory Committee?" Response categories included "often, occasionally, seldom, or never." The results are shown in Table III. Again, there is variation among the citizen advisory committees in the perceived responsiveness of public officials. Greater responsiveness is seen in the Walla Walla and Big Bend CACs, and lesser responsiveness in the Southwest and Yakima CACs.

THE IMPACT OF RECRUITMENT

The nature of the process by which CAC members are chosen has implications for the extent to which the CAC fulfills its goals. Recruitment methods may systematically include or exclude certain portions of the public, thereby influencing who in the public is represented. Citizen advisory committee members report four methods by which they were chosen: election at a public meeting, volunteering, being chosen by a specific group, company or agency, or being chosen by a public official. These methods differ in the extent to which they allow for the open involvement

Table III
The Extent to Which Public Officials are Perceived by CAC Members to Have Been Influenced by the Views of the Members of the CAC

How Often Influenced	Citizen Advisory Committee					
	Spokane	Walla Walla	Southwest	Yakima	Big Bend
Often	4%	27%	21%	12%	21%
Occasionally	50	50	21	41	51
Seldom	25	5	42	35	21
Never	4	5	5	6	3
No answer	18	14	11	6	4
Total	101%	101%	100%	100%	100%
N	(28)	(22)	(19)	(17)	(72)
Index[a]	+25	+67	−5	+10	+48

[a] Index score is the percentage in the top two categories (often, occasionally) minus the percentage in the next two categories (seldom, never).

of the public. The greater the number of CAC members chosen by public officials or selected to represent specific groups, companies or agencies, the more closed is the CAC to entry from the general public. The greater the number of CAC members chosen on the basis of an election or volunteering, the more open is the CAC.

Table IV presents the distribution of responses to a question about the method of selection for each of the CACs. There is some difference among citizen advisory committees. Three CAC recruitment patterns emphasize the more closed process; Spokane, Walla Walla, and Big Bend. Yakima and Southwest emphasized the open mechanisms of elections and volunteering. An index of recruitment openness was created by subtracting the percentage selected by a closed method from the percentage selected by an open method.

The question of present concern is whether these variations in the manner by which the CAC members were selected make any difference in the representativeness of the CAC members' policy preferences when compared to the policy preferences of the public. The original hypothesis stated that the level of representation should increase as the openness of the recruitment process increased. The rationale is that open recruitment processes should allow for the entry into the policy process, in this case the citizen advisory committee, of interests previously excluded. Estimations of the relationship between recruitment and representation are difficult because the study deals with only five cases, the five river basin citizen advisory committees. Thus, some statistical techniques appropriate for larger samples are excluded from use. The examination must be more intuitive. Figure 1 presents the representation scores (the average Gini Index of Inequality) for each of the five CACs along the vertical axis and the openness scored along the horizontal.

The pattern suggested by the average scores is curvilinear. The citizen advisory committee with the most closed recruitment process has an average index of *inequality* about as great as the two with the most open processes. Excluding the most closed CAC, the pattern is relatively regular, *but in a direction opposite to that hypothesized.* That is, after the most closed process is shown to be high on inequality of representation, inequality drops and then begins a regular increase as the recruitment process becomes more open.

Why should open recruitment processes result in less repre-

Table IV
Members' Reports on Methods of Selection to Citizen Advisory Committee

	\multicolumn{5}{c}{Citizen Advisory Committee}				
Selection Method	Spokane	Walla Walla	Southwest	Yakima	Big Bend
Election	0%	0%	74%	65%	4%
Volunteer	18	9	5	0	13
Selected by public official	32	50	11	6	42
By group, company	25	32	5	24	36
No answer	25	9	5	6	6
Total	100%	100%	100%	101%	101%
N	(28)	(22)	(19)	(72)	(17)
Index of openness[a]	−39	−73	+63	+35	−61

[a] The percentage in "election" and "volunteer" minus the percentage in "selected by group or company" and "selected by public official."

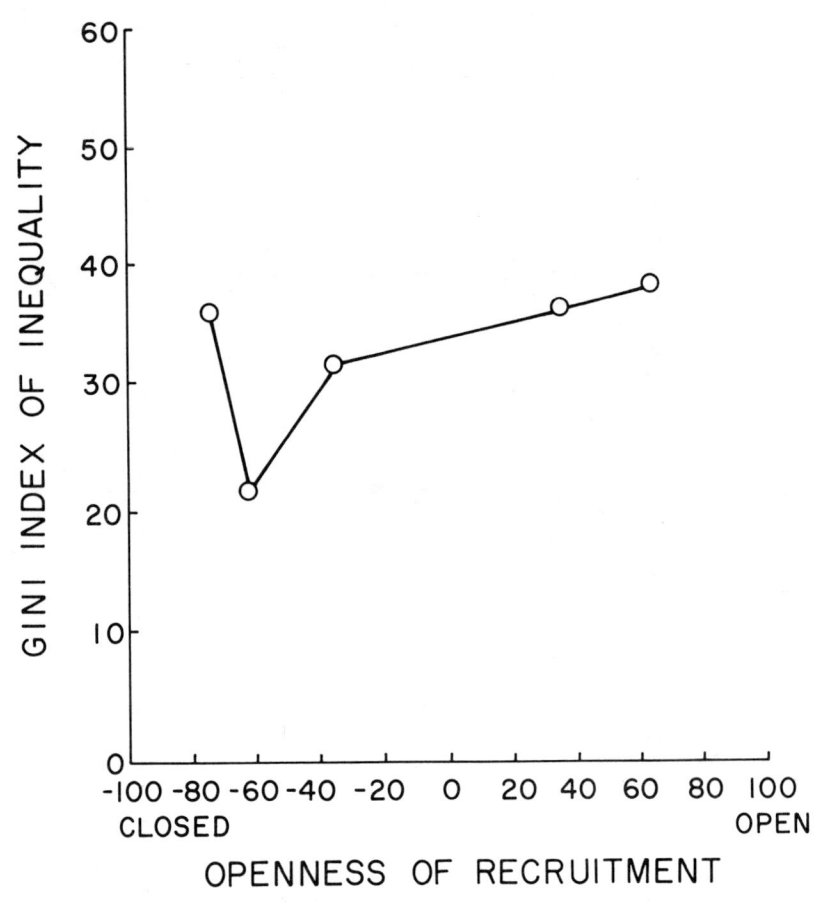

Figure 1. Scatterplot of openness index and Gini Index of Inequality.

sentation of the public's preferences (with the one exception, of course)? The answer is probably found in the nature of the closed and open processes themselves. In the closed processes the burden of choosing members of the CAC falls primarily on public officials or their representatives. They may approach that task with alternative orientations, ranging from a focus on specific, favored interests to one of trying to assure that all relevant interests are represented. These data indicate a tendency toward the latter. Based on their experience and perceptions of the distributions of interests in the river basin, including those interests not usually interacting with government, they may systematically recruit representatives of each of the alternative interests. Indeed, it is plausible that there are some interests with individuals who would be more likely to participate when recruited directly by policy-makers than when the process is open. They may include individuals with no direct economic interest in water or no intense commitment to a certain water resource value—consumers and the general public, as opposed to preservationists, farmers, and energy interests. At the same time, the open recruitment process may work in the other direction. Because attendance at public hearings, campaigning for elections, or volunteering require some level of interest and effort along with some self-perception of expertise, the open processes may allow for the selection of people already active in water politics. They may represent the organized interests that monitor water resource politics generally, and therefore be less representative of the entire public.

Figure 2 shows the relationship of recruitment and representation, controlling for the policy emphasis. In only one ranking, that of preservation, does the relationship differ substantially from the overall pattern of the means, thereby supporting the original hypothesis. Even for preservation, however, the pattern is curvilinear, with the level of *inequality* of representation the greatest for the Southwest CAC, which had the most open recruitment process. In the other four CACs there is a small but steady decline in inequality as recruitment openness increases. Citizen involvement pressures and participation in the water resource area most often have been linked to preservationist interests. Perhaps the noted activism of the preservationists allowed them to take advantage of the Southwest's more open recruitment process. Indeed, in the Southwest river basin, the average ranking of preservation by the CAC members is 3.39, the highest of any of the CACs or river basin publics. On the other hand, the Southwest public average ranking for preservation is 4.40, about the middle of the five river basin publics and lower than all but one of the CACs.

The second link of the citizen advisory committee model of public involvement is the relationship of CAC members and public officials. Do recruitment patterns make any difference in the way CAC members perceive the responsiveness of public officials? Figure 3 presents evidence to support the hypothesis that as the openness of recruitment increases the *perceived* level of

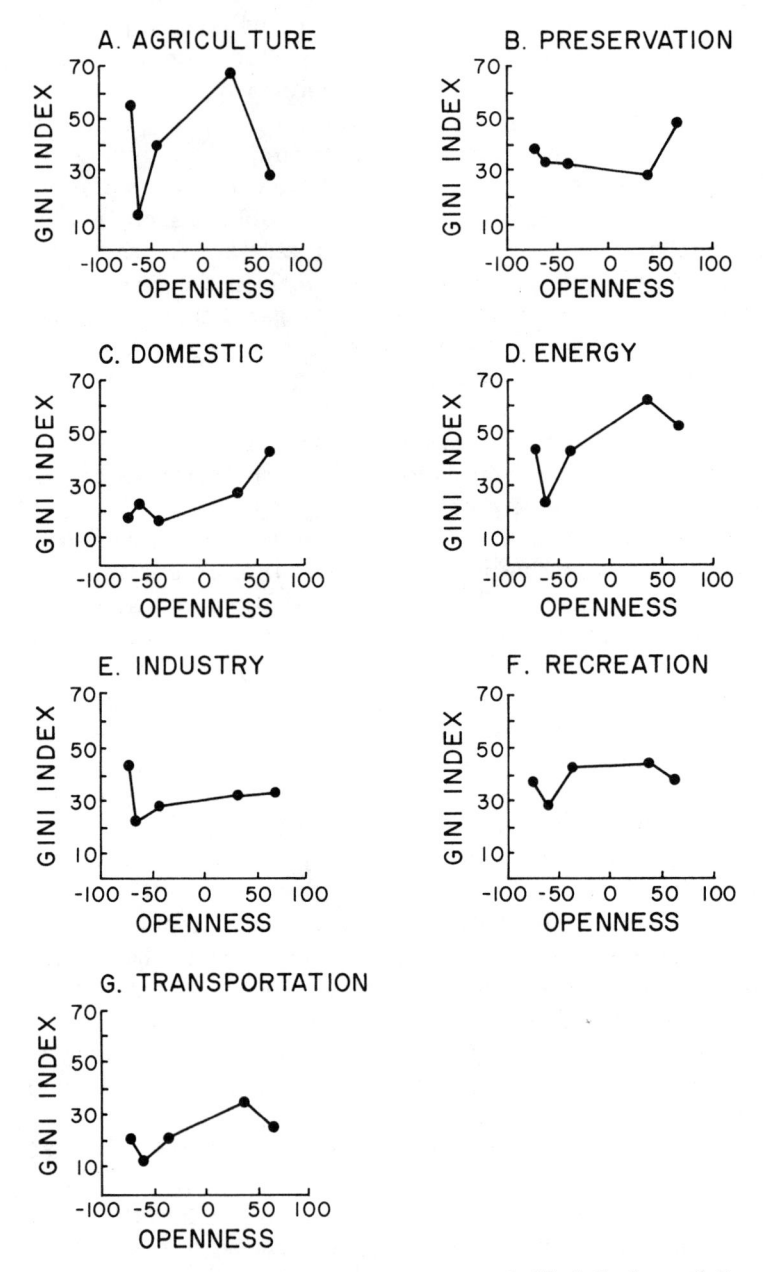

Figure 2. Recruitment openness and Gini Index of Inequality by policy preference.

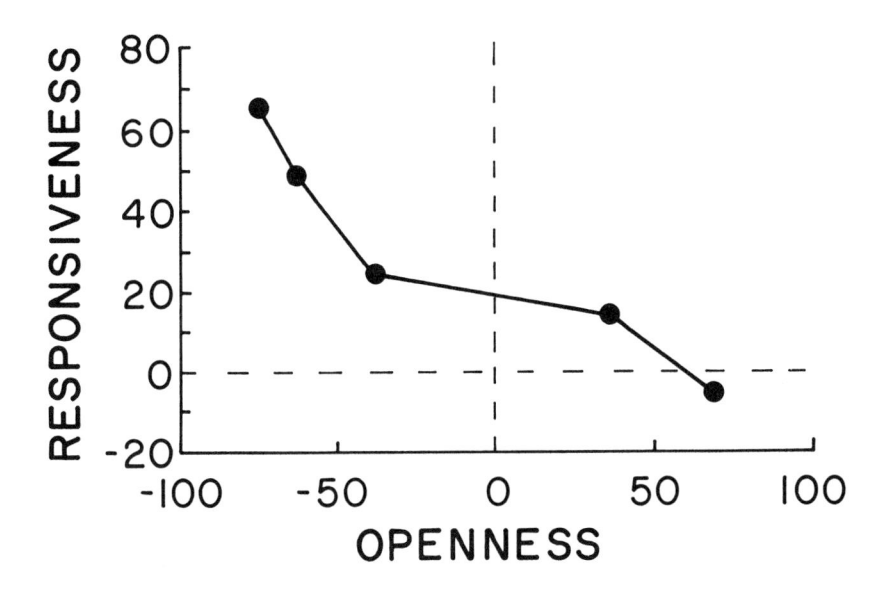

Figure 3. Recruitment openness and perception of public official responsiveness.

public official responsiveness decreases. Public officials are seen as most responsive in those citizen advisory committees where the entry to the CAC was more controlled. Public officials were seen to be the least responsive in those CACs where entry was more open.

Several explanations for the pattern of recruitment and responsiveness may be found. First, CAC members selected by public officials may simply take that selection as *prima facie* evidence that the officials are responsive to their views. On the other hand, because members selected through open mechanisms owe little to public officials for their CAC positions, it is reasonable that they would perceive public officials as less responsive to them. Second, representatives to CACs selected by public officials are more likely to have previously interacted with those officials, and to have a greater familiarity with the process and problems as seen by the public officials. Through time, the interaction builds shared values and norms, a process called "elite accommodation" (Presthus, 1974), even though policy preferences may differ. The actions of public officials may then be seen in a different, more familiar context, than seen by the new entrant to water politics.

CONCLUSION

This chapter has examined the relationship between the method of recruiting members of Citizen Advisory Committees on the one hand and those committees' levels of representation and perceived public official responsiveness on the other. Contrary to the original hypothesis, as the openness of the selection process increases, the level of representation of the CAC members compared to their respective publics decreases. The exception is the CAC with the most closed recruitment, which also is the least representative. Thus, the relationship is curvilinear. When controlling for specific policy emphases, only in the representation of preservation interests is there a positive relationship between the level of representation and the openness of the recruitment process. Concurrent with the original hypothesis, the openness of the recruitment process is inversely related to the perceived responsiveness of public officials. As the process becomes more open across CACs, the level of perceived public official responsiveness decreases. In summary, then, open recruitment processes in the CAC public involvement program tend to have a negative impact on representation and a negative impact on perceptions of public official responsiveness.

What do these results mean for the role of selection processes in the ability of citizen advisory committees' fulfilling their purposes? The answer depends on one's perception of the purpose of citizen advisory committees. If the purpose of CAC programs is to represent the actual distribution of water resource interests in the public, the more closed recruitment processes may be preferable. That is, public officials may be better able to select representatives of interests of varying levels of intensity for membership on the CAC, where through the open recruitment process certain kinds of interests may be excluded. They may be excluded because of either their own lack of interest and motivation, or because of some characteristic in the recruitment process. The policy process may provide insufficient information for them to be aware of the program or aware of its relevance to their own interests.

Yet, not all people would argue that the CAC programs should be judged in terms of the representation of interests. Rather, for some the important element is the *opportunity* for individuals and interests to be represented. Thus, the more open processes would be preferred because the process itself is more normatively acceptable, regardless of the impact of the process on the representation of interests. A number of observers of the water policy process argue that public officials design public involvement programs with the purpose of solidifying support for their own agency and its policies. If one takes the position of the public official, the closed recruitment processes would be most acceptable because in the more closed CACs members perceive public officials to be the most responsive.

The intensive search for ways to involve the public in water resource decisions has begun only recently. The citizen advisory committee is one of the many tactics in that search. Much remains to be discovered about the efficacy of the citizen advisory committees and the variables affecting their performance. As a beginning, this chapter has shown that the method of recruitment has some impact on the level of representation and the perceptions of public official responsiveness. Importantly, some of the findings are of an unexpected nature. This reinforces the need for continued research into the nature of citizen advisory committees, particularly with regard to some of their fundamental assumptions. Some of those assumptions, for example that more open recruitment will increase representation, are questionable and need to be considered in the light of the particular goals of any specific public involvement program.

ACKNOWLEDGMENTS

The research on which this paper is based was supported jointly by Washington State University and the U. S. Department of the Interior, Office of Water Resources Research as authorized under the Water Resources Act of 1964 (P.L. 88-379).

REFERENCES

Alker, H. R., Jr. *Mathematics and Politics* (New York: Macmillan, 1965).
Campbell, A., P. E. Converse, W. E. Miller, and D. E. Stokes. *The American Voter* (New York: John Wiley and Sons, 1960).
Dixon, R. G., Jr. *Democratic Representation* (New York: Oxford University Press, 1968).
Dodge, B. H. "Achieving Public Involvement in the Corps of Engineers, Water Resources Planning," *Water Resources Bull.* 9 (3), 448 (1973).
Felton, P. M. "Citizen Action in Water—Asset or Liability," in *Proceedings of the Fourth American Water Resources Conference* (Urbana, Illinois: American Water Resources Association, 1968).
Jewell, M. E., and S. C. Patterson. *The Legislative Process in the United States*, 2nd ed. (New York: Random House, 1973).
Pace, D. "Citizen Involvement in the Washington State Water Program," a report prepared for the Washington State University Cooperative Extension Service, Pullman, Washington (July, 1974), (mimeographed).
Pitkin, H. F. *The Concept of Representation* (Berkeley: University of California Press, 1967).
Presthus, R. *Elites in the Policy Process* (London: Cambridge University Press, 1974).
Schneider, A. L. "Measuring Political Responsiveness: A Comparison of Several Alternative Methods," presented at the annual meeting of the Western Political Science Association, Seattle, Washington (March 22, 1975).
Seligman, L. G., M. R. King, C. L. Kim, and R. E. Smith. *Patterns of Recruitment* (Chicago: Rand McNally, 1974).
Wahlke, J. C., H. Eulau, W. Buchanan, and L. C. Ferguson. *The Legislative System* (New York: John Wiley and Sons, 1962).
Wilson, R. L. *Towards a Philosophy of Planning: Attitudes of Federal Water Planners* (Washington, D. C.: Environmental Protection Agency, 1973).

Part IV

Annotated Bibliography

14. Public Participation in Water Resource Policy Making: Selected Annotated Bibliography

Kathleen M. Beatty

INTRODUCTION

The scholarly work on public participation in water resource politics is mushrooming. The purpose of this bibliography stems from the disparate locations in which the research results are found. Much of that recent work appears in water resource journals, in water resource symposia and conventions, and in water research center publications and project completion reports around the country. Most social scientists are unaware of those sources of information dealing with the problem of public participation in water resources. Likewise, the increasing interest of social scientists in specific policy areas also has resulted in publications and conference papers to which members of the water resource community are unexposed. Hence, the purpose of the bibliography is to generate an interdisciplinary sensitivity to shared interest and research, and to provide a sampling of the kinds of research currently taking place.

Thus, the bibliography is not intended to be complete and it omits some of the classics in the field in order to provide space for those with which scholars may not be familiar. An attempt was made to provide a cross section of topics, approaches, conclusions, authors, and sources. The hope is that the bibliography will be useful to the social science scholars and students interested in public participation in water resource politics, and to the water resource professionals who are sensitive to the political and social implications of water resource policy.

ANNOTATIONS

ALLEE, DAVID J., Ed. *The Role of Public Involvement in Water Resources Planning and Development*, Technical Completion Report No. 79 (Ithaca, New York: Cornell University Water Resources and Marine Sciences Center, 1974).

Results of an experimental educational program, aimed at encouraging wider and more informed public participation in water resources management in several river basins, are reported. An effort was made to encourage community participation in specified river basins between 1969 and 1971. The project presupposed the water management public to be composed of interest groups, some of which are latent and subject to stimulation. The leadership framework was presumed to vary from issue to issue; an intensive educational program, it was hypothesized, would develop "new leaders." The report includes guidelines for the role of public involvement in water resources planning, with particular emphasis on the role of the university in public education and public involvement.

ASHTON, PETER M. "Accountability of Public Water Resource Agencies: Legal Institutions for Public Interaction," *Proceedings: Conference on Public Participation in Water Resources Planning and Management*, James M. Stewart, Ed. (Raleigh, North Carolina: Water Resources Research Institute, University of North Carolina, 1974), pp. 51–75.

Possible legal remedies (*e.g.*, judicial intervention) for ensuring greater public involvement in agency decision-making activities are discussed. The author poses the question of whether increased public involvement, often based on ill-informed or emotional responses, is, in fact, desirable. It is suggested that legal remedies, allowing public agencies to perform technical tasks without harrassment and yet ensuring a, system of checks and balances for public protection, may be the ultimate solution.

BAUR, E. JACKSON. *Assessing the Social Effects of Public Works Projects* (Fort Belvoir, Virginia: Department of the Army Corps of Engineers, Board of Engineers for Rivers and Harbors, 1973).

This report attempts to clarify the problems involved with the assessment of the social effects of public works projects; it deals with the development of an inventory of social phenomena and a discussion of the problems involved in assessing the effects of public works on human society. Social effects are the results, in the form of altered human conduct, of interaction between an agency and the public. Analysis must include consideration of the kind and extent of public involvement in project planning and management and a developed list of social phenomena. Both quantitative and qualitative analysis may be needed. Moreover, the author suggests a continuing research program for determining *actual* social effects of completed projects.

BISHOP, A. BRUCE. *Public Participation in Water Resources Planning*. (Alexandria, Virginia: Institute for Water Resources, U. S. Army Corps of Engineers, 1970).

This report is intended to serve as a guide for the development of plans for public participation in water resources planning. Models are developed that offer the planner a range of choices for structuring a planning study. A number of procedures and institutional arrangements are explored at critical points in the planning process. Strategies used by planners, which determine how, when, and to what extent the public participates in water planning, are particularly important. Effective public participation can be achieved only after four objectives are met: legitimization of the planning process, community participation in planning, community definition of goals, and development of water resources plans that will augment other efforts to reach community goals. The focus of planning must shift from narrow end products to continuing attention to a broad range of societal goals.

BISWAS, ASIT K. "Socio-Economic Considerations in Water Resources Planning," *Water Resources Bull.* IX, 746–754 (1973).

Gradually, objectives other than economic efficiency have emerged in water resource development; these new objectives include regional income redistribution, environmental quality, and social well-being. The questions of how different objectives should be traded off against each other and of who (planners, politicians, or the public) should make the decision on the final mix of alternatives are raised. Increased public participation should be integrated into planning processes, but techniques for doing so are currently quite rudimentary. The author encourages the development of social science models for improvement of planning processes.

BOLLE, ARNOLD W. "Public Participation and Environmental Quality," *Natural Resources J. XI*, 497–505 (1971).

The "environmental crisis" calls for a new set of relationships between the public and environmental agencies at all levels. Citizen involvement in environmental decision-making should be encouraged; too often the reaction of administrators to the public is resentment. The U. S. Forest Service is cited as an example of the gap between stated policy favoring public participation and actual policy, which evidences resentment towards citizen participation. Effective public participation in all phases of the policy process is deemed vital to environmental quality.

BORTON, THOMAS E., KATHARINE P. WARNER, and J. WILLIAM WENRICH. *The Susquehanna Communication-Participation Study; Selected Approaches to Public Involvement in Water Resources Planning*, Report to the U. S. Army Engineer Institute for Water Resources (Springfield, Virginia: Clearinghouse for Federal Scientific and Technical Information, 1970).

An effort to undertake a public involvement program as part of a water resources planning study in the Susquehanna Basin is described. The objective was to develop and evaluate an approach for improving communication between the public and the governmental agencies involved in water resources planning studies. Public involvement efforts included a series of linked contacts between agency planners and local residents. Local opinion leaders were identified and involved in planning workshops. Later, series of public forums were held for all interested citizens. Interviews and questionnaires administered throughout the study demonstrated that the techniques used improved the understanding between agency planners and local representatives. Suggestions are made for the development of a communications and public participation program. A public participation model is also presented, relating public participation methods to: goal and objective determination, data collection, discussion of needs and systems for meeting them, development of alternatives, and presentation of formal plans.

BURKE, ROY, III, JAMES P. HEANEY, and EDWIN E. PYATT. "Water Resources and Social Choices," *Water Resources Bull. IX*, 433–447 (1973).

The problem of water resource management requires some type of "collective decision" mechanism. The current water resource decision process does not give explicit consideration to the larger social decision system, emphasizing instead technical and physical systems. This paper points out a need for blending technical planning activities with organized societal processes and then proposes a decision framework to satisfy this requirement. A bargaining arena, which links technical activities with the social process, is the key element in the new planning framework. It is emphasized that new planning processes integrating social and political factors into the technical planning process will make decision-making more difficult by opening up an array of possible alternatives and introducing subjective data. Nevertheless, the importance of considering social choices is stressed.

COPP, HOWARD D. *More Responsive Water Planning is Possible,* Washington State University College of Engineering Research Division Bulletin 330 (Pullman, Washington: Engineering Extension Service, 1973).

A new type of water resource planning, involving public participation, is discussed, and recommendations for assured public participation in water resource planning in the State of Washington are presented. Washington water planning has been inadequate in the past, due to a lack of readily available information (informing the public of water policy alternatives) and inadequate opportunity for public influence on water plans and decisions. Public involvement should be encouraged through general information dissemination, identification of interested groups, organization of local "sponsoring groups," selection of "contact groups," and conducting public workshops. Planners with a heightened awareness of public preferences can then formulate meaningful plan alternatives based on those preferences.

CURRAN, TERENCE P. "Water Resources Management in the Public Interest," *Water Resources Bull.* VII 33–39 (1971).

Water resources planning objectives have broadened to include social (as well as economic) goals; thus, the public must be involved in the planning process. This paper examines the role of the water resources manager in involving the public in decision-making and in pursuing the "public interest." Citizen involvement should be encouraged through public information programs, public hearings and meetings, and public opinion polls. The water resources manager should evaluate the technical feasibility of an array of alternatives, leaving the final decision to the political process.

DAVIS, ADAM CLARKE. "Information Response and Interaction-Dialogue Aspects of Public Participation," *Proceedings: Conference on Public Participation in Water Resources Planning and Management*, James M. Stewart, Ed. (Raleigh, North Carolina: Water Resources Research Institute, University of North Carolina, 1974) pp. 19-49.

The growing concern for public participation in water resources decision-making has left two basic questions unanswered: "Who is the public?" and "What is participation?" Concepts of the appropriate "public" range from "everybody" to interested "publics" to organized groups, while participation can mean anything from information dissemination to intensive public involvement in the planning process. A series of seven "decision-participation models," beginning with an information-generating or one-way model and culminating with a "plural planning model" (involving publics on a level equal to that of the planning agency), are presented and discussed.

DAVIS, ADAM CLARKE. *Public Participation in Water Pollution Control Policy and Decision-Making* (Chapel Hill, North Carolina: Water Resources Research Institute, University of North Carolina, 1973).

In this research project, an attempt was made to ascertain the extent of public awareness and concern about stream pollution and public hearings held by the Quality Control Commission of the North Carolina Board of Water and Air Resources. The extent and type of public participation in these hearings was also examined. Random sample surveys of households in areas affected by public hearings were carried out immediately following each hearing. Results showed that although respondents demonstrated concern over stream pollution, they had little knowledge about agencies responsible for controlling stream pollution. Respondents also showed little knowledge of public hearings and demonstrated a very low level of participation at hearings.

DODGE, B. H. "Achieving Public Involvement in the Corps of Engineers, Water Resources Planning," *Water Resources Bull.* IX, 448-454 (1973).

Rising public interest in governmental planning has opened

the question of the relative rights of the public versus the planner. Although the Army Corps of Engineers has for some time worked closely with "official representatives" of the public in its water resource planning activities, a new emphasis on public involvement has arisen since 1971. This paper describes the program of the Corps for obtaining direct public input to its water resource planning processes. The program centers around information exchange (two-way, between the Corps and the public), identification of publics that should be involved, and consideration of new approaches for communication. A program was developed and implemented for a Corps study area, and the experience there is discussed. Some basic problems that must be solved in any public involvement program are mentioned.

DOWNS, ANTHONY. "Up and Down with Ecology—the 'Issue-Attention Cycle,'" *The Public Interest* (summer, 1972), pp. 38–50.

Downs contends that there operates a systematic "issue-attention cycle" governing American public attitudes and behavior. That cycle has five stages: the preproblem stage, alarmed discovery and euphoric enthusiasm, realization of the cost of significant progress, gradual decline of intense public interest, and the postproblem stage. The author posits that environmental concern has begun to move toward the fourth stage (decline of intense public interest). Several factors working to sustain environmental efforts are mentioned. Nevertheless, the American public will become bored, however gradually, with environmental improvement, and the "issue-attention cycle" will run its course.

DREYFUS, DANIEL A. "Competing Values in Water Development," *J. Hydraul. Div. 99*, 1599–1604 (1973).

The public has begun to display increased interest in water resource management for many reasons; particularly notable have been the exponential growth of the nation's economy, imposing conflicting demands on resources and constraints on decisions, and the growth of the environmentalist movement. The "utility approach" to planning, which is based on trend projections, has been subject to attack, and the public has begun to insist on using water resource management as a tool to shape the future of society.

DYSART, BENJAMIN C., III. "Education of Planners and Managers for Effective Public Participation," *Proceedings: Con-*

ference on Public Participation in Water Resources Planning and Management, James M. Stewart, Ed. (Raleigh, North Carolina: Water Resources Research Institute, University of North Carolina, 1974) pp. 77–127.

This author hypothesizes that the prevalence of engineers among key persons with water resources planning and management responsibilities may partially account for the traditional (and frequently unsuccessful) "frontal assault" approach to public participation. Misunderstanding and conflict have characterized public participation in water resources planning. This research deals with factors related to the responsiveness of technical planners to the needs and desires of the public in the South Atlantic-Gulf-Tennessee Region. Research procedures included the following: identification of key planners and managers; determination of training, orientation, and capabilities of key planners and managers; determination of knowledge required by key planners and managers; determination of factors specific to the region; comparison of capabilities and needs; and preparation of a state-of-the-art review and recommendations for educational programs.

DYSART, BENJAMIN C., III, and ANDY H. BARNETT. "Determination of Public Environmental Preferences in Water Resources Planning and Development," paper prepared for presentation at the American Society of Civil Engineers' Annual and National Environmental Engineering Meeting, St. Louis, Missouri, October 18–22, 1971.

A technique was developed to measure the public's environmental preferences in matters relating to water resources development. In an expressed attempt to encourage the reflection of public desires in water resources planning, researchers developed "reliable, quick, and inexpensive" measurements for citizen preferences and willingness to pay for water quality improvement. A mail questionnaire was utilized to obtain data reflecting citizen attitudes on pollution in the Reedey River in Greenville County, South Carolina. The authors conclude that more acceptable and successful water resources planning can emerge from studies like this.

ERTEL, MARGE OLSON. *The Participatory Role of Citizen Advisory Groups in New England Water Resources Planning: A Preliminary Study* (Amherst, Massachusetts: Water Resources Research Center, University of Massachusetts, 1972).

Two related trends in public participation in water resources planning are identified; they are the rise of public environmental concern and the refusal of the public to accept governmental resource decisions blindly. One response to this changing public mood has been the rise in "citizen advisory committees." The existing literature on the use of citizen advisory committees in federally funded agencies' water resources decision-making is surveyed with an emphasis on the use of such boards in New England. Three types of New England advisory groups are identified and discussed: elective, "self-generating," and appointive groups.

FELTON, PAUL M. "Citizen Action in Water—Asset or Liability?" *Proceedings of the Fourth American Water Resources Conference*, sponsored by the American Water Resources Association, New York, November 18–22, 1968, pp. 304–309.

The author posits the question of whether citizen action in water development is a net asset or a liability. Several examples of the "helpfulness" of citizen associations in promoting water development and planning projects are cited. Yet citizen action groups are sometimes responsible for the termination of development programs "which our best agency planners endorse as necessary."

FINLEY, JAMES R. and ANTHONY A. HICKEY. *A Study of Water Resource Public Decision-Making* (Ithaca, New York: Cornell University Water Resources and Marine Sciences Center, 1971).

Through a series of open-ended interviews with leaders and key informants in the Eastern Susquehanna River Basin, the factors affecting public participation in water resource planning were identified and examined. Four subsystems (competing parties in the planning process) were identified: the reactive subsystem (threatened groups), the advocates, the interpreters (who provide "unbiased" information to the public), and the decision-making subsystem (high-level agency officials). Benefits and costs of public involvement for both agency and public are discussed. Individual participation, it is posited, will rest on rational assessment of utility. Negative and positive collective participation are both discussed and their effects analyzed. Conclusions include suggestions for structural change in water resource decision-making.

FRAUENGLASS, HARVEY. "Environmental Policy: Public Participation and the Open Information System," *Natural Resources J. XI*, 489–496 (1971).

The interrelationships between sophisticated management information systems and public participation in environmental management are explored. The new search by management for information from below is not to be construed as evidence of a new willingness to share decision-making authority with the public. Rather various methods, such as the creation of citizen advisory boards, the office of ombudsman, and formal adversary processes, have been utilized to *avoid* a full exchange of information with the public. Management must begin to utilize communications techniques, sharing with regional and local citizen groups the information of programs. The establishment of open communications between resource managers and citizen groups will lead to the formulation of reasonable alternatives for environmental action.

HENDEE, JOHN C., ROBERT C. LUCAS, ROBERT H. TRACY, JR., TONY STAED, ROGER N. CLARK, GEORGE H. STANKEY, and RONALD A. YARNELL. *Public Involvement and the Forest Service: Experience, Effectiveness and Suggested Direction*, Report from the United States Forest Service Administrative Study of Public Involvement, May, 1973.

An administrative study group assesses the relationship between the public and the Forest Service and suggests possible ways to improve that relationship. To achieve the overriding objective of public involvement, that is, better and more acceptable resource management decisions, foresters must consider involving the public at five stages of the decision-making process: issue definition, collection of public input, analysis of public input, evaluation, and decision implementation. Recommendations for an improved public involvement program are also offered. Several points stressed by the study are the needs to clarify objectives, develop comprehensive plans with broad public input (including consideration of a full range of alternatives), develop clear and consistent procedures, and provide full disclosure and feedback to the public.

HINES, WILLIAM W., and GENE E. WILLEKE. "Public Perceptions of Water Quality in a Metropolitan Area," *Water Resources Bull. X*, 745–755 (1974).

This study presents the results of a survey conducted in two counties in the Atlanta metropolitan area; the effects of communication behavior on the perceptions of water quality are assessed. A two-stage, stratified, cluster sampling design with sample size of 1,600 was used. Results indicated that a high percentage of the sampled population considered the water quality problem a serious one and favored stronger protective legislation and enforcement as well as increased expenditure for water treatment. Perceptual variables were of more importance than demographic variables. The authors indicate that findings show a need for timely dissemination of information about water quality to the public.

INGRAM, HELEN. "The Changing Decision Rules in the Politics of Water Development," *Water Resources Bull.* VIII, 1177-1188 (1972).

Traditionally, a set of decision rules have governed the politics of water development, minimizing the costs of water policy decision-making. This author conducted 63 interviews with water development practitioners, for the purpose of identifying the decision rules and indicating how and why they are changing. Traditional decision rules assumed the viability of water development projects, but such assumptions are frequently proving invalid. Several factors are cited in explanation of the breakdown of the traditional rules. Public support for water development is no longer a given; moreover, communities are beginning to question the values of growth and development. The rising number of active environmental groups and rising demands for consideration of environmental as well as economic consequences of development projects have also contributed to greater uncertainty and conflict in water development decision-making.

INGRAM, HELEN. "Patterns of Politics in Water Resources Development," *Natural Resources J.* XI, 102-118 (1971).

A model is developed representing the pattern of politics in water resource development as rational political action. The model includes the following components: the nature of the issues involved with water development; the activists who perceive the issues and the stakes; the political arena or locus of decision; consent-building relations among the people and groups with power; and the content of policy outcome. Water development has typically been a local issue, supported by locally oriented activists who have excellent access to all levels of government. Consent-building has traditionally been accomplished through "mutual noninterference" and magnification of needs and benefits. Water policy outcomes are, according to the model, rational ones given the localism of people's perceptions. Hence, effective alteration of water policy will be forthcoming only when water is viewed in other than local terms.

KASPERSON, ROGER E. "Political Behavior and the Decision-Making Process in the Allocation of Water Resources Between Recreational and Municipal Use," *Natural Resources J. IX*, 176–211 (1969).

A case study undertaken in Brockton, Massachusetts, provides data on the attitudinal and behavioral characteristics of participants in a water resource dispute and identifies a number of larger issues in the public management of natural resources. A survey of resource users in a recreational lake area, interviews with community political leaders, and local newspaper accounts of the water controversy provided the data for the study. Findings included a widespread lack of awareness and knowledge and general confusion about available alternative solutions to water problems. The author develops a typology of political participants in natural resources disputes, including private actors, civic actors, and ideological actors, and suggests that a distinction among motivations for participation may be useful for enlarging the role of the public. Group activity stimulates both knowledge and activity and thus may mobilize greater public involvement. Most crucial is the development of more adequate information systems for the improvement of the managerial process.

LEIFER, NANCY. *Public Involvement from a Public Perspective*, Report prepared for the Montana Department of Natural Resources and Conservation, February, 1974.

A pilot study of public involvement in water resource planning was conducted in conjunction with a river basin planning program in Montana's Flathead River Basin, with the objective of formulating a meaningful public involvement program. The Project Consultant conducted interviews with 300 area "opinion leaders" and administered a questionnaire through newspaper circulation. Two basic problems of public involvement were identified: a deep-seated mistrust of government and an inability of government agencies to communicate with the public. The author (project consultant) suggests that a heightened level of funding and expertise coupled with a "human interaction" approach to public involvement will facilitate meaningful public involvement. A procedural outline for encouraging public involvement, especially at the goal formation stage of planning, is included.

MCKENZIE, LINDA, Ed. *The Grass Roots and Water Resources Management*, Report No. 10 (Pullman, Washington: State of Washington Water Research Center, Washington State University/University of Washington, 1972).

The proceedings of a conference held in March, 1971, include statements from representatives of various interests in the State of Washington (including private citizens, organized groups, university professors, commission members, and public agency representatives) on "grass roots" involvement in Washington water resource management. Participation and nonparticipation in specific water management projects are discussed, as are the changing roles of the water resource planner and of the concerned citizen. Public involvement approaches used by both state and federal agencies are considered.

MORLEY, C. G. "Public Participation: A Right to Decide," *The Allocative Conflicts in Water Resource Management* (Winnipeg, Manitoba, Canada: Agassiz Center for Water Studies, The University of Manitoba, 1974) pp. 509–524.

A case is made for public participation in environmental decision-making, with public rights guaranteed and meaningfully defined by law. Public rights should be defined and carefully spelled out in legal codes. Not until the public shares environmental decision-making responsibility will the public understand the complexity of environmental decision-making.

PETERSON, JOHN H., JR., and PEGGY J. ROSS. *Changing Attitudes Toward Watershed Development* (State College, Mississippi: Water Resources Research Institute, Mississippi State University, 1971).

An attempt was made to assess the influence of water resource development projects on citizen attitudes and to identify the factors responsible for attitudinal changes over time. Survey data is presented from a 1965 survey of landowners with holdings adjacent to 36 proposed dam sites and from a 1971 resurvey of landowners adjacent to 6 of the original 36 sites. Attitudinal change of the population of landowners was measured with the following findings: implementation of water resource development projects leads to more favorable attitudes toward water resource development, particularly towards the proximate project-related experiences and perceived benefits. The authors recommended that water resource developers, in order to generate more favorable public attitudes, should carry out an initial development program favorable to the public.

Ross, Peggy J., Barbara G. Spencer, and John Peterson, Jr. *Public Participation in Water Resources Planning and Decision-Making Through Information-Education Programs: A State-of-the-Arts Study* (Mississippi State, Mississippi: Water Resources Research Institute, Mississippi State University, 1974).

This study asserts that the most important key to public participation in water resources decision-making is provision of information to relevant "publics." The principal research aim was to assess the "state of the art" of public information and education programs. Included in the report are a critical review of available literature and the findings of a small scale study of the information/education programs of agencies involved in water resources management in Mississippi. The data illustrate that although efforts designed to accomplish information objectives have been substantial, agency success in involving publics in planning activities and in securing public support for proposed projects have not been commensurate with the effort expended.

Schafer, Arthur. "Citizen Participation," *The Allocative Conflicts in Water-Resource Management* (Winnipeg, Manitoba, Canada: Agassiz Center for Water Studies, The University of Manitoba, 1974) pp. 487–508.

A theoretical analysis of the role of citizen participation in environmental decision-making leads to the conclusion that no policy of environmental protection is likely to succeed without substantial public involvement at all levels of decision-making. The author treats two theories of democracy and the interpretation of citizen participation found in each: democratic elitism, which accepts the political incompetence of the "masses," and participatory democracy, which holds maximum participation in political life to be essential to the full development of individual capacities. An argument is developed for acceptance of the latter (participatory democracy), or for the desirability and feasibility of extensive citizen participation in environmental decision-making.

SEWELL, W. R. DERRICK. "Environmental Perceptions and Attitudes of Engineers and Public Health Officials," *Environ. Behav. III*, 23–59 (1971).

Two studies were undertaken at the University of Victoria to determine how two groups of professionals involved in water quality management—engineers and public health officials—perceive the problems with which they deal and the solutions they recommend. Interviews were held with a sample of water resource engineers in 1967 and with public health officials in 1969. Included in the information sought were the attitudes of the two groups toward the proper roles of others (including the public) in dealing with problems of environmental quality. The author points out that both groups were quite skeptical of involving the public in policy-making. The solution to the emerging environmental crisis lies in adoption of a "holistic" approach to environmental problems, direct involvement of the public in the planning process, and administrative structural, legal, and policy changes. Such changes, however, will meet with vigorous opposition from environmental quality professionals.

SMITH, COURTLAND. *Public Participation in Willamette Valley Environmental Decisions* (Corvallis, Oregon: Water Resources Research Institute, Oregon State University, 1973).

Using four major types of data—surveys, interviews, record review, and observation—this author analyzes environmental decision-making in the Willamette Valley in Oregon. Environmental decisions there, he argues, have not resulted from pressure by environmental groups, but rather have emerged after long periods of debate during which Willamette Valley citizens and groups pursued their own self-interest. Each actor, whether group or individual, was energized by emotional commitment. These "privateers," acting in their own interest, were critical to the process of making choices among competing extremes in natural resource decision-making.

STEWART, JAMES M., and DAVID H. HOWELLS. *Perception of Water Resource Information Sources and Educational Needs by Local Officials and Special Interest Groups* (Chapel Hill, North Carolina: Water Resources Research Institute, University of North Carolina, 1971).

Although public interest in environmental quality has risen, it has not been accompanied by increased public knowledge of water resource programs and understanding of the public role in water resource decision-making. This study deals with the public perception of water resource information sources, presenting the results of a state-wide survey of seven local groups in North Carolina. Results, which show a marked deficiency in public information and education in the area of water resources management, should aid water resources agencies in assessing and planning public information programs.

THOMSEN, ARVID LEE. *Public Participation in Water and Land Management* (Albany, New York: New York State Sea Grant Program, State University of New York and Cornell University, 1973).

This study was designed to strengthen the relationship between engineering and social science in water and land management. The factors constituting the "social dimension" of water management are discussed. It is suggested that achievement of effective public participation will require an experimental approach including public information, feedback and dialogue with management, identification of participants, and continuous public participation in decision-making processes and other activities. A case study of the operation of an international regional agency, designed to manage the water and land resources of the Great Lakes Region, is presented. Recommendations concerning the appropriate public role in the conception, design, and operations of an international regional water and land management agency are given.

THUESEN GERALD J. *A Study of Public Attitudes and Multiple Objective Decision Criteria for Water Pollution Control Projects* (Atlanta: School of Industrial and Systems Engineering in Cooperation with the Environmental Resources Center, Georgia Institute of Technology, 1971).

Quantitative methods for incorporating public attitudes about water quality into water resource planning are investigated, with the purpose of emphasizing the nonmonetary factors of water that have impact on the public. Specifically, three questions are addressed: (1) how to develop an assessment structure for quantitatively considering the impact of water quality, (2) how to quantify the value of the information provided by the assessment structure, and (3) how to display the information and decide which rules to employ in assessing alternatives. Identification of publics includes classification of groups into water user types (*e.g.*, recreation, water supply).

TINKHAM, LESTER A. "The Public's Role in Decision-Making for Federal Water Resources Development," *Water Resources Bull.* X 691–696 (1974).

This article stresses the desire of the U. S. Army Corps of Engineers to promote public participation in water resource development planning and implementation. Water resource planners, according to the author, must move away from purely technical considerations, and join with interdisciplinary teams to consider contrasting points of view when evaluating development alternatives. Planners should consider public attitudes as measured by a number of techniques ranging from public hearings to circulation of study brochures. Public participation, although costly and time-consuming, should be initiated during early planning stages and continued for the duration of water resource development projects.

TUCKER, RICHARD C. "Planners as a 'Public' in Water Resources Public Participation Programs," *Water Resources Bull.* VIII 257–265 (1972).

The need for identifying urban and regional planners as one of the "publics" in any public participation program is discussed. Local planners, even those outside of the water resource area, are often intimately involved with local planning activities and knowledgeable about local attitudes. The efforts to establish a working-level public-planner contact, as part of the Susquehanna River Basin Study, are described, as are the benefits accruing from such contacts. The author maintains that a viable public participation program will include public information, provision of public forums, and meaningful public input.

WANDESFORDE-SMITH, GEOFFREY. "The Bureaucratic Response to Environmental Politics," *Natural Resources J.* XI 479–488 (1971).

There exists a crisis in American natural resource management. The author develops several ideas supportive of the notion that there are fundamental differences between the politics of natural resource management and the politics of the environment; thus a new theory of environmental administration, substantially altering administrative practices, may be required. Growing concern, on the parts of environmentalists with non-economic values, and with the value-systems and goals of natural resource planners demands adjustments in environmental administration. Moreover, official legislative demands for recognition of all relevant interests in environmental decision-making call for adjustments in decision-making processes.

WARNER KATHARINE P. *A State of the Arts Study of Public Participation in the Water Resources Planning Process* (Arlington, Virginia: National Water Commission, 1971).

This report is a "state of the arts" review of public participation in governmental planning studies, with emphasis on water resources management. The research was supported by the National Water Commission with the objective of synthesizing useful information on what types of public involvement activities have recently taken place, how these have been evaluated by planning agency personnel, civic leaders, and environmental leaders, and what programs and institutional modifications might be suggested for future use. Conclusions and recommendations include the following: increased availability of water resources information, public involvement in development of evaluation criteria and directional guidance, increased resource commitment by agencies to participatory planning, agency staff training geared toward participation by the public, joint (with other agencies) participation efforts, general technical assistance to local governments and groups for solving water problems, availability of planning funds to local and regional governments, compilation of a reviewable record of the public participation process, monetary support for participating publics, increased use of university resources, and further research on effective public participation.

WENGERT, NORMAN. "Public Participation in Water Planning: A Critique of Theory, Doctrine and Practice," *Water Resources Bull.* VII 26–32 (1971).

A new insistence on public participation and involvement in governmental planning and decision-making has emerged in recent years. Concern for citizen participation arises from a variety of concerns ranging from a commitment to democratic ideals to a reaction to the politics of confrontation. But although the desirability of citizen involvement is frequently voiced within the federal bureaucracy, there has been little evidence amassed supporting the idea that better programs emerge from administrative participation. In the area of federal water policy, agencies have traditionally tended to develop relationships with particular "publics," usually clientele and support groups, but their existing arrangements for public participation would hardly satisfy emerging criteria. One very important question remains to be addressed: what individuals and groups are likely to be affected by water policy? It should not be assumed, however, that involving these affected persons and groups will result in greater harmony and acceptance of government plans.

WILKINSON, KENNETH P., and R. N. SINGH. *Generalized Participation of Voluntary Leaders in Local Watershed Projects* (State College, Mississippi: Water Resources Research Institute, Mississippi State University, 1969).

This investigation focuses on the relationship between the extent of leading actors' involvement in watershed development projects in Mississippi and the extent of their involvement in their local communities. The objective was to address the question of how "linkage between a limited interest activity and the generalized interests of local community can be established in a more gainful way." To that end a questionnaire was administered to Board members of Water Management Districts. Relationships between participation in Watershed Boards, Soil Conservation Districts, and broader community activities were examined. Findings indicate that Board Members were also active in other natural resource-related activities. The relationship between watershed participation and general community involvement was found to be less pronounced and to warrant further research. The authors suggest that maximum local participation in watershed programs might better be encouraged by restructuring those programs to utilize existing networks of community leadership.

WILSON, RAYMOND L. *Toward a Philosophy of Planning: Attitudes of Federal Water Planners* (Washington, D. C.: Environmental Protection Agency, 1973).

This study examines the attitudes, opinions, and perceptions of field level planners and their supervisors in three federal water resource agencies. The study helps to explain some of the reasons for current patterns of federal water management and identifies areas where policy changes and altered planning practices may be desirable. Seventy federal water planners were surveyed in a wide range of hydrologic regions. Attitudes toward planning objectives, personal roles, and socio-political structure, time and the environment were the subjects of the survey. Although some planners indicated limited willingness to involve the community in plan development, most held very low opinions of the public's ability to aid their plans; public involvement was desired primarily to expedite acceptance of the planner's ideas.

Index

Accountability, 270
Administrative process, 30
Aggregation, 26, 81, 107, 114, 162, 241
Appeal, 52, 53
Arrow's Paradox, 94
Arrow's Theorem, 78
Atomic Energy Commission, 201

Benefit-cost analysis, 71, 235
Benefit-cost ratio, 6
Bureaucracies, 39, 230, 236, 243, 245, 286
Bureaucratic backlash, 203, 273
Bureaucratic model of linkage, 15
  direct accountability of, 15
Bureaucratic resistance, 227

Citizen Advisory Committees, 11, 54, 123, 172, 248, 249, 277
  linkage models, 12
  recruitment process, 123, 249
  representativeness and responsiveness, 123, 249
Citizen inputs, 30
Citizen involvement, 34, 109. See also concerned citizens
Citizen opinion, 109
Citizen Power Scale, 214, 240, 242
Citizens
  affected, 39, 135, 146, 287
  interested, 39, 136, 146, 202, 272
Civic Duty Scale, 240, 242, 243
Cleveland-Akron Study, 215, 236, 240, 242
Codinvolve, 121, 122, 137, 145
  analysis, 146, 150, 153, 157
  codebook, 155
  decision implementation, 147
  development, 149
  evaluation, 146, 150
  issue definition, 146
  public input analysis, 152
  public input collection, 146
  public input processing, 151
  summary form, 155
  survey of input, 154
Columbia Interstate Compact, 14
Communication, 32, 54, 56, 87, 128, 228, 232, 272, 275, 279
Comparative analysis, 57
Concerned citizens, 281
Congress, 134, 161, 162, 225, 233, 243, 246
Conservation, 5
Constituencies, 108, 110, 245
Correspondence, 54

Decision-maker, characteristics of, 66
Decision-making
  incremental, 64
  stages, 31
  process, 71. See also participative decision-making; U.S. Army Corps of Engineers; water resources decision-making
Democratic elitism, 282

289

290 INDEX

Demographic characteristics, 26
   representativenes, 143
   variables, 279
Direct participation, 9, 14, 43, 225
   initiative, 10
   public opinion polling, 10
   referendum, 10, 43
   town meeting, 10

Elections, 52, 53, 87, 107, 230, 258, 261
Elite accommodation, 264
Environmental
   awareness, 234, 236, 240, 245
   concerns, 40, 67, 71, 217, 218, 275, 277
   crisis, 6, 272
   improvement, 30
   impact statements, 64, 153, 156, 232, 233, 244
   movement, 36, 275
   quality, 271, 283
Environmentalists, 185, 187, 191, 207, 209, 214, 221, 225, 228, 229, 232, 238, 242, 244, 246, 279
Escapes, 78
   intensity, 78, 83
   preference limitation, 78, 81
   probabilistic, 78, 80
   technical, 78, 79
Evaluation of Planning Scale, 215, 221, 240, 242
Evaluation of Project Scale, 215, 221, 240, 242
Executive Branch, 229

Federal Advisory Committee Act, 133, 134
Federal Register, 133
Flood control, 31, 37, 63, 72, 229
Freerider problem, 123, 226, 227, 238, 245

Gini coefficient, 113
Gini Index of Inequality, 253–255, 258, 260, 262
Goal congruence, 205. *See also* instrumental goals

Ground water flow, 35
Group choice, 75, 84
Groups, 122, 128, 226, 273, 281, 283, 284, 287. *See also* interest groups
   affected, 56
   interested, 56, 129, 131
   surrogate, 46

Historical analysis, 57
Hydroelectric energy, 36, 75, 169

Idaho Primitive Area Study, 158
Identification, 60
   self-identification, 60, 61, 185, 187, 191, 239–241
   staff identification, 60, 61. *See also* publics, identification of
Incrementalism, 65
Indirect participation, 11
Information, 26, 59, 128, 136, 244, 249, 265, 269, 273, 275, 279, 280, 282, 284–286
   costs of, 67, 69
   in value conflict, 68
   of consumption, 68
   opportunity, 68
   politics of, 63
   timing, 67
   utility of, 70
Institute of Water Resources, 203, 208
Instrumental goals, 182, 184
Interest groups, 5, 55, 229, 232, 270
Interviews, 140, 272, 277, 280, 283
Intransitivities, 77, 78, 81
Iron law of oligarchy, 7, 8
Irrigation, 36, 63, 92, 93
Issue-attention cycle, 6, 275

L-15 Levee Study, 236, 237, 240, 246
Land use planning, 125, 152, 164
League of Women Voters, 50
Legislative Branch, 229
Legislative professionalism, 87

INDEX 291

Legitimation, 30
Linkages, 5, 13, 210, 211, 218, 219, 250, 256, 287
  electoral model of, 13
  processes, 4, 9. *See also* bureaucratic model of linkage; Citizen Advisory Committees; pressure group model of linkage
Lorenz Curve, 111, 113

Majority method, 80, 104, 106, 150
Majority rule, 76, 77, 80, 83
MR-GO Study, 236, 240, 242

National Environmental Policy Act (NEPA), 231, 236
National Environmental Policy Act of 1969, 43
National Forest, 125, 126, 142, 145
National Reclamation Association, 5
National Rivers and Harbors Congress, 5
National Water Commission, 4, 286
National Water Resources Council, 4, 67, 71
Natural resources, availability, 17
Navigation, 31

Office of Management and Budget, 133
Ombudsman, 278
Opinion polling techniques, 37. *See also* public input collection techniques; public opinion

Pareto principle, 75, 80
Participation. *See* direct participation; indirect participation; public participation; water policy public participation; water politics participation
Participation
  stages, 31
  thesis, 122, 204
Participation levels, 33
  functional, 33, 36
  geographic, 33, 36
Participation patterns, 121
  evaluation of, 121
Participative decisionmaking, 206, 209, 212, 216, 217
  questionnaires, use of, 211–213
Participatory democracy
  thesis, 204, 282
Path-independence, 80
Petitions, 52, 53
Planning process, 67, 203, 211, 213, 221, 230, 231, 235, 283. *See also* U.S. Army Corps of Engineers planning process
Pollution problems, 36
Power to the People, 29, 211
Preference order, 75, 81, 82
  aggregation of, 75
Preferences
  individual, 75, 81. *See also* public preferences; water use
  policy, 26, 183, 258, 264
  ranking, 189, 190, 196
  single-peaked, 82, 105
  social, 77, 79, 80
Preservation, 5, 261, 264
President, 158, 161, 246
Pressure group model of linkage, 12, 15
Principles and standards, 67
Protest, 52, 53
Public
  attitudes, 123, 275, 282, 286
  definition of, 34, 38
  hearings, 12, 52, 53, 57, 168, 172, 230, 232, 246, 261, 273, 274
  input, 30, 31
Public input collection techniques, 126
  ad hoc committees, 127, 128, 132, 133

292 INDEX

advisory boards, 127, 128, 133, 134
agency reports, 128
credibility, 129, 133, 134, 141, 151, 203, 205
day-to-day contacts, 128
direct mail, 128, 134, 135
distortion of input, 130
field trips, 128
interviews, 128, 131, 272, 277, 280, 283
issue definition, 126
key contacts, 128, 134
local, 142
mailing lists, 128
mass media, 128
national, 142
opinion leaders, contacts with, 127
opinion polls, 127, 146
petitions, 127, 146, 150
presentation to groups, 128
public forum, 127, 129
public meetings, 125, 128, 130, 134, 146, 202, 215, 230, 233, 235, 237, 241, 251, 256
regional, 142
questionnaires, 128, 136, 138, 160, 161, 171, 181, 214, 236, 239, 253, 272, 276, 280, 287
suppression of viewpoint, 130
surveys, 109, 127, 146, 204, 274, 281, 283
workshops, 127, 128, 130–132, 134, 146, 202, 231, 232, 237, 241, 272, 273
written, solicitation of, 136
Public interest, 11, 243, 273
Public involvement, 26, 29
Public opinion, 122
 polls, 273
Public participation, 3, 7, 29, 43, 210, 228
 compromise, 210
 expanded model of, 210
 in federal agencies, 229
 in water policy, 75
 institutional constraints, 7, 8

legitimizing, 7
rationality, 229
reasons for, 7
Public preferences, 11, 16, 26, 30, 51, 69, 76, 260
 measurement of, 44, 122
Public works, 52, 202, 203, 207, 228, 245
 planning, 61
 projects, 41
Publicity, 52, 53, 142, 143, 244
Publics, affected, 59, 60, 146
Publics, identification of, 43
 components, 46
 demographic characteristics, 44, 48
 field interviews, 58
 geographic characteristics, 44
 interests, 47
 rules and roles, 49
 self-identification, 52, 55
 social characteristics, 47
 technique selection, 53, 54
 theoretical considerations, 45
 third party identification, 52, 54, 55, 60

Referenda, 41, 97
Representation, 26
 measurement of, 110
Resource development agencies, 71
Responsivenes, 27, 30, 94, 113, 114, 276
 as concurrence, 27, 89, 92
 as opinion, 103
 community preferences, 97
 concurrence index, 91–93, 95, 97, 98, 102, 113
 concurrence scores, 89, 93, 99, 107, 108
 definition of, 105, 113
 index of opinion-policy congruity, 103
 matching, 94
 measurement of, 99
 political, 87, 90, 91
 scores, 103, 104, 107, 113, 114
Rivers and Harbors Act of 1970, 43

Roadless Area Review, 125, 138, 141, 156
Role orientation, 14

Salmon River Proposal, 158 160, 164
San Pablo Creek Study, 236, 237, 240, 241
Self-identification, 185, 187, 191, 239–241
Self-interest, 167, 283
Self-selecting process, 11
Silent majority, 39, 142, 148
Snoqualmie River Study, 236, 237, 240–242
Social choice, 82, 226, 228
Soil Conservation Service, 51, 71
Suit, 52, 53
Survey research, 51. *See also* public input collection techniques
Susquehanna Study, 4, 37, 38, 231, 272, 277, 285

Tennessee Valley Authority, 40
Transitivity, 79
Trustees, 15
Tyranny of expertise, 7, 8

U.S. Army Corps of Engineers, 4, 22, 23, 37, 40, 54, 58, 69–71, 78, 201–204, 207–210, 212, 214–218, 222, 226, 228–231, 232, 235, 236, 238, 239, 242–246. *See also* Evaluation of Planning Scale; Evaluation of Project Scale
   Chief of Engineers, 202, 230, 243
   model of participatory decision-making, 206, 210, 213, 216, 217
   utility, 235, 236
   model of public participation, 204
   orientation toward Corps Scale, 214, 221, 239, 241
   participation thesis, 204, 206, 207, 215, 220
   planning process, 203, 204, 207, 210, 211, 213, 214, 220, 221, 236, 238, 243, 271
   legitimization of, 271
U.S. Bureau of Reclamation, 4, 40, 69–71
U.S. Census, 56
U.S. Forest Service, 69, 121, 125–127, 132, 134, 138, 139, 141–143, 157, 158, 160, 164, 272, 278
   Recreation Research Projects, 126
U.S. House of Representatives, 14

Washington State Department of Ecology, 252
Washington State University Cooperative Extension Service, 252
Washington State Water Program, 252
   data collection, 253
   impact of recruitment, 256
   Index of Recruitment Openness, 258
   measurement of representation, 253
   public official responsiveness, 256
Washington State Water Resources Act of 1971, 252
Water allocation problems, 10
Water development, 35–37
   agencies, 63
   projects, 13
Water policy, 3, 16, 75, 122, 167, 170–172, 179, 180
   -making, 5, 13, 15, 279
   process, 265
   public opinion about, 179, 181, 182, 199
   public participation in, 75
   satisfaction with, 170

Water politics, 63, 261, 264
 information sources and content, 63, 66
Water politics participation, 167, 168, 175, 176
 average levels of, 175
 rationality of, 167, 168, 170
Water Pollution Control Act 1972 Amendments, 43
Water resources, 3
 development, 6, 30, 31, 39, 40, 71, 271, 276, 279, 281, 285
Water Resources Council, 71
Water resources decision-making, 6
Water resources interests, 250
 agricultural, 250
 energy, 250
 industrial, 250
 preservationist, 250
Water resources planning, 3, 43, 47, 49, 50, 52, 55, 56, 58, 239, 270–273, 276, 277, 280, 284
Water resources policy, 25, 27, 258, 269
 beneficiaries of, 39
Water resources politics, 16, 25, 87, 121, 122, 249, 250, 269
 rationality of behavior, 122
Water use, 179, 182
 agricultural preference, 183, 195
 business preference, 194
 domestic preference, 183, 193
 energy preference, 181, 195
 preservation of, 183
 preservation preference, 183, 192
 public preference, 179, 181
 terminal values, 182
 transportation preference, 182, 183, 194, 197
Water users, 184
 identification, 184. *See also* self-identification
 values of, 184
Wild and Scenic Rivers Act of 1968, 158, 162
Wilderness Act, 158